TRANSCENDENTAL HERESIES

TRANSCENDENTAL HERESIES

HARVARD AND THE MODERN

AMERICAN PRACTICE OF UNBELIEF

DAVID FAFLIK

UNIVERSITY OF MASSACHUSETTS PRESS
Amherst and Boston

Copyright © 2020 by University of Massachusetts Press
All rights reserved
Printed in the United States of America

ISBN 978-1-62534-489-2 (paper); 488-5 (hardcover)
Designed by Deste Roosa
Set in Adobe Garamond Pro and Univers
Printed by Maple Press, Inc.
Cover design by Frank Gutbrod
Cover art by Sirma Krusteva/Unsplash

Library of Congress Cataloging-in-Publication Data
Names: Faflik, David, 1972– author.
Title: Transcendental heresies : Harvard and the modern American practice of unbelief / David Faflik.
Description: Amherst : University of Massachusetts Press, 2020. | Includes bibliographical references and index.
Identifiers: LCCN 2019042715 | ISBN 9781625344885 (hardcover) | ISBN 9781625344892 (paperback) | ISBN 9781613767344 (ebook) | ISBN 9781613767351 (ebook)
Subjects: LCSH: Transcendentalism (New England)—History. | Irreligion—United States—History.
Classification: LCC B905 .F34 2020 | DDC 141/.30973—dc23
LC record available at https://lccn.loc.gov/2019042715

British Library Cataloguing-in-Publication Data
A catalog record for this book is available from the British Library.

for brother Jonathan . . .

CONTENTS

Acknowledgments ix

INTRODUCTION 1

CHAPTER 1
Emerson and the Evolution of Belief in New England 15

CHAPTER 2
Henry David Thoreau, Village Atheist 49

CHAPTER 3
Transcendental Women "Losing" Their Religion 93

CHAPTER 4
Transcendentalism, Urbanism, and Unbelief 147

AFTERWORD 187

Notes 193
Index 235

ACKNOWLEDGMENTS

This book has been many years in the making. During that time, the author has received a good deal of help and encouragement along the course of what's been a long and winding road. I hardly exaggerate when I say that this book would not have been possible without the generous support it received at each stage in its development. The author Henry David Thoreau famously wrote that every book, in the final analysis, was more or less concerned with the "I" who composed it. Yet it's only natural that I should acknowledge the "we" who, in one way or another, lent a hand in the shaping of this monograph.

Given the central place this study affords the educational seat of Harvard, it seems fitting that I should begin these acknowledgments with a tribute to the teacher from whom I learned the most about New England transcendentalism. Those who know Philip F. Gura as a scholar of the American nineteenth century recognize him as a researcher and writer whose vision of history is as incisive as it is comprehensive. Those who have studied under Professor Gura, as I have, know a person whose pedagogy is surpassed only by his generosity, which in my own case has been limitless. The graduate seminars I took with Philip at the University of North Carolina (UNC) at Chapel Hill in the late 1990s and early 2000s were very much a rite of passage for me. They were, in fact, a coming-into consciousness that led me, some ten years ago, to begin to work in earnest on this present volume. I am beyond fortunate to have had such a mentor, much as I benefited from Chapel Hill's being, throughout the time of my stay there, a kind of sacred transcendental ground. In a course at UNC on antebellum modernity with Charles Capper, the transcendentalist Margaret Fuller's biographer, I began to have a better appreciation for the critical traditions through which one must pass in the historical study of transcendentalism. And, in a subsequent course on the thought and writings of the

American psychologist William James, taught by the Emerson and Thoreau biographer Robert D. Richardson, I was provided a glimpse of the extraordinary intellectual arc that transcendentalism has figured since its beginnings. Additional encounters in Chapel Hill with some of transcendentalism's most distinguished scholars—Lawrence Buell, Joel Myerson, Ronald Bosco—lent further encouragement as I was finding my way toward this study. I thank all of these teachers for making me feel less lost.

I'm no less thankful for the institutional support I have received during the life of this project. In 2014 an Andrew W. Mellon Foundation Fellowship from the Massachusetts Historical Society allowed me to make great archival headway in the book that became *Transcendental Heresies*. I am particularly grateful to the society's former research coordinator Kate Viens and its former director of research Conrad E. Wright for believing in a book about unbelief. More recently, a Marjorie Harding Memorial Fellowship from the Thoreau Society enabled me to make use of the Raymond Adams and Henry S. Salt Collections at the Thoreau Institute. I have been the beneficiary of the Walden Woods Project generally in my work on Thoreau, and I am indebted to Jeffrey S. Cramer, curator of collections, for making my stay at the institute as enjoyable as it was meaningful. I could say the same of my research trips to the Concord Free Public Library, where Leslie Perrin Wilson, former curator of special collections, went out of her way to show me the lay of the land that was Thoreau's native town. In addition, a 2018 summer research grant from the New England Regional Fellowship Consortium (NERFC) opened up a host of archives that have been invaluable to my writing the book I eventually wrote. I thank the staff of the Schlesinger Library, at the Radcliffe Institute for Advanced Study, as well as at Harvard's University Archives, Houghton Library, and Widener Library, for opening their doors to me. Support from the NERFC also permitted me to conduct research at the Boston Athenaeum, and, in numerous separate excursions, I benefited greatly from my access to the special collections of the Andover-Harvard Theological Library and the Boston Public Library. A subvention award in 2019 from the Ralph Waldo Emerson Society helped to offset some of the production costs of this study.

Closer to home, I received crucial support from the University of Rhode Island (URI). This support has taken many forms: a Project Completion Grant from the Division of Research and Economic Development, a Faculty Career

ACKNOWLEDGMENTS

Enhancement Grant from the Council for Research, a Faculty Research Grant from the Center for the Humanities, and, with the backing of my departmental chair in English, Professor Travis D. Williams, and the dean of Arts and Sciences, Jeannette E. Riley, a semester's sabbatical leave in the spring of 2018. The former director of the URI Center for the Humanities Annu Palakunnathu Matthew has been an advocate of my work of long standing, and I can only hope this book meets the elevated standards of the humanities that she has fostered on our campus in Kingston over the course of many years. Her directorial predecessor Galen Johnson has been equally supportive of my work, as well as the resident philosopher I needed to ask the timeliest of questions about this project. I am trying to imagine, finally, how I might have researched this book without the assistance of Emily Greene, the interlibrary-loan librarian at URI's Carothers Library. Only modesty would prevent her from admitting how much, and how often, she has contributed to my research.

Only sincerity leads me to thank those who have helped just by listening, suggesting, and reassuring or otherwise sharing and disseminating their own work on transcendentalism. Among the former I must thank Matt Becker, my editor at the University of Massachusetts Press. His instincts and counsel about what this book could be have only ever been right. Among the latter I must include Dean Grodzins, who, in repeated e-mail correspondence, did his best to set me straight in my thinking on the transcendentalist minister Theodore Parker. Furthermore, my work on the transcendental women who appear in this book, in chapter 3, would have been unthinkable without the example of Jana L. Argersinger and Phyllis Cole. Their edited collection, *Toward a Female Genealogy of Transcendentalism* (2014), has been a model of scholarship that I have tried my best to follow. All of which brings me to David M. Robinson. The scholarly example he's set with several decades' worth of research and writing on transcendentalism has been both the inspiration and the motivation behind my own foray into a field that he in many respects defined. Those of us who work these fields do so knowing why the earth has proved so fertile.

Of all my good fortune, I have benefited most from knowing a real transcendentalist, Rachel Boccio. In reading and commenting on the entirety of this book in its manuscript form, Rachel has been a reliable source of insight as I've written and revised this study. In being the beautiful person she is, she's given me so many reasons to believe.

I gratefully acknowledge permission to republish materials from the following archival collections:

Parker, Theodore, 1810–60. Papers, 1836–62. bMS 101/3 (1). Andover-Harvard Theological Library, Harvard Divinity School, Cambridge, Massachusetts.

———. Series II, bMS 101/5 (1). Andover-Harvard Theological Library, Harvard Divinity School, Cambridge, Massachusetts.

Twenty-Eighth Congregational Society, Boston. Records, 1845–89. bMS 7/1 (10). Andover-Harvard Theological Library, Harvard Divinity School, Cambridge, Massachusetts.

Unitarian Universalist Association. Minister files, 1825–2010. bMS 1446 / 107. Andover-Harvard Theological Library, Harvard Divinity School, Cambridge, Massachusetts.

TRANSCENDENTAL HERESIES

INTRODUCTION

"Unbelief was not something that *happened to* religion," the historian James Turner writes in his pioneering study *Without God, Without Creed: The Origins of Unbelief in America* (1985). "On the contrary, religion caused unbelief." Since Turner made this claim almost forty years ago, the conscientious observer of religion in the West has had to question the causal relation that has long been thought to exist between secularization and modernization. While acknowledging that, from the time of the Enlightenment forward, a series of related changes in science and social commerce exerted unprecedented pressures on the human inclination to believe in a supernatural (and superintending) power, Turner makes the unsettling suggestion that it was, in fact, "the defenders of God" who "slowly strangled Him."[1] The leading suspects in this hypothetical murder were, for Turner, the mainline denominations of Reformed Protestantism—Presbyterian, Congregational, Unitarian, and liberal Methodist and Baptist—that became the cornerstones of organized faith in an emerging American nation over the course of the eighteenth and nineteenth centuries. None of these churches was complicit with the forces of *secularization* per se, a term that we might define as the weakening hold of religion on the general social and intellectual life of a given people. Instead, Turner contends that the putative defenders of a widely shared Protestant faith were so intent on accommodating belief to the changes associated with modernity that they effectively killed it.

Any thoroughgoing representation of New England transcendentalism must complicate this narrative. While our usual portrayals of transcendentalism as a regional moment (some would say outright *movement*) have made much of participants' involvement in everything from liberal spiritual renewal to philosophical German idealism to principled social reform, we have rightly highlighted the transcendentalists' religious commitments in explaining the motives and shared mind-set of this generation of mostly young, middle-class, earnest intellectual-activists as they came of age in the 1830s and 1840s.[2] As a religion, in other words, transcendentalism was waxing at the precise moment when Americans' supposed stake in belief was waning. With that being said, transcendentalism did place great strain on the accepted understanding of belief in these years. Many a follower of this not so easily classifiable faith would have endorsed the views of its leading light, Ralph Waldo Emerson, who complained in 1846 that a "corpse-cold Unitarianism" was being promulgated from area pulpits.[3] Emerson spoke for those among his region's believers who, like him, were unmoved by the denominational conventions of the religious establishment in New England. Eight years earlier, the defenders of those conventions had gone so far as to characterize Emerson's similarly tending remarks before the Harvard Divinity School as "the latest form of infidelity," to borrow the theologian Andrews Norton's famous formulation for a religious position that struck him as anything but. From a certain conservative perspective, transcendentalism thus not only gained prominence as a public religious controversy resulting from private spiritual complaint, but was also felt by many to be incompatible with all orthodox expressions of religion, as we might anticipate from Turner's now classic interpretation.

But if transcendentalism truly did qualify as another predictable instance from the era of "unbelief," then it also represented the life-sustaining choices of the members of a loosely affiliated group who yearned for a more expansive conception of belief than was available to them within the religious status quo in New England at that time. Or, in keeping with Turner's views, we can say that transcendentalism as a religious dispensation represented less the "*available ideas* in the culture" than it did the wholesale patterns of outlooks, practices, and behaviors that distinguished the transcendentalists from their contemporaries.[4] That those practices included open spiritual questioning, expressed misgivings about traditional notions of divinity, and a flouting of religion's customary forms only underscores how unstable the forces of modernity had made the historical distinction between belief and unbelief. Indeed, that the transcendentalists should have proved so adept at finessing this distinction suggests just how modern they were. Much of what experience had taught the mass of Americans in the middle decades of the nineteenth century to dismiss as *ir*religion the transcendentalists themselves embraced as the renewable basis for a faith they could actually live.[5] The paradoxical nature of that embrace is the subject of this book.

According to this alternative reading, transcendentalism's alleged heresies figure an instructive counternarrative in comparison with religious histories that presuppose belief's diminishing returns over time. There was, for example, something strangely "spiritual" about the embattled religious climate that enveloped Emerson in the aftermath of his emergence as the spokesperson for what were known as the "New Views." The challenges he posed to the Unitarian order of New England ranged well beyond the finer points of theology or religious discourse to which his opponents (and sometimes his supporters) retreated, as if by instinct. By these lights, even such long-standing local practices as the noncompliance of Harvard's undergraduates with the college regulations governing attendance at daily prayers and Sabbath services could be seen as contributing to an area trend toward religious reform, of which transcendentalism itself was a conspicuous instance. To be sure, within the nonconforming context that Emerson and others of analogous religious tendencies made possible, a critical distance from conventional religion—even a disregard for religion, period—could count as a *kind* of spiritual responsiveness, once we loosen our preconceptions about what constitutes a proper "religious demonstration," in the memorable phrase of transcendentalism's leading twentieth-century commentator, Perry Miller. We might say the same of the practical experiments in spiritual expression that were conducted in Concord by Emerson's protégé the writer and reformer Henry David Thoreau. If he did not quite qualify as the proverbial "village atheist" of New England legend—and he well might have, as we will see—the contrarian moralist Thoreau did give religion a new face at a time when the accepted forms of faith and infidelity increasingly seemed coterminous. Thoreau was, in many ways, the "active soul" whom Emerson envisioned in his "American Scholar" address, from 1837. He was the believer as *doer*, but he was also, as was typical of Thoreau, the worshiper as naysayer. As an author, Thoreau embodied a certain skepticism. As an artist, he compiled a body of work that reads as an inspirational statement on such religious paradoxes as the transcendentalists had individually perfected. What we're permitted by a revisionist account of the respective spiritual styles of transcendentalism— as evidenced by the likes of Emerson, Thoreau, and others of their extended circle—is a better appreciation of the degree to which such contradictions as these devotees evinced in their everyday lives could be considered a religion in their own right. At a cultural moment when the decision to position oneself, somewhat equivocally, between the inherited conceptions of belief and unbelief was defensible in a way that it never had been before, the transcendentalists together exhibited what was to become the quintessentially modern religion: affirmative in the personal faith it performed, "negative" in the tired conventions it rejected, and activated by a sincere desire to reattach the sacred to the profane.

RETHINKING TRANSCENDENTAL RELIGION

The religious culture of transcendentalism surpassed any single person, practice, or place. This is not to say transcendental religion lacked a center. As subsequent chapters will show, that center was Boston, where the "demonstrations" that marked transcendentalism's diverse array of spiritual responses assumed recognizable shape. Of equal importance in the formation of religious transcendentalism was the college in Cambridge, Harvard. This present study is no more intended to be an institutional history than it is an intellectual one. At the same time, it needs to be emphasized that Harvard was implicated in nearly all of the most recognizable aspects of transcendentalism's religious flourishing. It was here where many of the ideas associated with transcendentalism were incubated and later translated into action. Daniel Walker Howe is not wrong when he states that "a certain frame of mind . . . prevailed at Harvard" from the turn of the nineteenth century up until the start of the U.S. Civil War.[6] Yet as the very existence of the transcendentalists (so many of whom either studied at Harvard or else held some sort of connection to the college) suggests, the mind frame that prevailed on the main campus in Cambridge was maybe more flexible than the majority of the school's dyed-in-the-wool administrators and faculty would have cared to acknowledge.

There is no denying that Harvard's official religious standard of enlightened liberal Protestantism must factor into any historical account of transcendentalism. But we would also do well to remember that those restless souls who lived through the "moment" were stirred as much by the insular workings of the religious mind (whether their own or that of some trusted authority) as they were by the gratifying sense of acting on religious impulses that didn't have to align with such moral and philosophical principles as a Unitarian fortress like Harvard chose to uphold. The study of a transcendental religion for this reason alone requires more than a grounding in the Unitarian conscience. It calls for a canvassing of the space that exists "between faith and unbelief," since, as Elisabeth Hurth observes, the "tendencies toward atheism were inherent in transcendental thought."[7] That, at least, would have been the view of transcendental religion from an orthodox Unitarian vantage, conditioned as it was to a particular Christian order that bore more than a negligible resemblance to the usually tranquil scenes in Harvard Yard. One of the primary aims of this book is nevertheless to monitor transcendental thoughts to the point where they became behaviors. Whether and how these qualified as heretical in the eyes of critics is immaterial, inasmuch as we are interested in transcendentalism as a religion to the extent that it multiplied, rather than removed, the available spiritual possibilities among New Englanders. Those possibilities did not invariably lead back to Harvard, but they frequently began there in the thoughts—and, more important, the deeds—of real people, who passed through Cambridge either in person or else in sympathetic absentia in a number of different capacities: seekers, seers, even nonbelievers.

The Unitarian stronghold they met with there had not always been so formidable. Until the passage of the so-called Religious Freedoms Act of 1811, the Congregational Church of the Commonwealth of Massachusetts enjoyed de jure status as the state's solely supported religious establishment. The enhanced legal status that was afforded religious dissenters with the passage of the above act ended this preferential arrangement, thereby strengthening the standing within Massachusetts of competing denominations that had long since operated under de facto conditions of sufferance both by scattered local townships and by the state legislature in Boston. Whatever previous advantages the Congregational Church received from earlier taxpayer support were further eroded by the Unitarian schism that had divided the church's followers since the closing decades of the previous century. The increasing ranks of Unitarians within the state virtually ensured that any planned repeal of the act of 1811 would be politically impossible. And so, from this point forward, the various denominations of Massachusetts would ostensibly operate on more equitable terms. All of which developments put in place the legal parameters necessary for Unitarianism to gain ascendance within certain portions of the state and for transcendentalism, in turn, to emerge as a viable religious option to Unitarianism. The acceptance of religious difference would in fact be legally mandated in 1833, with the formal disestablishment of the state's Congregational Church.

As a faith, Unitarianism rested precisely on faith in human reason. Its worshipers in New England were the regional descendants of the "Old Light" Congregationalists who, in the face of the "New Light" religious revivals that coincided with the Great Awakening of the 1730s and 1740s, resisted what they believed to be the unwarranted intrusion of "heart" feeling into religion. The Old Light emphasis on a rational religious sensibility held strong until the end of the eighteenth century, by which time those who pledged a "reasonable" Protestant faith had come to be known as "liberal" Christians. By the start of the nineteenth century, "Unitarian" was the preferred term. It was also the preferred faith among many of the educated and upwardly mobile classes of Boston and its interconnected outlying communities. For a people who set great store by their own worldly success—the result, it would have been easy to believe, of their sensible and sustained earthly labors—the Unitarian rejection of a Trinitarian deity (a bedrock belief of the emotionally radical, yet scripturally conservative New Lights) composed of a Father, Son, and Holy Spirit held great appeal. From a Unitarian outlook, it was offensive to reason to worship Jesus Christ as an inscrutable figure of divinity from biblical myth. It made far more sense to regard Christ as separate from the Godhead proper, and so esteem him as representative of the surpassing goodness a human being could achieve on earth. The Unitarians who subscribed to these beliefs made great inroads within the state, in what had only recently been uncontested country for Trinitarian Congregationalists. Unitarians secured the additional sanction of prestige, if not numerical advantage among congregants, with the appointment in 1805 of the Unitarian minister Henry Ware to the Hollis Chair of Divinity at Harvard. That is to say, several years prior to disestablishment, Harvard had already turned liberal Christian, a change that drew fire at the time from Congregationalists. Charges of "infidelity" against Unitarians were not uncommon in these years. Nor was the new Andover Theological Seminary, founded in the wake of Ware's appointment, shy about its having been created to offer a Trinitarian alternative to Harvard for some of the nation's most promising seminarians. In time, the transcendentalists themselves would provide an alternative to Unitarianism of their own, albeit as a progressive choice to pair with the conservative one offered by Congregationalists. But, by the start of the new century, Unitarians in Massachusetts no longer resisted the religious establishment; they *were* the religious establishment.

Any assurances the Unitarians received from occupying a position of newfound privilege were more apparent than real. In New England, as elsewhere in the United States, the first half of the nineteenth century might have been a time of denominational realignment, but it also marked the continuation of what Turner describes as a historical pattern of spiritual defeatism that he likens to a "religious lineage of unbelief." Turner's rationally minded Reformed Protestants were as responsible as anyone for the modern decline of the "transcendent mystery within the divine design." So, too, were the evangelicals behind the Second Great Awakening, given that they had traded, in Turner's view, their severe acceptance of an inscrutable Providence for a weakened religion offering them the promise of a God within human reach. Neither of these responses, the rational or the revivalist, allayed the pervasive spread of "secularism" in the antebellum United States. Yet, as John Lardas Modern explains, "secular" under these circumstances did not have to mean a complete turning away from the spiritual; it meant an expansion of the very category of the religious, to the point where one's spiritual choices could include everything from "reverence" to "hostility" to "indifference." Charles Taylor elaborates that religion in this "secular age" did not always amount to "subtraction." It also involved "addition," of the kind that would have made the charges of "infidelity"—from the Latin *infidelitas,* for a lack of faith—that were levied against Unitarians and transcendentalists alike something of a logical (and semantic) impossibility. By Taylor's terms, the secularists of the nineteenth century could be "with" religion as much as they were "without" it. None of which assisted the causes of New England's Trinitarians, Unitarians, or transcendentalists. In the last of these religions, Turner says, "the orthodox sniffed incipient atheism." But in a secular age, any such suspicion would have been misplaced, for the region's growing acceptance of an expanding variety of spiritual responses made the mutual supposition of infidelity that sprang from one or another interdenominational conflict something of an anachronism. In many respects, the heterogeneous secularism of the American mid-nineteenth century already admitted of what we today have named the *postsecular.*[8]

If the transcendentalists cannot be classified as either believers or nonbelievers, slack Unitarian rationalists or open-hearted revivalists, neither can transcendentalism be bracketed into discrete categories of belief and praxis. As a vernacular religion, transcendentalism combined a conflicting mix of beliefs and behaviors that drew, on the one hand, from the scriptural, theological, and critical influences of transatlantic romanticism and found expression, on the other, within the context of the unique folkways and material conditions of Boston and its environs.[9] The result of these combinations, whereby the life of the mind intersected with the cultural world of customs, habits, and practices, was a welter of a religion consisting of a plurality of distinctive spiritualisms. Many of the uninitiated may have miscomprehended this religion as so much mysticism, pantheism, or atheism. But for the initiated, transcendentalism imparted spiritual meanings as profound as they were pedestrian.

CHAPTER OUTLINE

Transcendental Heresies begins with a chapter-length examination of the transitional religious culture that was both a cause and an effect of transcendental religion. That Harvard helped to foster this culture in the 1830s and 1840s is the premise of "Emerson and the Evolution of Belief in New England," but this is not to argue that Harvard was somehow responsible for producing "infidels" in the period, of a transcendental pedigree or some other. Rather, we are trying to recapture the conditions under which those who already possessed a dedicated faith were able to rediscover religion on their own college-assisted terms. One of the recurring charges made against the transcendentalists and other alleged nonbelievers was that they were beholden to a "negative" faith. The suggestion was that whatever they opposed from the Christian tradition outweighed whatever it was they "believed," assuming they believed anything at all. To be fair, many of the transcendentalists were unrepentant critics of the religion in which they had been raised. That religion more often than not was Unitarianism. But the transcendentalists were also, this opening chapter suggests, the most constructive of critics. As such, they often distinguished themselves by their capacity to depreciate the liberal Protestant standards of the day even as they raised the prospective replacements for religious convention high enough in the estimation of many that being "without" religion suddenly no longer designated as precarious a position as it once had. Not every religious critic of this era was a transcendentalist. Yet the very essence of transcendentalism was one's willing adoption of what we might name a *critical* religion, that is, a religion that allowed for an undogmatic survey of what the Harvard psychologist and philosopher William James would later name, at the turn of the twentieth century, "the varieties of religious experience."[10]

It was the rare Harvard undergraduate who turned transcendentalist as a direct result of his exposure at the college to such religious ideas as made a spiritual life outside of mainstream Unitarianism seem possible, let alone desirable. The critical spirit that permeated transcendentalism did penetrate through to the religious culture on campus, however, so that student life itself began to take on the trappings of what it meant to "be" transcendental. The nonattendance or inattentiveness at twice-daily prayer meetings, the breaking or disrupting of Sabbath-day services, a relaxing of interest in theological study: each of these was representative of the average religious experience for much of the undergraduate class at Harvard before, during, and after transcendentalism's passing. Chapter 1 resurrects this experience with an illustrative account of students' required course of study, while providing some sense of the increasing dereliction of religious duties that accompanied their usual progress (or regress, their elders said) through the college. Heretics were, of course, even rarer at Harvard than self-identifying transcendentalists. Mostly, we're intent on describing rather than stigmatizing the space that existed between these respective religious positions.

Much as the life and writings of Ralph Waldo Emerson inform chapter 1, the person and ritual practices of Emerson's disciple Henry David Thoreau determine the contents of chapter 2. Thoreau began his career in the critical tradition that Emerson had made synonymous with his religion. Opposition came naturally to Thoreau, and he, too, would reimagine contrariness in the religious terms of conversion, while making "negativity" the formal basis—at once an image, theme, and structuring device—for much of the prose he produced in the 1840s and 1850s. First and last, Thoreau was a writer of the sacraments. The spiritual experiments in rowing, walking, eating, reading, thinking, observing, and resting that he undertakes in such works as *A Week on the Concord and Merrimack Rivers* (1849) and *Walden* (1854) portray the implied author as worshipful actor. Here, Thoreau's narrative persona approaches ever closer to a higher ground of belief, through the private ceremonies of subsistence that he performs *against* whichever conventions inhibited his coming into a centered state of religion. Thoreau's religious arrival was never complete. But, in incompletion, this next-generation transcendentalist raised the critical tradition passed down to him by Emerson into both a functional art form and a usable faith.

The title of this chapter, "Henry David Thoreau, Village Atheist," suggests the nature of the reception extended to Thoreau by the residents of his birthplace, Concord, Massachusetts, as a result of his sacramental eccentricity. For all his obstinacy, Thoreau partook of spiritual practices that were far from qualifying as atheism. A Unitarian by virtue of his family upbringing and educational training at Harvard, Thoreau demonstrated, as much as any of the transcendentalists, the more than residual traces of faith that could be found in nonconformity. Yet whether in transposing his given first and middle names, accidentally setting fire as a young man to a large stretch of Concord's woods, or practicing an anomalous (and dangerous, some locals felt) domesticity on the shores of nearby Walden Pond, Thoreau forever seemed to be thumbing his nose at his neighbors. They responded, in kind, by greeting Thoreau as a sort of honorary infidel, one whose criticisms of their most cherished conventions could sometimes prove offensive. As far as we know, there was never a movement afoot inside Concord to ostracize the idiosyncratic "Henry." All of the evidence suggests that Thoreau was mostly respected among his contemporaries, liked by many of his fellow townspeople, and adored by a chosen few friends and intimates. But at a time when the so-called village infidel of a more uniformly Reformed Protestant past would have represented less striking an aberration from communal norms than before, Thoreau with his store of pet criticisms became a serviceable substitute for the oddball "atheist" of New England lore. With chapter 2, we revisit the tradition of the village atheist within Concord's history, the better to gauge the ways in which Thoreau's neighbors regarded his peculiar behaviors as a form of unbelief.

The women who found religion in transcendentalism were no less well versed in undermining convention than was Thoreau. In chapter 3, "Transcendental Women 'Losing' Their Religion," we explore the critical nature of these women's own oppositions and whether and how their beliefs served them as a vehicle for spiritual expression. The reform work of a number of women who were immersed in the transcendental "moment" is well known and encompassed the organized advocacy for change in abolition, education, and political representation. A celebrity intellectual such as Margaret Fuller, meanwhile, drew notice for the Boston-area "Conversations" she held with a following of eager subscribers for her wide-ranging Socratic dialogues on life, literature, and philosophy. I touch briefly in this chapter on the convictions that led women into these activities, but dedicate a greater share of my attention to the inspirations of lower-profile women in the surrounding countryside. Moved as they were by the transcendental spirit, a particular class of these women quietly came to assert the spiritual longings that had failed to find an outlet under one or another of New England's previous orthodox regimes. Some of these women wrote of their renewed religious awakenings under transcendentalism in private journals and letters. Others took steps to share their spiritual discoveries with close companions or even strangers, articulating on their own terms a transcendental vision that had more often than not been imparted to them by men.

If they were "minor" players in the moment, the women of transcendentalism's second and third waves were far more influential than their abbreviated place in the historical record would indicate. They are noteworthy, to begin, for having managed to weave religion into the fabric of their everyday lives. For many women in this period, those lives consisted of household and family responsibilities, a perhaps less than ideal setting for the kinds of spiritual concerns that motivated them. Yet this aspect of women's experience touches on just one of the mistaken assumptions that we might make about the spread of a transcendental religion. The domestic sphere proved most conducive to "spirit"; the routine work that occurred there encouraged a certain receptiveness to unconventional forms of worship, which might not have been possible in more public surroundings. Moreover, although not a few women made their first contact with the ideas and attitudes of transcendentalism in the city (more on which below), they often *practiced* transcendentalism outside of Boston, in what remained the more familiar domestic setting of the autonomous single-family home. This circumstance was more coincidental than causal. Despite the sharp antebellum increase in city living during the 1830s and 1840s, most New Englanders at midcentury continued to live in rural or modest "urban" settings of fewer than twenty-five hundred people, even though large-scale industrialization had begun to transform the traditionally pastoral qualities of regional settlements as early as the 1820s.[11] In the analysis presented here, transcendentalism depended less on "nature" than nurture, of the kind that would have been encountered in such mundane household arrangements as had conspired to make the lives of women "separate" from those of men. It was precisely the shortcomings—practical, emotional, and spiritual—of conventional domesticity for some women of a comparatively less urbanized New England that enhanced for them the unconventional appeal of religious transcendentalism.

The city of Boston loomed large in the life of transcendentalism nonetheless. From a practical standpoint, Boston really was the regional hub; it stood as the nation's third-largest city as of 1850 and thus served as the geographic, commercial, and cultural link for many of the people of New England. From a religious perspective, Boston was also the area crucible of unorthodoxy, in the sense that the city's relatively dense population, engaged citizenry, and intricate institutional networks were well adapted for supporting the weird spiritualisms that were a recurrent feature of the metropolis in the antebellum period. However far transcendentalism might have traveled into the countryside, it depended for its dissemination on the Massachusetts capital's ferment of religious innovation and busy information flows. Spiritually speaking, what happened in Boston didn't stay in Boston.

Chapter 4, "Transcendentalism, Urbanism, and Unbelief," restores the city of Boston to the story of transcendentalism as a religion. The narrative on offer here unfolds in three stages. The first of these highlights Abner Kneeland, the last person to be prosecuted in Massachusetts on charges of blasphemy. Before he was brought to trial (several trials, in fact) in the mid-1830s, the former Universalist minister turned freethinking preacher Kneeland was holding weekly religious meetings in Boston for the members of his First Society of Free Enquirers. These meetings drew audiences that counted into the thousands for Sunday-morning and Wednesday-evening lectures at the city's Federal Street Theatre, beginning in 1831. Similarly, the newspaper that Kneeland edited, the *Boston Investigator,* had raised his local profile to the point that the free thought he espoused could no longer be so easily dismissed as designating the lunatic fringe of religion. A transcendentalist like Emerson would go so far as to sign a legal petition in Kneeland's support, despite not endorsing all of the reputed "atheist's" more divisive views. Kneeland and his ministry, in any case, invite a closer consideration of the ways in which the city itself—its available public venues and integrated communications channels, its vibrant street-side cultures and pockets of radical chic—was an aid to religious dissent in the years in which transcendentalism was germinating. Much the same could be said of the religious stirrings caused by Theodore Parker in the 1840s. Parker would play his part in the religious controversies that Barbara Packer says "absorbed" much of transcendentalism's "energy" in that decade and the one preceding.[12] He, too, would be on the receiving end of the charges of "infidelity" that Emerson, no less than Kneeland, had incurred. Yet the ordained Unitarian clergyman Parker was no unbeliever; if anything, his was a transcendental variety of unbelief, heretical only to the extent that his religion, from a Unitarian perspective, was unidentifiable as such. More to the point, Parker's separate residencies at Boston's Melodeon Theatre (beginning in 1845) and, later, at the city's Music Hall (beginning in 1852) became celebrated occasions, noted in the local press as much for the crowds they occasioned in an urban array of modern performance spaces as for the provocative content of the sermons on offer. Concluding this survey of transcendental religion in the city is a selective examination of the Free Religious Association. Founded in the Boston home of the Reverend Cyrus A. Bartol on October 29, 1867, the association was among the more obvious shelters for religious liberals in the years following transcendentalism's decline. Emerson was listed as a member, as were Rabbi Isaac Mayer Wise, the Quaker reformer Lucretia Mott, and the Harvard-educated Francis Ellingwood Abbot, whose postgraduate reckoning after he left the college with the evolutionary thought of Charles Darwin had led him to try to reconcile religion with science. It was Boston that made any such reconciliations as the association might have dreamed conceivable, in theory and in practice.

In the end, it is this imaginative basis to faith that emerged in Greater Boston midway through the nineteenth century that underpins this study. At a moment in modernity when the requirements of belief and unbelief were both being renegotiated in unexpected ways, transcendentalism allowed for a more creative approach to spiritual questions than might have been possible in less "liberal" times. The ensuing pages follow this creative impulse to its outermost bounds, where the lines between religion and irreligion were not always clear.

CHAPTER 1

Emerson and the Evolution of Belief in New England

> Yet, what is my faith? What am I?
>
> —Ralph Waldo Emerson, "The Transcendentalist"

Writing in his early essay "Spiritual Laws" (1841), the Massachusetts-born Unitarian minister turned transcendentalist agitator Ralph Waldo Emerson helped give voice to a religion that spoke to the divided spiritual experience of nineteenth-century New England. On the one hand, Emerson was alive to what he called the "intellectual obstructions and doubts of his age."[1] Among these he counted the "theological problems" that Emerson says continued to beset the region's "young people," whom he describes as being preoccupied by their abiding concerns with "original sin, origin of evil, predestination, and the like" (*CW,* 2:77–78). On the other hand, the inborn Yankee in Emerson remained very much in touch with the "practical life" that transpired around him in such places of his native Commonwealth state as Concord, Cambridge, and Boston (78). This life, too, qualified for Emerson as part of what he named our "spiritual estate" (84). Whether "we come out of the caucus, or the bank, or the Abolition convention, or the Temperance meeting, or the Transcendental club," Emerson wrote, and no matter if we were "farmers," "poets," "women," "laborers," or "children," we must find that "a little consideration of what takes place around us every day would show us, that a higher law than that of our will regulates events" (79–81). "Belief and love" are ours, Emerson seems sure. "The whole course of things goes to teach us faith. We only need obey" (81).

But "faith" was not as simple a matter as Emerson imagined. In his private journal, he admitted to being out of step with the religious norms of his contemporaries. "They call it Christianity. I call it consciousness," Emerson confided in the summer of 1838, just three weeks prior to delivering a contentious address at the Harvard Divinity School that outlined what he regarded as the compromised spiritual condition of New England in these years. At the same time, even though Emerson might have testified to a religion of the *mind,* or what he otherwise liked to call "consciousness," he was also steadfast in his conviction that thought, as such, was necessarily coextensive with action. "Man Thinking," Emerson remarked in his historic "American Scholar" lecture to Harvard's Phi Beta Kappa Society on August 31, 1837, is capable of all kinds of "creative actions." Not the least of these is that he "can read God directly," Emerson said. His suggestion—a disputable one, in that day—is that "belief" was an undertaking for the "active soul," rather than the "idle" abstraction of someone "obstructed, and as yet unborn."[2] By his own calculus, believing was doing for Emerson; *not* doing was a form of aborted faith. And still, the confidence of these assertions notwithstanding, the always active Emerson was less than secure in the condition of his own spirit, so much so that he would ask, in his lecture "The Transcendentalist" from 1841, "Yet, what is my faith? What am I?" (214). These were questions that largely defined the transcendentalist milieu in which Emerson played so prominent a part.

The historian Nathan Hatch writes of the "democratization of American Christianity" in the nineteenth century, a time when "renegade" denominations like the Methodists, Universalists, Freewill Baptists, and Mormons openly testified of their belief that salvation was available to converted sinners of any social background, should they reconcile themselves to the teachings of Christ's gospels.[3] These "restless" popularizers of religion were a different breed of believer than a transcendentalist like Emerson. For the latter, belief represented less the obedience to any creed than it did the acceptance of a world-embracing faith that originated *within* (Hatch, 4). Transcendentalism would thus be no more easily squared with the heated fervor of Protestant populism than it was with the genteel traditions of American Christianity, whose followers were often left to wonder at what they felt were the transcendentalists' glaring improprieties. Indeed, it was in keeping with the spirit of transcendentalism that its subscribers disagreed on a host of spiritual principles on which Unitarians, especially, were inclined to see eye to eye. These included the historical veracity of the Christian scriptures, the credibility and significance of Christ's miracles, the meaning to be assigned to Jesus's role as a mediator, and the importance of religious institutions generally. What the transcendentalists did share was a conviction that there could be no clear distinction drawn between natural and revealed religion. In their view, which ran counter to the position of such deists as denied that revealed religion even existed, "divine" revelation was natural and at least in theory universal, not a miraculous dispensation given to a few. If such a religious outlook was democratic, then it was also ambivalent in a way that positioned transcendentalism, problematically, somewhere between the affirmation of a natural faith the transcendentalists deemed sacred and a negation (of everything else) that was nothing if not spiritually motivated and sincere.

Not every American was prepared to appreciate such nuances, at a time when the stability of Christian belief already seemed to have been shaken. "God save us from a negative religion, for it is almost worse than none at all" (270). That's how the Unitarian clergyman Noah Worcester surveyed the condition of liberal Protestant Christianity inside the dominion of his native New England in 1836. The occasion for the Brighton, Massachusetts–based minister's remarks was his published sermon *A Review of Atheism for Unlearned Christians,* which Worcester's associates in the American Unitarian Association had printed for distribution on his behalf. Worcester was hardly alone among Americans in his concern for the spiritual state of the nation in these years. Like countless commentators before him, he regarded the radical free thought of the French Revolution, in particular, as marking a perilous moment in the religious existence of the West. As Worcester wrote, it had become possible, in the aftermath of the unsettling events that closed out the eighteenth century in Europe, for men who might have earlier entertained genuine religious unbelief only privately now to "become Atheists in heart, in opinion, and in practice" (3). Thus, Worcester could complain of the apparently familiar example of a man's (he neglects to mention women) "habitually saying, that 'he is not a religious man'" (57).[4]

Despite raising the specter of irreligion in his sermon, Worcester was in fact troubled by something other than an outright *atheism,* the etymological roots of which word suggested someone who was wholly "without God." Instead, he would caution his audience against the reputed believer who "assumes for himself this negative character in religion" (58). That is to say, Worcester was making a devotional point that resonated close to the home of his own denomination. What he most wanted, in his own words, was to see "Unitarianism losing the indifference that has too often palsied, and the dry, negative form that has too often cramped it" (366). The professed pacifist Worcester harbored no "hatred or ill will toward the Atheists" (3). Far more pressing a matter than any perceived *opposition* to religion, at least in the mind of this prominent member of the Boston area's Unitarian establishment, was the personal *orientation* toward religion of those within Worcester's own religious community. It was not, finally, an elusive "Atheism" from which the pastor would "save" his contemporaries. Worcester was seeking salvation from what he named "a negative religion," which by implication posed an even greater threat to his "religious culture" than no religion at all (57).

This chapter considers the historical implications of Worcester's search. The "negative religion" that he identifies in his *Review of Atheism* provides us with an alternative perspective on the contours of liberal Protestantism in New England's religious past. As it turns out, "negative religion" (or, at least, a widespread perception of the same) was a characteristic feature of the spiritual life in and around antebellum Boston. The phrase had a special relevance for the sequence of high-profile controversies involving a so-called transcendentalism that emerged in the vicinity in the early middle decades of the nineteenth century. Speaking, for example, to an audience of former students (some of them his own) of the Harvard Divinity School in Cambridge, the leading Unitarian theologian of the day, Andrews Norton, would bemoan the "revolutionary and uncertain state of religious opinion, existing throughout what is called the Christian world" (4). Norton was of course making these remarks a year after Ralph Waldo Emerson had delivered his own Harvard "Divinity School Address" in July 1838. The conservative response to that epochal statement on what the celebrated Concord intellectual regarded as the spiritual impoverishment of the religious status quo is well known: it is encapsulated in the title of Norton's uncompromising lecture, *A Discourse on the Latest Form of Infidelity* (1839).[5] There, Norton announces that "the latest form of infidelity is distinguished by assuming the Christian name, while it strikes directly at the root of faith in Christianity, and indirectly of all religion" (11). More telling than the ostensible content of Norton's objections to an unnamed transcendentalism is the "form" he assigns this "latest form of infidelity."[6] "Next to intolerance in religion," he states, "I hate that negative, destructive spirit which would take from us all that the past has handed down, and leave us nothing but barren negations instead. Enough of negation!" (27).

Whatever we make of Norton's opinions of "the new school of infidelity," we should recognize that, in certain respects, Emerson himself came to share them

(42). Only several years after issuing his famous generational statement on what his biographer Robert D. Richardson calls "positive religious feeling," Emerson, too, would interpret transcendentalism in a "negative" light, as he makes plain in a subsequent address from December 23, 1841, "The Transcendentalist," which he delivered as the centerpiece of an eight-part lecture series called "The Times" at Boston's Masonic Temple.[7] Emerson opens "The Transcendentalist" in a glow of seeming appreciation, as he posits a transcendentalism that he'd done so much to help establish in the northeastern United States in the most favorable of terms: "The Transcendentalist adopts the whole connection of spiritual doctrine. He believes in miracle, in the perpetual openness of the human mind to new influx of light and power; he believes in inspiration, and in ecstasy. He wishes that the spiritual principle should be suffered to demonstrate itself to the end, in all possible applications to the state of man, without the admission of anything unspiritual" (*CW,* 1:204). Notwithstanding his generous appraisal of a transcendentalism epitomized, for Emerson, by its idealist commitment to "spiritual principle," he proceeds to take the transcendentalists to task over the style as much as the substance of their general religious outlook. They "betake themselves to a certain solitary and critical way of living," he says (207). They "hold themselves aloof" in their "tendency" to be "the most exacting and extortionate critics" (207, 209). They reside, as a result, in what Emerson describes as an "Iceland of negations" (214). Transcendentalism might have been redeemed for him by its essentially religious nature, inasmuch as Emerson recognized that adherents had mounted a laudable resistance against "a spirit of cowardly compromise and seeming, which intimates a frightful skepticism, a life without love, and an activity without an aim" (211). But, as Emerson also observes, the cost of this resistance was that it effectively negated what little of "life" had been left transcendental believers. They were content to "complain that everything around them must be denied," he decides (215). For his part, Emerson aspired to something other than "the attestation of faith by my abstinence," even as he acknowledged transcendentalism as "the Saturnalia or excess of Faith" (212, 206). And therein lay the heart of the paradox that transcendentalism figured for the area's forward-looking religionists. Depending on one's point of view, transcendentalism could signify either too much or too little spiritual expression. Yet as a religious *disposition,* as a holistic way of orienting oneself to a catholic religious life, transcendentalism was supposed by an array of contemporary commentators—including, on occasion, its own sympathizers—to align a person by necessity in a *negative* way "against" religious norms.[8] Amid the fallout from Emerson's "Divinity School Address," the transcendentalist Theodore Parker would defend his friend against the improbable charge of being *"religious, yet an atheist,* of which is a contradiction to be without God—and yet united to God."[9] None of which would spare Parker and the other transcendentalists of his acquaintance from suffering a similar imposition. Sooner or later, most of them would find themselves having to reduce transcendentalism to the lowest of terms: as a state of being extravagantly with or egregiously without religion. Even as staunch a supporter of transcendentalism as the progressive Unitarian minister James Freeman Clarke would characterize the outspoken Parker as "the expounder of Negative Transcendentalism," while he considered the exemplary "Mr. R. W. Emerson . . . the expounder of Positive Transcendentalism."[10] Given the immediate context of a religious conversation that tied transcendentalism by *negative* association to atheism, skepticism, infidelity, and what Noah Worcester called spiritual "indifference," these were hardly academic distinctions.

A CRITICAL RELIGION

The "religious quest" that David Robinson holds to be the key to Emerson's writings was, as the Concord philosopher wrote in his essay "Circles" (1841), a primary drive that leads us "eagerly onward to the impersonal and illimitable" (*CW,* 2:186).[11] At the same time, because the dialectical nature of Emerson's thought usually compelled him to pair his premises with their seeming opposites, he also maintained, as Robinson states, that "the largest affirmation always provides the easiest access to doubt" (23–24, 28). It was consistent with Emerson (as pertains to his notions of consistency and his personal experience of religion) that faith and "doubt" should occupy positions along a single continuum of belief. It comes as less than a surprise, then, that Emerson, after his initial enthusiastic outpourings in the 1830s, should have undertaken a cycle of purposeful encounters with skepticism in the following decade. Nor was his youthful tangle with unbelief in the 1820s out of keeping with someone whose spiritual pendulum was always swinging. Emerson is generally assumed to have adopted a less ecstatic, more sustainable religious bearing in the aftermath of the first mature articulations of his transcendental vision. There are reasons to support this reading, which informs Robinson's account of how Emerson offset the painful onset of a "double consciousness" brought on by the dispiriting disparity between everyday life and transcendent ecstasy through the dramatic performance of his "spiritual crisis" in the public forum of his writings and lectures (54, 57). We might nevertheless qualify our appreciation of the pivotal role that *negativity* played in the unfolding of Emerson's religious consciousness. In his essay "Compensation" (1841), Emerson himself would announce, "Being is the vast affirmative, excluding negation, self-balanced, and swallowing up all relations, parts and times, within itself" (*CW,* 2:70). This is, as Robinson acknowledges, the "profoundly affirmative" Emerson whose popular optimism underwrites the legacy of "Positive Transcendentalism" that James Freeman Clarke was among the first to apotheosize (20). But, as Robinson also reminds us of Emerson, "the existence of an affirmative necessarily implies a negative" (23–24), so that we can only fathom the one in his work as it relates to the other, and vice versa. Indeed, we can go so far as to say that *negativity* is less the antithesis of positivity in Emerson's transcendental spiritualism than it is the synthesis of the promiscuous religious dispensations that he was, in most instances, prepared to receive. Or, to invoke Emerson's own image, *negativity* is not the circumference but the center of his "Circles," the provisional position from which a religious life begins, only to begin again.

The "negative" connotations of *negativity* notwithstanding, Emerson derived a curious comfort from acts of resistance. As Branka Arsić explains, Emerson took close note of the human urge to "protect boundaries, mediate ruptures, minimize changes, and safeguard . . . restfulness." In the face of this overwhelming evidence of "negation," Emerson instead conceived of life as restlessness, such that the opposition he offered to the instinctive longing for stasis—the opposition by which he validated the idea of "fluctuation" on which he founded his philosophy—might be construed as a contrary example (that is, an ambidextrous example of contrariness) of what Arsić describes as Emerson's insistence on an "affirmation of existence."[12] Similar gestures of creative negation appear throughout his early career. To begin, Emerson seriously began to reimagine religion at the start of the 1830s, we know, after he resigned his ministry upon finding the Unitarian mainstream wanting. Even earlier, on a trip to the coastal U.S. South in 1827 to restore his flagging health, he had discovered reason to "love & honour this intrepid doubter" in the person of the visiting Achille Murat, the son of one of Napoléon's marshals, whom Emerson credited as the only "consistent Atheist" he had ever known. Of his new acquaintance, a man avowedly "without" God, Emerson would write in his journal, "I have connected myself by friendship to a man . . . with as ardent a love of truth as that which animates me[,] with a mind surpassing mine."[13] And, more memorably, Emerson would stage his final confrontation with organized religion as a refutation by ambivalence in the shape of the lecture he presented at Divinity Hall in Cambridge in the summer of 1838. Addressing a graduating class of Harvard Divinity School students, Emerson undertook to shake the Unitarian complacency of a sizable share of his audience. In doing so, he anticipated the "spiritual history," rendered in "the optative mood," of which he makes explicit mention three years later, as part of his eponymous profile of the "seething brains," "unsocial worshippers," and "admirable radicals" who populate "The Transcendentalist" (*CW,* 1:207–8). None of this would have qualified as "negative" in Emerson's eyes.

A portion of the original listeners who attended Emerson's "Divinity School Address" are on record as having regarded the lecture as a false positive; they met it as an offensive attempt to make a spiritual *something* out of the "nothing" of an atheism they were unafraid to mention by name afterward.[14] Others, presumably, could have interpreted the address in the distinctive spirit in which it had been delivered: as the promulgation of a religion that the speaker giveth to the degree that he taketh away. Bearing in mind the "restlessly critical and self-critical" mandate that Bruce Ronda says typified transcendentalism in New England, we can begin to recast "The Divinity School Address" as the life-giving rejection of convention it was intended to be.[15] Like much of Emerson's canon, his remarks in Cambridge cut (at least) two ways. They construct through deconstruction. In the context of the transcendental critique with which this chapter begins, this and so many of Emerson's acts of negation—in the above case, of a religious establishment whose rituals and traditions, he was sure, had proved hollow for the liberal Christians of a rising generation—signal a faithful effort at regeneration.

For all its contrary tendencies, "The Divinity School Address" has garnered a rough consensus among modern interpreters. Most commentators today highlight the radical propositions the talk makes plain. For example, in contrast to what the majority of Christians believed, nature is not fallen, Emerson says. It's "refulgent" and promises a "crimson dawn" of days to come (*CW,* 1:76).[16] Still more radical was Emerson's account of Christ's mission on earth. "Alone in all history," he insists, only Christ has "estimated the greatness of man" (81). This statement may seem innocuous enough according to the Protestant traditions in which it was made, but in fact this outsize affirmation reverses the typical Christian cosmology. Man, *any* man, Emerson implies, should be understood to stand at the center of the universe, not Christ. In addition, Emerson also reprises with his address the miracles controversy that had rocked the Unitarian community just several years earlier—the question of whether Christ's miracles, as recorded in the Bible, were a literal and necessary component of Christian belief—only to afford himself a platform for an unceremonious dismissal of miracles as such. It is incumbent upon us to behold the common miracle of everyday, *any* day, Emerson maintains, rather than rest dependent on Christ's performance of some prodigy. Philip Gura likens "The Divinity School Address" to "an aspirational call to arms," issued to a new generation of ministers whom Emerson would see lead their congregations with nonconformist courage. Yet the address was also, as Gura points out, "a studied insult to the assembled clergy."[17] Hortatory on the one hand, rudely defiant on the other, "The Divinity School Address" is the signature instance of Emerson pairing a positive, constructive conception of religion with what many of those assembled would have sworn was a negative indictment of religion as it was known in the region. Of one thing Emerson's audience could be certain: they suffered the speaker's comparison at their own expense.

Negativity was not simply a rhetoric for Emerson; it was a religion in its own right. His message with "The Divinity School Address" was his medium in that the affirmation he makes of transcendental faith—a revelation based on individual intuition alone—finds expression in a lecture that reads as an extended exercise in negation.[18] From first to last, Emerson summons hopefulness from nothingness, with an address that repeatedly makes the unlikeliest of retrograde leaps at belief.[19] Richardson writes that the "counterweight" the lecture offers to formal religion is "not atheism but a personal religious consciousness . . . a belief not so much in pantheism as hypertheism" (288). In other words, "The Divinity School Address" would appear to propose a healthy dose of spiritualism as the remedy for a religion that increasingly had left worshipers depleted. We can detect an opposite process at work as well inside a lecture that depends equally on reversals of figure, form, and faith to achieve its purposes. In his introductory passages, Emerson situates us amid the "almost spiritual rays" of nature, the better to counteract the "gloom" and "shade" of unawakened belief under which so many people slumber (*CW*, 1:76). Here, he speaks of the religious impulse itself, which in his estimation obtains from an innate "moral sentiment" that he calls "the essence of all religion" (77). It's this moral sentiment that enables us to recognize the world as a virtuous whole. It's furthermore this same "sentiment" that "successively creates all forms of worship." "All things proceed out of the same spirit," Emerson says, "and all things conspire with it" (79). Yet convinced as he is that "good is positive," Emerson seems no less certain that "evil is merely privative, not absolute: it is like cold, which is the privation of heat" (78). At first blush, the suggestion of the schema Emerson represents here would seem to be this: that what's "positive" is all pervasive, and any occasion to the contrary is "merely" a momentary lapse in the normal (religious) order of things. But it is precisely our departure from what's "positive"—this, and a belated invitation from the Harvard Divinity School's seven graduating seniors—that has brought Emerson to Cambridge in the first place.[20] Because religion is "intuition" for Emerson, "it cannot be received at second hand." And because of the "defect" of the "historical Christianity" emanating from such redoubts of liberal Protestantism as the Divinity School—where, Emerson believed, the accepted standard of belief "shows God out of me," not "in me"—the birthright assurance of our "divine nature" had been "forgotten." Or, as Emerson summarizes, "the absence of this primary faith is the presence of degradation." Now that the "doctrine of inspiration is lost" and "denied to all the rest," a "base doctrine" had been substituted in its stead (80).

There is no denying that such terms as Emerson uses as "absence," "loss," "base," "defect," "privation," and "degradation" more than hint at the *negation* with which he was charged by his detractors. Nor does Emerson's pointedly naming what he took to be Christianity's two great shortcomings—a mythologizing preoccupation with Jesus and a fetishistic embrace of the Bible that effectively cast revelation in the past and left God for "dead"—help much to demonstrate his stated belief that "good is positive" or to dispel his "sad conviction," as he says, "of the universal decay and now almost death of faith in society" (*CW,* 1:84). "The Divinity School Address" does amount to an affirmative testament of faith, however, one that makes *negativity* "the breath of new life" that Emerson asks "be breathed by you through the forms [of religion] already existing" (92). "O my friends," he declares, "there are resources in us on which we have not drawn" (91). Indeed, there would have to be, or else Emerson's faith in the infinitude that he sees inside each of us would be unfounded. Finding a shortage of spiritual "resources" around him, Emerson therefore turns to the plentitude *within* him, much as he would encourage the rest of us "fainting hearts" to do if we, too, would welcome a "new hope and new revelation" (92). Swept up as we are (or taken aback, as many of his listeners in Cambridge could only be) by such statements, we might well miss the implications of this critical disposition. The subjective turn that Emerson recommends—the hallmark of his vision for a transcendental religion—is made possible by a general religious condition of insufficiency. Even if, as Emerson maintains, "evil is merely privative," the same cannot be said of "privation" itself. The presence of "absence" is palpable in "The Divinity School Address." The modern world described here lacks faith (but not forms), conviction (but not creeds), the "seer" and "sayer" (but not the preacher) (84). Even the "bold village blasphemer" has the lay of the land, while the "true conversion," the "true Christ," escapes us, waiting as it does "to be made, by the reception of beautiful sentiments" (87). What those "sentiments" are, and when they will come, Emerson doesn't say. What he does suggest is that the *something* of intuitive religion will naturally come from "nothing," because "nothing" is the contemporary norm that transcendence will sooner or later replace.

Emerson's effrontery in these matters concealed the debt that transcendental religion owed, in its earliest iterations, to the emotional pietism and post-millennial assumptions that informed Unitarianism, as is evident in the hurt responses the address drew from those of the staunchly Unitarian members of the Harvard faculty who turned out for the occasion. As a group, the transcendentalists were by no means unified in their religious views, but they did share, as Robinson observes, a "critique of Unitarianism" that was "at times critical to the point of hostility."[21] The school's hierarchy received Emerson's address accordingly. Dean John G. Palfrey, head of the Divinity School, didn't mince words when he remarked that the part of the lecture "which was not folly, is downright atheism." Others were even more forthright. Theodore Parker, in attendance for what was supposed to have been an informal ceremony, reports one dissenter in Divinity Hall shouting, "The Philistines be upon us," while he relates that another exclaimed, "We be all dead men." Meanwhile, Henry Ware Jr., Emerson's ministerial predecessor at the Unitarian Second Church in Boston, and at that moment the Divinity School's professor of pulpit eloquence and pastoral care, offered a careful critique of the critic. In a sermon titled *The Personality of the Deity* (1838), delivered at the Divinity School that September, Ware reminded parishioners that the deity was more than just an *idea*, as an unidentified Emerson had insinuated. To contend otherwise was, in Ware's words, "a virtual denial of God."[22] Andrews Norton's angry reaction was more typical among strict Unitarians. Writing in a Boston newspaper in late August, the retired Dexter Professor of Sacred Literature denounced the "new school" for its "incapacity for reasoning" and "an equal contempt for good taste," while remonstrating with transcendentalism's disciples for presuming to "announce themselves as the prophets and priests of a new future." Norton would have none of it. As he read Emerson's address, "the author professes to reject all belief in Christianity as a revelation." What's more, he accused Emerson of resorting to such "antic tricks" with "our common language" as "inversions, exclamations, [and] anomalous combinations" in order to obscure the meaning of words—"God, Religion, Christianity"—that, for Norton, were unchanging but had been "abused in modern times by infidels and pantheists."[23] In his aforementioned *Discourse,* Norton would measure the offense that Emerson had given by tracing (somewhat speciously) the religion of "The Divinity School Address" to a source among the "nominally Christian theologians" of Europe, whom he "allied" with "atheism, with pantheism, and with the other irreligious speculations" (10). He would even go so far as to challenge Emerson to a public debate, which the instigator in question respectfully declined. In his journal, Emerson gave vent, in turn, to his own wounded feelings, writing that "the feminine vehemence with which . . . A[ndrews]. N[orton]. of the *Daily Advertiser* beseeches the dear people to whip the naughty heretic is the natural feeling in the mind of those whose religion is external."[24] Courting controversy, Emerson had received it, with interest.[25]

Still, "The Divinity School Address" was no more grounded in feelings (Emerson's or anyone else's) than it was the lifeless forms of worship that Emerson discounts in his lecture. As Sharon Cameron explains, the religious experience that Emerson heralded throughout his corpus of work might have placed great weight on the cultivation of a responsive, intuitive self, but it also aspired toward an "impersonal" freedom from feeling, since, as Emerson wrote in "The Over-Soul" (1841), "we do not yet possess ourselves" (*CW,* 2:165). Thus, the ravishment that Emerson's address performs is less a powerful fulfillment of feelings—especially such "positive" feelings as hope, gratitude, and joy, any one of which "implies the possibility of its opposite," Cameron notes—than it is a self-annihilation, or what Cameron calls an "extrication from emotion." In some respects, Emerson wanted (and accomplished) with his lecture to elicit an impassioned response. But ultimately, his religious ideal was not zeal but, rather, the "emptying of reaction" that Cameron likens to "an alternative to moods." Conversion would come when the affect of self-awareness was flat. Religion would be revealed when individual subjects were decentered, the better to partake of the state of grace that attended spiritual holism. "Faith makes us," Emerson proclaims at the end of his address, "and not we it" (*CW*, 1:92). In the religious terms "The Divinity School Address" makes available, this was *negativity* to a contradictory tee: a *transcendence* that at once required the cultured reception, and containment, of such feelings as many of Emerson's peers were clearly intent on resisting.[26]

THE NEW NONCONFORMITY IN CAMBRIDGE

If Emerson was the "infidel" that Norton took him for, then the acknowledged spokesman for transcendentalism in antebellum New England would have found himself in good company in Greater Cambridge in these years. Harvard, in particular, was no bastion of Christian heresy. The school had been functionally Unitarian since the turn of the century. As such, the college combined the rational emphasis of natural religion with the more respectable strains of emotional expression associated with evangelical pietism to continue what Josiah Quincy, Harvard's president from 1829 to 1845, called the founders' "crusade against ignorance and infidelity."[27] This official post-Calvinist commitment to Protestantism notwithstanding, the school's intellectual history, campus climate, and core curriculum helped nurture in Emerson and a number of other influential transcendentalists the proclivity for religious questioning and experimentation that led many of them to a spiritual state of *negation*. Harvard closed its ceremonial doors to Emerson for thirty years following his appearance at the Divinity School in 1838. Yet the radical religionist whom they rebuffed was in some respects the one they had made, insofar as Emerson and countless additional graduates of the college and Divinity School proper (founded in 1816 as the Theological School, with the cooperation of Harvard's Society for Promoting Theological Education) received from their alma mater initiation into the critical religious reckoning that was then occurring in much of the West during the first half of the nineteenth century. James Turner writes of this midcentury period that "unbelief emerged as an option fully available within the general contours of Western culture, a plausible alternative to the still dominant theism." This was the result, Turner explains, of people's uncoordinated attempts to accommodate their various beliefs to the moral, socioeconomic, and scientific challenges posed by the forces of modernity. The argument of the preceding pages has been that New England transcendentalism fits within this same tradition of ironic modern outcomes. Put simply, as the spiritual response of a loose band of regional believers to the insufficiencies of traditional faith, transcendentalism inadvertently served to undermine the "positive" basis for belief. Here we can advance a similar claim about the institution of Harvard. The members of the school's corporate board, like much of its faculty, sowed the seeds of unbelief among students and the surrounding community in spite of their sometimes fraught defense of the religious conventions of their milieu. At worst, *negativity* preceded Emerson's appearance at Harvard. At the very least, the school helped to create the cultural conditions in which Worcester's "negative religion" could take root and flourish.[28]

Late in the nineteenth century, one of transcendentalism's early historians, the reform-minded Unitarian pastor Octavius Frothingham (Harvard College class of 1843, and a graduate from the Divinity School in 1846) remarked that "unbelief is more widely spread now than it ever was." He was similarly convinced, unlike Andrews Norton (Harvard College class of 1804), that unbelief could take any one of multiple forms. "Unbelief is of all kinds," Frothingham said:

> It is wise and simple; learned and ignorant; thoughtful and loose; philosophical and popular; deep and shallow; it is the unbelief of far-sighted men [again, no mention is made of women] who see behind the letter into the spirit, and it is the unbelief of short-sighted men who simply stumble over the letter; it is the unbelief of those who worship and believe more, and it is the unbelief of those who worship and believe less; it is refining, eloquent, lofty, dignified; it is coarse, vulgar, rude, violent and mean. It carries itself like a king, stately and calm, and it grovels in the dirt like a scullion.

"Most of it," Frothingham went on to say of unbelief's origins, "springs probably from unquestioning indifference to ideal things, that is peculiar to our generation and our peoples."[29] He fails to mention whether this assessment included the transcendental idealists whose cultural impact he, among other Americans, was still weighing as the century drew to a close. It likely did not, as Frothingham only two years earlier had characterized transcendentalism as a "gospel," premised on a belief in "the living God in the Soul, faith in immediate inspiration, in boundless possibility, and in an unimaginable good."[30] At the same time, although Frothingham does not track unbelief by name to his own

Harvard, he does implicate the "philosophical" and "far-sighted men" one encountered there in the traffic in such "attitudes" as had made a religious stance of unbelief more widely available than it had ever been before. Never more than a religious minority in Frothingham's United States, the unbelievers whose presence he almost certainly inflated to enhance the pulpit effect of his sermon were nevertheless not disqualified, in his estimation, from occupying positions of privilege in society.[31] However "rude" unbelievers might have appeared in everyday life, however much they might be rebuffed by their pretended betters, unbelief itself presumably did not discriminate by social rank, strictures of courtesy, or one's level of education.

The conflicted status of religion at Harvard in the first several decades of the nineteenth century bears out Frothingham's contentions regarding the diversity of unbelief in New England. Given the unpredictable nature of the forms that unbelief could take, as well as when and where it might manifest, unbelief could conceivably show itself among even the learned professors of the Unitarian faith in Cambridge, Massachusetts. Visiting the United States in the 1830s, the Frenchman Alexis de Tocqueville observed that Americans overall professed the "doctrines of Christianity from a sincere belief in them," although he supposed that at least some citizens did so from fear of being "suspected of unbelief."[32] His remarks correspond with the spiritual state of affairs that existed at Harvard at this time.

Just a few years earlier, in the first of a series of *Annual Reports* issued by the college, the school's Committee of the Overseers unwittingly betrayed the extent to which religious difference and doubt were an ingrained feature of campus life. This was a time of momentous change at Harvard. The school had just approved sweeping alterations to its statutes and laws in June 1825, allowing for much tighter administrative oversight by the committee of Harvard's president and its instructors. In thus transforming the immediate governance of the college, the committee equally indicated a "tendency to distance Divinity," the result of what the historian George H. Williams says were the clearer lines of demarcation that were now to obtain between the faculty of the college itself and the separate—both physically and institutionally speaking—Divinity School, which was located down the road from Harvard Yard.[33] Germane to our discussion of the religious atmosphere at the college are the overseers' above-named reports, the bulk of which consist of short descriptions of the instruction offered in all of the school's undergraduate and graduate courses (in the present instance, for the academic year 1824–25), as well as outlines of the duties accruing to each of the endowed professorships in the college and professional programs alike.[34] These catalog-like descriptions naturally speak to Harvard's official stance on instruction; they represent the administration's highest expectations for education, rather than reflect what was inside the heads and hearts of students. The summary provided for the Alford Professor of Natural Religion, Moral Philosophy, and Civic Polity is revealing in this respect. According to the report, "The said Professor shall read his lectures on Natural Religion to all the four classes of undergraduates; those on Moral Philosophy, to the two junior classes; and those on Civil Polity to the Senior class only" (44). As an added stipulation, the officers of the college, resident graduates, and "such other gentlemen as the Corporation shall permit" could also attend these lectures (44), the content of which can be surmised from this account given of the Alford Professor's "principal duty":

> . . . by lectures and private instruction to demonstrate the existence of a Deity or First Cause, to prove and illustrate his essential attributes, both natural and moral, to evince and explain his providence and government, and together with the doctrine of a future state of rewards and punishments; also to deduce and enforce the obligations which man is under to his Maker, and the duties which he owes him, resulting from the perfections of the Deity, and from his own rational nature; together with the most important duties of social life; resulting from the several relations which men mutually bear to each other; and likewise the several duties which respect ourselves, founded not only in our own interest, but also in the will of God; interspersing the whole with remarks, shewing the coincidence between the doctrines of Revelation and the dictates of reason, in these important points; and lastly, notwithstanding this coincidence, to state the absolute necessity and vast utility of Divine Revelation. (43)

Since at least the middle decades of the eighteenth century, Harvard had been warmly hospitable to the natural religion of the Enlightenment. Then college president Edward Holyoke defined this religious worldview in 1755, in the first installment of a recently endowed annual lecture cycle called the Dudleian Lectures on Natural Religion, as the "regard to a Divine Being or God which men arrive at by mere Principles of Natural Reason, as it is improvable by Tho't, consideration, and Experience, without the help of Revelation."[35] Such context would help to explain the Alford Professor's continuing obligations, as specified above, to "the dictates of reason" that we'd associate with the previous century's scientific revolution, much as the college's intervening evolution to Unitarianism—a relatively hybrid form of religion, steeped as much in controlled feeling as enlightened reason—would account for the reawakened appreciation accorded the "vast utility of Divine Revelation." In the language of the report, it is incumbent upon the Alford Professor to "shew [sic] the coincidence between the doctrines of Revelation and the dictates of reason." The suggestion, no doubt unintended, is that "reason" and "Revelation" were otherwise somehow at odds, which of course they were from a certain transcendental perspective.[36]

Emerson, for one, complained in his journal of the "coolness" of "absolute skepticism and despair" that he saw in "the corpse-cold Unitarianism & Immortality of Brattle street & Boston," remarks occasioned by his attendance on April 30, 1846, at Edward Everett's inauguration as Harvard's new president.[37] In any case, what the Committee of the Overseers had made evident, well before Emerson issued his transcendental challenge at the Divinity School, was that, far from being "natural" and self-evident or else "revealed" by an unfathomable Deity, the alleged truths of religion could be interpreted differently. Some looked to earthly signs for external confirmation of their religious beliefs; others were content to await the day when the reassuring knowledge of a superintending spirit would be divulged from on high. Apparently, there was no "right" way to believe, when even Harvard had hedged its interpretive bets. Then, too, the committee's *Annual Report* left the unnerving impression that religious "truth" needed to be instilled in students by the pedestrian, if well-intentioned, members of a faculty who were paid for that otherworldly purpose. College "lectures and private instruction" were *necessary* "to demonstrate the existence of a Deity or First Cause." Lessons were required "to prove and illustrate his [the Deity's] essential attributes." Students (along, perhaps, with college officers, local alumni, and assorted "gentlemen" from the neighborhood) were assumed to be incapable, on their own, "to deduce and enforce the obligations which man is under to his Maker." None of which boded especially well for the liberal wing of the Protestant revolution at midcentury. As Emerson later wrote "of a period of belief" that had been "followed by an age of criticism," "Luther would cut his hand off sooner than write theses against the pope if he suspected that he was bringing on with all his might the pale negations of Boston Unitarianism."[38]

Irrespective of their denominational attachments, the students at Harvard in these decades blew hot and cold in their belief. One graduate from the turn of the nineteenth century assured a correspondent in 1843 that "Cambridge has, for many generations, been viewed with unsuspicious eyes by the self-styled orthodox."[39] Trinitarian Congregationalists would have disputed this claim; in fact, area Calvinists actively campaigned in the 1830s against what they regarded as Harvard's insupportable liberal religious principles, warning parents of the sorry fate that would befall their children should they enroll at the college. Still, even though, as Stephen P. Shoemaker explains, Harvard would "get out of the theology business" by the middle of the next decade, with the phasing out of its theological course requirement for undergraduates, the school remained committed to delivering a thoroughgoing Protestant education.[40] As of October 1824, undergraduate applicants at Harvard were regularly tested in their knowledge of the New Testament, in addition to being examined in other traditional subject areas as well. For those who matriculated, moreover, the members of all four undergraduate classes, as we have seen, were required to enroll in course work in natural religion, with junior classmen undergoing an especially intensive encounter with theology up until the time of the quiet modifications in course requirements that took effect in 1845. Religious readings rounded out the entire curriculum, however. During freshman year, students worked their way through *De Veritate Religionis Christianae* (1620), the Latin version of a poem written by the Dutch Calvinist Hugo Grotius. Sophomore year brought an extended turn with the Enlightenment moral philosophers John Locke and Dugald Stewart. The natural theology of the Englishman William Paley's *View of the Evidences of Christianity* (1794) featured during the junior year. Reinforcing this important work were students' introduction to Hebrew grammar, the Hebrew Bible, and the Greek Testament. So-called senior sophisters received no reprieve from religious instruction in the classroom, either. Throughout their final academic year, they took several courses that treated the relation between church and state, while also reading Joseph Butler's *Analogy of Religion, Natural and Revealed* (1736). Undergraduate instruction in theology concluded with a collective rite of passage for the entire graduating class: one-hour lectures on the New Testament (at the close of the 1820s, offered twice a week, on Monday and Friday, at 11:00 a.m.) by the Reverend Henry Ware Sr., Hollis Professor of Divinity.[41]

It is difficult to say with any certainty whether the elevating intentions of such instruction were met. What is certain is that college life, for most students, included a considerable share of the mundane that perhaps might have struck interested parties as being at cross-purposes with the school's earnest religious commitments. Even a precocious Theodore Parker, while enrolled in the three-year course of graduate study (which he completed in 1834) at the adjoining Divinity School in Cambridge, could write of religion with some levity to his nephew before reverting in the same family letter to matters decidedly unspiritual. "You inquire about my belief—I believe in the *Bible*. Does this satisfy you!" Parker begins, only to abruptly pick up the trail of a more terrestrial topic, his early struggles for subsistence. "I am now boarding myself upon *dry bread,*" he relates. "It will cost about $ ½ a week—think of that, for your belly."[42] Parker would long prove adept at mixing the sacred and the profane. In his lecture "Transcendentalism" (1849–50), he spoke in one breath of a "Transcendental Theology" of "intuition, or spontaneous consciousness," while in another, drawn years earlier in his published masterpiece *A Discourse of Matters Pertaining to Religion* (1842), he testified to the "negative work" of all Protestant reformers, Unitarians included.[43] But it did not take an apprentice doctor of divinity to fly in the face of official religion at Harvard. As an undergraduate member of the Pythologion society, the charter for which spoke to the club's dedication to the "principal arts" of "speaking and writing," an irreverent young Ralph Waldo Emerson (Harvard College class of 1821, Harvard Divinity School class of 1829) would sign off from his brief term as club secretary in May 1820 with what he described as "a stroke of the pathetick [*sic*]." Invoking the impertinent words of "the ever illustrious Falstaff," the future class poet rejoiced, "Here ends my catechism!!!"[44] One gathers from such drollery that not every student shared the college's religious priorities.

Dereliction of religious duty was, in fact, a popular pastime at Harvard, noticeably in the decades before and after transcendentalism's emergence. Andrew Preston Peabody (Harvard College class of 1826) recollected that the "much wider latitude" given to notices at daily prayers at the close of the previous century—he tells of one occasion when "the Faculty had sat in solemn deliberation over a keg of rancid butter"—did not always enhance the gravitas of the chapel experience that was a foundational part of everyday life at the college. Nor did it help that the old Holden Chapel (which opened in 1744), Harvard Hall (completed as a replacement for Holden in 1766, with an interior chapel for religious purposes), and even University Hall (where, for the first time in the school's history, the college accommodated Sunday worship on campus) were all multiuse facilities combining classrooms, kitchen, buttery, commons, chapel, and living quarters for domestic staff in one building (figure 1). Henry

Lee (who was elected to Harvard's Board of Overseers in 1867) liked to say that University Hall "was symmetrically and philosophically arranged to supply the daily cravings of body, mind, and soul." Yet he also allowed that the floors of the new chapel "were sanded,—a questionable arrangement, as many a chilly or abstracted student has thus got into a scrape while he little dreamed of it." Most damning of all in Lee's remembrance, however, was his evocation of the august clergyman Henry Ware Sr., who for many years presided over morning prayers and chapel service on Sundays. "A learned, earnest, and most guileless and benevolent man," "Old Sykes," as Ware was known, "never dreamed of the apathy or weariness of his hearers."[45]

The disciplinary records of Harvard's undergraduates in this period reveal what Ware couldn't recognize. Although there is no easy case to be made for students' irresistible slide toward the secular, let alone the "infidelity" with which at least one of them was later charged by the Unitarian establishment, we can say that the "gentlemen" of Cambridge offered much resistance to the prescribed practice of religion that was then in effect at the college. Unlike the universities of Oxford and Cambridge in England, where religious tests for degree aspirants continued to be administered until 1871, Harvard made no formal insistence on belief (for students or faculty) as such. Instead, it *presumed*

Figure 1. University Hall, Harvard College. From *The Harvard Book: A Series of Historical, Biographical, and Descriptive Sketches* (Boston: Houghton, Osgood, 1875).

as much on the strength of the college entrance requirements, course work, and prayer rituals that contributed to set a uniform tone for the religious life of students from the very beginning to the very end of their undergraduate careers. The presumption was that anyone who successfully ran this gauntlet of rigorous Christian observance would have to have been more than a token professor of the faith. Compiled for the first time in 1642, and revised at intervals thereafter, the Harvard laws that governed all facets of life at the college nevertheless attempted to ensure a faithful decorum among students by making certain stipulations about religion. The sheer existence of this code of conduct suggests that the behaviors associated with belief were not entirely voluntary. These laws were still less universally obeyed, which in itself indicates at least a variance in belief.

With the publication, in June 1825, of a revised code of 153 laws in thirteen chapters—the first such update of the century—the Corporation and Overseers of Harvard ushered the college into a new era. What followed was, by their own tacit admission, a false dawning. The corporation decreed one thing (several things, actually) regarding religious observance; students pursued others or often none at all. Even before the transcendentalists began to disseminate their message of an intuitive faith, Harvard undergraduates had frequently shown the temerity to find their own religious way. Chapter 3 of the revised code of laws, "On Devotional Exercises and the Observance of the Lord's Day," specifies what was expected from students in terms of their spiritual conduct. In the language of the code, "The Students shall constantly, seasonably, and with due reverence, attend prayers in the Chapel every morning and evening, and publick worship at the assigned place on the Lord's day, on the days of the annual publick Fast and Thanksgiving, and of the Dudleian Lecture, and at such other times as they may be required." In addition, "Every student is required, on the Lord's day and the evening preceding, to abstain from visiting and from receiving visits, from unnecessary walking, from using any diversion, and from all behavior inconsistent with that sacred season" (1825 *Annual Report,* 10). Practically speaking, this meant that students, across the forty weeks (three terms) of Harvard's academic calendar, were required, Monday through Saturday, to attend morning and evening prayers for a total of thirteen times per week (evening prayers were omitted on the Sabbath eve), with attendance at both morning and evening Sabbath exercises also required on Sunday. All such services were held in the campus chapel located inside University Hall, which had opened to much fanfare in 1815.[46] Previously, daily prayers had been held in the multipurpose Harvard Hall, while Sunday services had been held at the First Church in Cambridge. But not even the added convenience that resulted from on-campus services made an appreciable difference in the habits of worship for most students. A fancy new pipe organ was installed in University Hall's chapel in 1821. At the time, it was the only one in Cambridge and one of just several in the Boston area. In July 1833, the corporation would additionally approve a major renovation of the chapel itself, which was housed in what had been the first stone building (it was constructed of Chelmsford granite) on campus. But quite simply, even though the chapel had been built, the students didn't come.

Harvard's *Annual Reports* between the years 1825 (when the school abandoned the practice of issuing fines and instituted a new disciplinary system of admonishments) and 1850 duly include a separate section titled "Omissions and Punishments of the Students." Here appears quantitative proof of the religious "indifference" against which so many observers had warned. During the academic year after Emerson delivered his "Divinity School Address," for example, the number of total absences from daily prayers and *unexcused* absences from Sabbath exercises rose high enough to suggest that the "omission" of formal religious observance was less an anomaly than a regression to the mean. Each college freshman out of a class of fifty-five students averaged seven absences from daily prayers *per term,* which is to say for a period that represented one-third of the forty-week school year. The numbers for the other classes tell a similar story. Some fifty-four sophomores together averaged eight absences per term. The forty-five members of the junior class, which, we'll recall, bore the heaviest brunt of religious instruction, averaged three absences per term. Rounding out this list are the seniors, whose average of twelve absences represented the highest total for this year, as it did for nearly all years. One conclusion that we might draw from the data is this: either the overt signs of devotion among students or the fear of the punishments stemming from accumulated absences—or both— diminished over the course of an undergraduate's tenure at the college. The same pattern held for Sunday services. Again using the school year 1838–39 as a baseline, we find that the freshman class averaged a sizable fifty-one absences per term from the twice-daily Sabbath exercises. The numbers for sophomores stand at thirty-nine, for juniors just ten, and for those brazen scofflaws the seniors a robust fifty-five. One extenuating circumstance to factor into this equation is the permission granted to matriculating Episcopalians—in all likelihood, members of southern slaveholding families—who were allowed to attend services at what the *Annual Report* called "that Church" when they submitted a written request to do so (1825 *Annual Report,* 10). Yet barring a bumper crop of southerners among any given class, the attendance figures for Sunday worship among Harvard's undergraduates are shockingly low, so much so that one wonders how the chapel seats that were assigned students (with freshmen and sophomores sitting at the sides of the pulpit facing north and south, juniors and seniors facing east) presented even the appearance of compliance. The annus horribilis for daily prayer and Sabbath attendance at chapel occurred either in 1840–41 or 1841–42, during the golden age of transcendentalism in New England. As the table below indicates, the average number of absences in these years is sobering (table 1). In individually averaging 15.5 absences from daily prayers per term in this two-year period, seniors were effectively foregoing an entire week's worth of such attendance as was required of them during the course of each academic term. That comes to an average of three weeks out of the total of forty weeks for a school year. Sophomores and juniors lagged not far behind, with even the more easily cowed freshmen registering an average of 7.5 absences. Noteworthy among the compiled numbers for Sabbath exercises are the absences recorded by juniors and seniors for the year 1841–42. For the comprehensive year, the juniors missed eighteen whole days of the twice-daily Sunday services; seniors missed 20.5 in the aggregate of the same.

Even worse were the alternatives to nonattendance, in terms of what they showed about the low esteem in which religious demonstrations were held. According to a special report produced in the aftermath of the historic student disturbances that swept across campus in 1834, "the worship of the Almighty God" had been interrupted on several occasions by "the indecencies of irreverend and riotous noises at the time and place of daily worship" (figure 2).[47] It was rare that anything but these blatant displays of students' disregard for authority should eventuate in their suspension, dismissal, or "rustication," to use the parlance of the college. Yet there is additional mention made, for the academic year 1831–32, of punishments being handed out as a result of "disorders having occurred in the Chapel."[48] There were subtler indications of a waning respect for religion as well. Starting with the academic year 1840–41, the customary "Tabular View of Hours of Recitation and Lectures" from the *Annual Report* began to list students' afternoon schedules numerically (for example, 1:00–2:00,

TABLE 1. AVERAGE ABSENCES FROM DAILY PRAYERS AND SABBATH EXERCISES, HARVARD COLLEGE

YEAR	CLASS SIZE	DAILY PRAYERS REQUIRED	ABSENCES FROM DAILY PRAYERS	ABSENCES FROM SABBATH EXERCISE
1838–39	Freshmen 55 Sophomores 54 Juniors 45 Seniors 63	Freshmen: same Sophomores: same Juniors: same Seniors: 11 per week x 40 weeks * morning and evening	Freshmen: avg. 7 a term (per student) Sophomores: avg. 8 per term (per student) Juniors: avg. 3 per term (per student) Seniors: avg. 12 per term (per student)	Freshmen: 51 unexcused (avg. ½ day per) Sophomores: 39 unexcused (avg. ¾ day per) Juniors: 10 unexcused (avg. ¼ day per) Seniors: 55 unexcused (avg. ½ day per) * 2 required each Sunday x 40 Aggregate totals / (per student avg.)
1840–41	Freshmen 62 Sophomores 71 Juniors 63 Seniors 45	Freshmen: same Sophomores: same Juniors: same Seniors: 11 per week x 40 weeks * morning and evening	Freshmen: avg. 10 a term (per student) Sophomores: avg. 10 per term (per student) Juniors: avg. 12.5 per term (per student) Seniors: avg. 15 per term (per student)	Freshmen: 6 unexcused (3 whole class) Sophomores: 13 unexcused (6.5 whole class) Juniors: 12 unexcused (6 whole class) Seniors: 11 unexcused (5.5 days' service for the whole class) * 2 required each Sunday x 40
1841–42	Freshmen 57 Sophomores 60 Juniors 68 Seniors 52	Freshmen: same Sophomores: same Juniors: same Seniors: 11 per week x 40 weeks * morning and evening	Freshmen: avg. 5 a term (per student) Sophomores: avg. 14 per term (per student) Juniors: avg. 15 per term (per student) Seniors: avg. 16 per term (per student)	Freshmen: 10 unexcused (5 whole class) Sophomores: 16 unexcused (8 whole class) Juniors: 36 unexcused (18 whole class) Seniors: 41 unexcused (20.5 days' service in year for whole class) * 2 required each Sunday x 40
1846–47	Freshmen 66 Sophomores 82 Juniors 57 Seniors 62	Freshmen: same Sophomores: same Juniors: same Seniors: 11 per week x 40 weeks * morning and evening	Freshmen: avg. 5 a term (per student) Sophomores: avg. 8 per term (per student) Juniors: avg. 8 per term (per student) Seniors: avg. 7.5 per term (per student)	Freshmen: 0 unexcused whole class Sophomores: 0 unexcused whole class Juniors: 2 unexcused whole class Seniors: 0 unexcused * 2 required each Sunday x 40

Figures taken from the *Annual Reports of the President of Harvard University to the Overseers, on the State of the Institution* (1825–50).

3:00–4:00, 4:00–6:00, etc.), whereas in earlier years the afternoon hours bore explicit reference to their relation to evening prayers ("2 ½ h. before prayers," "1 ½ h. before prayers," and the like). By the next year, the undergraduate attendance at lectures and recitations in Hebrew had become strictly voluntary. By the school year for 1846–47, meanwhile, the regular listing in the report of "Academical Departments" now found theology moved from its customary position of first in the ranking to fourth. More important, one year prior it was announced that students were now "permitted" to absent themselves from attendance at the Saturday-evening prayers they were already skipping, a shift in semantics, if not in policy, that goes some way to explaining the sharp drop in absences for both daily and Sabbath worship that appears for this year in the above table. Not only would absences be construed more loosely from this point forward, but "permitted" absences would not be included in the reported totals at all. It was almost as if "don't ask, don't tell" were becoming an unofficial guideline for monitoring the religious spirit on campus.[49]

The officers of the college were fully aware of these trends and took what steps they could to reverse them. After he assumed the duties of the office of the

Figure 2. In this early drawing from the occasional Unitarian minister Christopher Pearse Cranch (Harvard Divinity School class of 1835), we see an example of generational irreverence at Harvard. Before a divided audience of alumni, Andrews Norton, "Prof. A. N.," is shown rehearsing the errors of "infidels" who somehow "profess themselves to be Christians!" From Christopher Pearse Cranch, *Illustrations of the New Philosophy,* ca. 1837–39, MS Am 1506 (4), Houghton Library, Harvard University.

president of Harvard in February 1846, Edward Everett (Harvard College class of 1811) would write in his second *Annual Report* of a marked improvement, in relation to previous years, in "the attendance on the devotional exercises and literary duties of the institution." "The number of unexcused absences was perhaps never less," Everett said, maintaining that this was not simply an outcome of "greater laxity in enforcing the laws" (1846–47 *Annual Report,* 16). Still more encouraging was what the new president detected in the "deportment" of the students in University Hall. In the first of his *Annual Reports,* issued for the academic year 1845–46, Everett had named as one of Harvard's "most pressing wants" the "erection of a chapel exclusively consecrated to the religious exercises of the University." He wrote that "a place of worship . . . appropriated to that object, possessing all the associations congenial with it," would be much preferred to the then current mixed-use facility, which had become a sanctuary for "various practical evils and inconveniencies . . . eminently unfavorable to the attainment of the great object for which a chapel is required" (1845–46 *Annual Report,* 14–15). Everett would retire in frustration from the presidency in 1848, some ten years before the completion of Harvard's new Appleton Chapel. But this did not prevent him from reframing, before he stepped aside, the accepted picture of the religious life at Harvard at midcentury. In remarks that rival the *positive,* "optative" portion of Emerson's portrayal of the early transcendentalists, Everett did his best to depict an undergraduate body of "decorous" attenders, if not sincere believers:

> The President would especially record his satisfaction at a marked improvement, in reference to the attendance and deportment of the Students in the chapel and morning and evening prayers. Without adverting to the higher considerations which belong to this subject, he would observe that, in respect to the quiet and order of the seminary, he believes the first object to be attained is a regular and decorous attendance of the whole body of the Students at the daily devotions of the academic family. Where this exists, the institution will almost invariably be found to prosper in every other department; while great and habitual deficiency here will be felt throughout the whole system. Much of his attention has accordingly been given to this object; and, notwithstanding some serious obstacles and some discouragements, he is happy to say on the whole with gratifying success. But there is much room for farther improvement. (1846–47 *Annual Report,* 20)

However high were his standards for religious observance at the college, Everett reiterated in his *Annual Report* the following year his conviction that a strict enforcement of institutional rules and regulations was insufficient for achieving "the softened temper and gentle spirit which nothing but a religious principle can create" (1847–48 *Annual Report,* 19). A better check on what he described as "youthful levity and thoughtlessness" would be a concerted effort to "make the chapel services interesting and duly affecting." To this end, Everett made a number of recommendations. First, "the aspect and arrangements of the chapel should invite to meditation," he said. Second, he urged that "the organ and a solemn chant of a select portion of the psalms . . . should be united with the reading of the Scriptures and the offering of prayer." "A service of this description," Everett continued, "conducted by a chaplain of the University, whose exclusive duty it should be to promote the spiritual culture of its members, would, by the blessing of Providence, do more to increase its usefulness merely as a place of education, than an indefinite multiplication of means and appliances merely secular" (1847–48 *Annual Report,* 20). Perhaps reflecting Everett's lessened emphasis on religious discipline, the *Annual Reports* for 1848–49 and 1849–50 removed the usual section called "Omissions and Punishments," wherein students' yearly lapses in behavior were tallied. After almost a quarter century of endorsing a disciplinary system based on correction, the highest level of administration at the college was now advocating for a different index of religion altogether.

It was not until 1855 that a more decisive move away from religious forms ensued. In the end, the changes that Everett called for ultimately pertained to the adornments of worship at Harvard. His recommendations concerning devotional music and psalmistry, especially, represented something of a reversion back to the trappings of conventional worship, not least as they compared to Emerson's earlier "refusal," as Robert Richardson writes, "to put form first" (291). Some six years before the start of the U.S. Civil War, however, Harvard started down a religious path that, in retrospect, feels far more "revelatory" in its foremost considerations than anyone familiar with the school's long affiliation with a rational natural religion would have predicted. In establishing an endowed position in support of what the overseers named a "Preacher to the University and Plummer Professor of Christian Morals," Harvard's administrators indicated a shift in their priorities toward the religious "affections" of students. Hence their full announcement for a "Professor of the Philosophy of the Heart and of the Moral, Physical and Christian Life in Harvard University." Said professor would be solely responsible for leading daily devotions in the college chapel, as well as presiding over Sabbath worship. This would mark the discontinuance of an established practice whereby the various faculty of the Divinity School shared these duties between them. The Plummer Professor would furthermore, in the words of the Overseers' report, not only provide "moral and religious instruction to the undergraduates" but also "promote among them an earnest Christian faith and life" by exerting "a more direct religious influence in the College." To do this, the report continues, Harvard's new "Professor of the Philosophy of the Heart" would not work solely "through the medium of recitations and lectures, by which the intellect only should be sharpened and disciplined for religious speculation and theological controversy." Rather, he would employ "such exercises and appeals as should reach the heart and the life, promoting generous affections, manly virtues and Christian conduct and character."[50]

From this retrospective vantage, the debates in Cambridge surrounding transcendentalism in the 1830s might have seemed more the stuff of myth than retrievable memory. Yet the overseers of the college made it clear that they had not forgotten the religious controversies of the last several decades. In the final analysis, their forecast for Harvard's religious future bore an inverted resemblance to Harvard's recent embattled past. What they were calling for was "Christianity, and not sectarianism; pure and undefiled religion, and not dogmatic theology; the faith of the gospel of Christ, and the virtues which are its legitimate fruits, and not scientific creeds or human ceremonials" (1855 *Report on the Rules*, 9–10). These demands were understandable, given the bitterness of religious divisiveness that had come before. And, at a time when students' compliance with official creeds was unquestionably on the decline, and when the share of the recipients of the Harvard A.B. degree who elected to pursue special ministerial-theological study had reached its lowest point of the century, the desire for a "pure and undefiled religion" that could help offset a rise in undergraduate apathy would have represented for many within the community an admirable, even attainable, goal.[51] Those of a more *negative* mind-set might have begged to differ.

AN INCREASE IN INFIDELITY

"Infidelity!" intoned the Unitarian minister Hasbrouck Davis in a sermon to the Independent Church at Waltham, Massachusetts, in September 1853. "How rife it has become lately among us!" Like many of his religious brethren, Davis was alarmed as much by the extent as he was by what he called the "subterfuge" of unbelief in his day. Not only was it "much easier," he mused, "to call men Infidels, and denounce them as such, than it is to show their mistake and unchristianness of their doctrine." It was also the case, for Davis, that the type of the modern infidel could be "denounced" only if he was first exposed. This required some effort. As Davis explained, citing as the source for his remarks a recent article in the *New York Independent* newspaper, the "skepticism" of the age "is not a peculiarity alone of the radicals and fanatics: many of them [the infidels] are men of calm and even mind, and belong to no class of ultraists." Indeed, Davis was willing to admit that the accepted constructions of belief were probably negotiable, if the curious instances of religious "doubt" that he'd met with were any kind of benchmark. "There is a certain kind of 'Infidelity' which a man may be proud of," he says, "when it is a relaxation of old creeds for a more thorough and extensive search after truth." In short, even with "infidelity" all around him, Davis was preoccupied less by its apparent pervasiveness than the strangeness of the different aspects it wore in public.[52]

That was not a distinction—between the size and shape of unbelief—that many of the self-appointed monitors of religion in New England were especially sensitive to at this moment in time. In the predominant discourse of the day, the question of *what* infidelity was had attached to *where* it could be seen spreading. And, in the estimates of many, unbelief was just about everywhere; where it wasn't, it soon would be. This exaggerated sense of infidelity's historical (dis)proportions is crucial to how we apprehend the contemporary reception afforded transcendentalism. Whatever might have been the state of the religious spirit in Cambridge, where the institutional bearings of Harvard's sanctioned Unitarianism factored heavily into the heightened levels of awareness that prevailed there in relation to all manner of religious difference, the broader acculturation of traditional Christians in the region to the idea that "infidels" were already in their midst meant that their response to transcendentalism, when it came, would have been in some respects predetermined. The *negative* reaction that many of them had to what was widely purported (in the press, as well as from the pulpit) to be a *negative* religious display for this reason seems all but inevitable in hindsight. It represents the fulfillment of a critical religious prophecy, made by and on behalf of believers, that was itself based on a culture's fearful overreaction to the creeping reach of unbelief. *Negative* or not, transcendentalism was bound to provoke the adversarial response that it did.

The frequency with which New Englanders confronted infidelity in these decades is therefore less remarkable than we might imagine. In an era of domestic religious revivals, foreign revolutions, and ubiquitous movements for reform, even modest departures from the accepted norms of faith and worship could become magnified by a population that was already watchful against what many would have regarded as an incipient anomie. Hence the rash of reported discoveries of unbelief that occurred in this period. Religious commentators uncovered exactly what they had been prompted by an anxious society to look for: "infidelity," on their very doorsteps. In his journal the autumn succeeding his "Divinity School Address," Emerson would ask, "It is plain from all the noise that there is Atheism somewhere. The only question is now, which is the Atheist?" (*JMN,* 7:112). It was a question that others were asking as well. Before the full flowering of transcendentalism as a cultural phenomenon in the late 1830s, many Americans had already concluded that it was "dreamy, mystical, crazy, and infideleterious to religion," as the Philadelphia writer Charles Godfrey Leland remembered. Leland himself decided that transcendentalism's principal philosophers were "not men tremendous in spiritual truth."[53] His was a restrained response by the standards of that day. If an observer of an equanimous mind, say, the New England author Nathaniel Hawthorne, could describe the character Holgrave from his novel *The House of the Seven Gables* (1851) as the prototypical modern man "in his faith, and in his infidelity," then the mass of antebellum witnesses of the religious scene in the Northeast were by and large more excitable by comparison.[54] At the close of 1834, for example, the editors of the monthly *New-England Magazine* ran a two-part article titled "Atheism in New-England." Its author, the physician and abolitionist Samuel Gridley Howe, asserted that the number of Americans who "fearlessly avowed" atheism had climbed over the previous decade. And while he could reassure readers that "atheism and absurdity are to us synonymous," Howe was also convinced of the "danger" posed by those who "worship the great nothing."[55] These were commonplace views within a context of religious criticism in which a surge in unbelief was taken for granted. In a lecture before Boston's Trinity Church on March 15, 1848, the Episcopal bishop Thomas Clark took to itemizing the discernible "features" of what he called "the popular skepticism of the day." In the bishop's eyes, "modern infidelity" threatened not despite but because it tended "to regard itself . . . rather than God." It is "often intensely fervid," he said, "poetical, and, therefore, to many minds, attractive."[56] The Unitarian minister Nathaniel Hall intuited something no less corrosive in unbelief. "Infidelity," he warned in an ordination sermon at Danvers, Massachusetts in January 1846, touched "the heart" as much as it did the "intellect," and so "it chills the affections; it narrows the sympathies; it checks all generous enthusiasm; it hinders all admiring and reverential homage; it withholds from all noble endeavor."[57] Such was the vigilance stimulated by the general pursuit of the unbeliever that even the "editors and patrons" of the flagship journal of Unitarianism, the *Christian Examiner*, were described by a journalist in Boston in 1834 as being "confounded with infidels, scoffers, and atheists" because of their comparative willingness to wrestle with difficult theological questions.[58] This was the environment into which transcendentalism was introduced to the God-fearing (some of them, at any rate) people of New England.

It is fitting that Harvard's Divinity School should also have treated the matter of unbelief directly. Having been the unlikely site of a contentious religious quarrel that followed in the wake of Emerson's address, the theological school in Cambridge continued, well into the 1840s, to parse the questions that Emerson had raised in his last formal visit there. During this time, at least three students of divinity composed essays for their course work that arose from the writers' attempts to probe infidelity with greater thoroughness. One of these, Amos Smith, wrote to deflate the growing concerns attending unbelief. After defining the "infidel" as one who was "indifferent to all religious truths," he confessed that "genuine skeptics" did not constitute "any considerable class of individuals . . . in our time." Francis Charles Williams not only located but named modern infidels. "Literary men," he called them, as he explained that the unproductive "leisure" the members of this class enjoyed often led them back to "the falseness of their own hearts." From this unstable basis, Williams maintained, unbelievers willfully denied religion's "great principles." Augustus Woodbury, finally, came to the question of infidelity reflexively. For him, "the uncertain and skeptical state of religious opinions at present existing throughout Christendom" inhered in the "false ideas" of doctrines that were "abhorrent to every true and devout emotion of the soul." Given the prevalence of such doctrines, Woodbury said, which are "contrary to reason and common sense," "the wonder is that there is so little infidelity existing." But if infidelity itself, for Woodbury, posed comparatively little threat to the general public, there was a related matter that he recommended we examine more closely. What Woodbury called "disbelief" was at last a question that spoke to the means by which one's beliefs about belief were constituted within a cultural setting where so many people wore their beliefs on their sleeves. From this outlook, to believe or not to believe was no more at stake in the discussion of infidelity than the content (or even the form) of what a person did or didn't believe. What counted was the self-consciousness with which one occupied the ground of either religion or "indifference."[59]

Transcendentalism, too, had been predicated on spiritual self-awareness from the start. As we have seen, the personal journeys of many of the converted led them away from the liberal religious tradition of Unitarianism, which the writer, editor, and reformer Orestes Brownson was only one among many to characterize as "negative, cold, lifeless."[60] Thus, the transcendental search for something vital often began with an inventory of sorts, whereby the would-be communicant took stock of his given religion—for Brownson and other critics of Unitarianism, what they effectively maintained was an empty vessel—before relinquishing it altogether. But as Emerson made clear in the visionary statement that organizes *Nature* (1836), a work that lays plausible claim to being the touchstone text of American transcendentalism, our compulsion for religion is not so calculating (not so "negative," or so reflexive) that it can rest comfortably with what he calls "a too trivial and microscopic study of the universal tablet." Critical self-awareness might have been prized in places like Cambridge. Yet the corrective that Emerson recommends for anyone experiencing a shortage of spirit is to remember the "end" of religion rather than "immerse" himself "in the means" (*CW,* 1:36). Restated, Emerson's transcendentalist was keenly conscious of religious consciousness, but he was also proudly *un*conscious of "the pure and awful form" that religion takes in a world that Emerson says we can best access through "the splendid labyrinth" of our "perceptions" (36–37). However many faults transcendentalism found with Unitarianism, then, it "sees something," Emerson insisted from the beginning, "more important in Christianity than . . . the niceties of criticism" (36). Without question transcendentalism itself fits within a tradition of religious criticism to the extent that Emerson was offering to "interrogate," in his own words, what a religion "by revelation" would look like in a century that had problematized the distinction between too much religion, not enough religion, and no religion at all (7). But as a "form" of religious criticism, transcendentalism was no less a critical religion, with this difference: what its opponents read as a contradiction in terms—transcendentalism's opting *into* religion by opting out of it—was far more than an excuse for suspecting "unbelief" in others. It was the basis on which transcendentalism had earned such authentic spiritual currency in New England.

Emerson recognized as much and placed this seeming paradox at the heart of his "Lectures on the Times" from 1841 to 1842. In the fourth of these eight lectures, "The Transcendentalist," Emerson accounts for the "sincere and religious" propensities of his self-named subject, we'll recall, by endowing him with what appear to be polar impulses (*CW*, 1:208). Emerson's transcendentalist is identified in part by his "Faith," or what the speaker describes as his "Idealism," as well as the deference he pays to his "intuitions" and the "extravagant demand" he makes "on human nature" (206–7, 209). At the same time, Emerson's transcendentalist is prone to "complain" (215). His "heresy" was not only to express his "unconcealed dissatisfaction" with a world that, he was convinced, "must be denied" (208, 210, 215). The transcendentalist also acknowledged that "there must be some wide difference between my faith and other faith," a position on belief that some conservative Christians would have regarded as a logical (and spiritual) impossibility (213). Even the editors of Emerson's *Collected Works* regard "Lectures on the Times" as a statement of the speaker's moving *away* from religion. They read the entire series as marking a "transition . . . from the secular preacher to the professional lecturer, from the enraptured idealist to the benevolent skeptic, from the forensic persuader to the dialectic philosopher" (161). The assumption in this reading is that the critic and the "skeptic" are categories of equivalence, when in fact the *critical* component of transcendentalism is just that: a "dialectic" part of a religious pairing that depends just as much on "positive" thoughts and feelings as it does "negative" ones.

This is the difference (of fine distinction) that Emerson alternately splits and resolves in his "Introductory Lecture" in the series "The Times" from December 2, 1841. He begins his address on a downward note. The "times" are troubled, he says, for "a new disease has fallen on the life of man." And the "torment" that our society finds most distressing, Emerson continues, is "Unbelief," which he goes on to define as "the Uncertainty as to what we ought to do; the distrust of the value of what we do, and the distrust that the Necessity (which we all at last believe in) is fair and beneficent." Up to this point, the speaker sounds like someone very much in the Cambridge mold of religious commentators. He cannot and does not dispute that "Uncertainty," "distrust," and "Unbelief" have arisen among New Englanders in his day. Where Emerson parts ways with the critics of Cambridge and neighboring parishes is in the "value" that he places on criticism itself. "Our religion assumes the negative form of rejection," he states. "Out of love of the true, we repudiate the false: and the Religion is an abolishing criticism" (179). On its surface, these assertions would seem to reinforce the dejected opening of Emerson's lecture. His is an age when religion amounts to "rejection," when the will to "believe" now "assumes" the form of what it is not. But, as Emerson is careful to explain in "The Transcendentalist," the "Idealist" who has conviction enough to obtain his "faith" from his "intuitions" has resources of affirmation at his disposal to complement the "negative" energies of an "abolishing criticism" that has exceeded its own utility. Criticism, skepticism, and faithful idealism don't have to be mutually exclusive in Emerson's "times." In the transcendental religion that he envisioned, they're not.

CHAPTER 2
Henry David Thoreau, Village Atheist

> There is no infidelity as great as that which prays,
> and keeps the Sabbath, and founds churches.
>
> —Henry David Thoreau, January 1, 1842

Religious unbelief in nineteenth-century New England was not just a matter of concern for the students, faculty, and residents of Cambridge, Massachusetts; it also weighed heavily with the people of neighboring Concord, too, where the transcendentalist challenge to liberal Protestantism became as noteworthy a feature of the local spiritual landscape in the 1830s and 1840s as it did at Harvard. Whether Concord was any more representative than Cambridge of the general religious temper of New England in these years is a question that lies beyond the scope of this chapter. Concord was and remains associated in the popular imagination with antebellum transcendentalism, and for this reason alone it warrants the attention it receives here. Concord was the place where Emerson settled in 1835. Concord was the spot where many of the like-minded gathered—often at the household of the master himself—during the course of their personal religious unfolding. And Concord was, accordingly, the setting for what became one of the most conspicuous sites in contemporary New England for an honest evaluation of unbelief in the first half of the nineteenth century. The town of Concord held this distinction less because of anything that the rising celebrity intellectual Emerson might have said or done than for the timely provocations made by Concord's chief resident skeptic, Henry David Thoreau, against the area's religious establishment. What was arguably the distinguishing characteristic of that establishment is that it was less than uniform in its conception and practice of religion, a circumstance that must factor into any assessment we should make today of who did and did not qualify as an "infidel" according to the local understanding of belief.

To designate Thoreau, as the present chapter title does, the "village atheist" of his own hometown of Concord is both more and less than an attention-grabbing gesture. Thoreau was *more* than an atheist in the sense that he wasn't one. Whatever Thoreau did or did not believe, he was hardly without religion, as commentators in recent decades have made clear.[1] Thoreau's religious sensibilities ran deep, not least into the natural surroundings of Concord. At the same time, Thoreau was *less* than an atheist to the extent that his rejection of religious convention demands an altogether different calibration of religiosity than that afforded by our usual standards of measurement in such matters. To take the full measure of Thoreau's belief, we have to do more than merely add up the customary signs of a man's faith. Addition must begin in this instance by subtraction. After all, Thoreau began his transcendental journey toward belief by dispensing with many of the customs that were peculiar to his Protestant nation, his Unitarian region, and his local denomination, Concord's First Parish Church, where, Alan Hodder reminds us of this last location, "he was born, baptized, catechized, and even buried."[2] What Thoreau's religion was can be defined in part by what it was not. And what is was not was readily identifiable by only the most superficial religious norms of Concord in that day. Thoreau might not have been an atheist, unbeliever, or infidel, but for all intents and purposes he just as well could have been, when we consider the immediate context of the socioreligious conditioning by which the members of his community had determined—even as they debated—what counted as a legitimate spiritual form. If Thoreau was equally subject to this conditioning, he was also committed to questioning, on principle, any and all forms, including those fluctuating quantities of religious sentiment, observance, and expression that were unique to the Concord in which he came of age.

Thoreau's life and writings make plain that he did not always exist comfortably inside the religious boundaries that Concord, like Cambridge, had drawn from the colonial period forward, but he was seldom so far removed from convention that his unorthodoxy—perceived or real—positioned him beyond the pale of what was thought spiritually possible within his local religious environment. Among his neighbors, Thoreau was more inclined than most to test the limits of what was permissible with respect to spirit. That is to say, he was prepared to travel where many of his fellow townspeople dared not tread, most notably in public. Yet even one local farmer, contemptuous of Thoreau's decision on graduating from Harvard College in 1837 to transpose the order of his given birth names—"His name's Da-a-vid Henry," this sturdy citizen insisted, "and it ain't never been nothing but Da-a-vid Henry"—had to concede that Henry's (or David's) cherished habit of "standin'" and "lookin'" and "gazin'" the live long day in the vicinity of his beloved Walden Pond carried a religious purpose, "as if he," Thoreau, "was thinkin' about the stars in the heavens."[3] It is indeed the case that some of the friends of the uncompromising author of *A Week on the Concord and Merrimack Rivers* (1849) and *Walden; or, Life in the Woods* (1854) knew him as "that terrible Thoreau," in what Robert Gross describes as "a double-edged tribute to the 'dangerous frankness' of his relations with them."[4] But this is not to say, as the scholar Raymond Adams did midway through the previous century, that Thoreau suffered in his maturity from a stigmatizing process of "village vilification" by the people of Concord.[5] From the strenuous demands he makes (on all of us) to raise our respective expectations for individual accountability to the dogged defense he staged for his personal independence, Thoreau could, without question, rankle those who were close to him. The point is that people did, in fact, draw close to Thoreau, his undeserved reputation as a "hermit" notwithstanding. It was precisely from such proximity that he was able to frustrate those who entered into his familiar circle of experience. Geographically speaking, Thoreau rarely strayed for too long outside the town of Concord. He stood on literal terms at the very center of things, residing for much of his short lifetime in a series of separate domiciles along the busy corridor of Main Street.[6] Sympathetically speaking, Thoreau remained well within the orbit of what most Concordians were prepared to think and feel, especially as relates to the anxieties that continued to attach to religion in the historical interval before the Civil War.

By this reckoning, Thoreau was a model of religious contradiction in a town already mired in spiritual paradox. On the one hand, and as we will see, he adopted forms of worship that, if they struck certain observers as formless, were nevertheless faithfully enough subscribed to by their progenitor to constitute a religion in their own right. To suggest otherwise is to find fault with Thoreau for failing to conform to this or that prescribed religion, rather than to demonstrate his having renounced anything we might broadly construe as "religious." On the other hand, despite the occasional condescension with which they treated Thoreau, most of the critics inside Concord who saw fit to judge what was, in their eyes, his unusual spiritual commitments were no more able to boast of a privileged connection to the town's religious culture—a culture that was far from homogeneous, it bears repeating—than he was. In some cases, they simply protested too much, and so exposed their private spiritual uncertainties while arraigning their neighbor for his supposed eccentricities. In others, they betrayed a perhaps conflicted willingness to follow in Thoreau's religious footsteps, as they strained to allow themselves enough license to entertain alternatives of faith that ostensibly had been proscribed by the regional dictates of orthodoxy. However much Thoreau might have been "without" religion, then, he never wanted for company in Concord. At least a few of Thoreau's neighbors were transcendentalists in name. More than a few of them were what we might call honorary transcendentalists in practice, contributing just as much as he did to the ongoing negotiation in New England between belief and unbelief.

The religious climate of Concord belongs less in the background than it does in the foreground of any discussion that should ensue from that negotiation. We can therefore begin this study of Thoreau's complicated relation to faith with an examination of his town's prolonged period of spiritual discontent, which dates for our purposes to the aftermath of the American Revolution and runs up to and through Thoreau's late adulthood. Although he was never shy about striking up an opposition, Thoreau was also living within a community that had been at odds with itself over religion for several generations. Some of the people who lived right there beside him in Concord could claim a share of the responsibility for sustaining and deepening these rifts. Others were, at best, unwitting participants in helping to perpetuate divisions over religion that traced back longer than anyone would have cared to remember, had they first admitted to even having a religious "problem" that any comparable town in the Commonwealth didn't share. So often a leader in questions of conscience, Thoreau was thus something of a follower when he joined in the religious controversies that were well and truly under way in Concord at the time of his announcing himself a contrarian.

Regarding the content—and form—of unbelief, Thoreau was far more influential in the way that he articulated a religion of contradiction in his writings. In fact, he would go so far as to reveal the underlying spiritual properties of such oppositional positions as had been declared "negative," null, and void because of their too close association with transcendentalism at the moment this complex religious response was earning an increase in local notoriety for being anathema to faith. With his first full-length work, *A Week,* for example, Thoreau proposed a form (both literary and religious) of worship that ran around all of the days of the entire calendar week. The author's "Sunday" chapter, in particular, has received a great deal of attention for the forthright statements its narrator makes *against* conventional religion. What invites further consideration is what does and does not transpire during the rest of *A Week,* spiritually speaking. Most notably, the nonformal, everyday practices of worship that occur outside of "Sunday" appear to constitute the book's main "religious" talking points. It is here that Thoreau discovers a reliable basis for the sacramental in what we could identify as the quotidian aspects of his life. Such a discovery served as a reminder for the rest of Concord (if the town needed reminding) that the prospect of attaining a "heaven" on earth was not the impossibility it might have seemed. We can perform a similarly revisionist religious inquiry by revisiting the inimitable "I" that introduces and orchestrates the narrative of Thoreau's most celebrated work, *Walden*. As much as that book's narrator assumes the qualities of a singular individual, he reverts to a formulaic type over the course of his account. With each passing page, in other words, the "I" of *Walden* takes on the qualities of the classic "village atheist" figure from New England letters. This figure might pretend to march to the beat of a different drummer, but, for the most part, he conforms to a posture—at once rhetorical and religious—that the sometimes silent (and sometimes not) dissenting majority of Concord would have known all too well. In and around Concord, Thoreau was not the only one to believe in the necessity of diverse forms of belief. He was, however, the one self-selected member from among the ranks of the disaffected to be so moved by the beauty of that necessity as to feel called on to offer his townspeople a new revelation, in writing. Such a scripture as *Walden* was the people of Concord had never seen before. Such of the book's religious views as ran counter to convention many of these same original readers would have known by heart, since they had lived, on their own terms, what Thoreau had written.

FAMILIES, FARMERS, AND OTHER INFIDELS

"At the present day, when religious sects and controversies are evidently increasing . . ." That is how the pseudonymous "O" began his front-page letter to the editor of the *Yeoman's Gazette* on Saturday, September 16, 1826. Typically, the columns of this Concord weekly newspaper could be counted on to carry the recurring headline features that were more or less mainstays at most small-town serials in the period. Among other topical categories, these features included hard news ("Domestic Intelligence," "Foreign Intelligence," "Concord"), local miscellanies ("Sheriff's Sales," "Married," "Died," "Public Auction"), literature ("Poetry," usually of a sentimental variety), agriculture ("Feeding Cattle," "Selection of Seed Corn"), and back-page advertisements ("New Goods," "Indian Purgative Oils," "Concord Livery & Stable," "Stoves! Stoves!!"). No less typical in Concord was the column space that was regularly allotted to religion, the substance of which, on this occasion—on most occasions, actually—amounted to a matter of opinion. The writer of the present editorial, who presumably would have been interested enough in his subject to side one way or another as relates to the "controversies" he mentions at the start of his missive, assumed a more noncommittal posture than his occasion for reaching out to a public audience might have suggested. Writing neither to argue nor to amuse, he appears to have taken up his pen with the sole purpose to instruct.[7]

Concord, as "O's" readers were no doubt aware, was in the midst of a religious schism that had led a group of sixteen parishioners from the town's liberal First Parish Church to withdraw and organize their own congregation. A shorthand description of this impasse would relate it as a contest between old-line Trinitarians and modern Unitarians. "O" was demanding more than a shorthand description. He wanted doctrinal niceties explained in detail. "It is not only proper but needful," he wrote, "that the people at large should understand the peculiar tenets of each sect, and the particular subjects of controversy. For want of knowledge in these things, we frequently hear persons contending for sects whose real principles they do not believe, and ranking themselves under a denomination to which they do not in reality belong." Assisting "O" in his effort to inform the "people at large" was the American author Hannah Adams, whose book *A View of Religions* (1791) our editorialist cites by name. Herself a comparative religionist of latitudinarian views, Adams had divided the second edition of the work at hand into three sections: "An Alphabetical Compendium of the Various Sects Which Have Appeared from the Beginning of the Christian Era to the Present Day"; "A Brief Account of Paganism, Mohammedanism, Judaism, and Deism"; and "An Account of the Different Religions of the World." With a "world" of religious dispositions before him, "O" chose to be particular where Adams was expansive. He duly settled into what was, for him, a question of urgent concern, involving the "five points of doctrine" (by Adams's tally) on which "Calvin and Arminius disagreed." The resulting list spelled out in language that churchgoers in Concord would have comprehended what, exactly, it meant to be a "Calvinist"—or a "Trinitarian," as the seceding parishioners of Concord self-identified—or an "Arminian," as Unitarians throughout New England had come to be known for the resistance that they, like the sixteenth-century Dutch theologian Arminius, offered to such strict tenets of Calvinism as predestination and unconditional election. It was, apparently, as important to "O" to untangle theological differences as it was to establish clear lines of doctrinal allegiance. Yet he was ultimately motivated, in his own words, by a desire to offset what was, for him, a disturbing local trend that saw *"persons contending for sects whose real principles they do not believe"* (emphasis added). For all his technical talk about Reformed Protestantism, "O" was most concerned that the people of Concord "believe" what they believe and denominate themselves accordingly.

"O's" editorial is instructive in ways he could not have foreseen. To begin, his remarks give some indication of just how capacious and just how narrow the religious perspectives of New England could be in the second quarter of the nineteenth century. Even before that time, a notable local author, Hannah Adams, had been able to see past the religious horizons of her upbringing in the outskirts of Boston to take heed of a whole globe's worth of spiritual outlooks, many of which were markedly different from her own. The internal disputes of Concord's First Parish probably would have seemed small to her by comparison. What "O" also suggests is that a transcendental religion in New England, which his letter to the *Gazette* anticipates by at least a decade, arrived in the Massachusetts interior at a moment when the paper's readers—the laboring farmers, tradespeople, and families who accounted for much of Concord's population—were already predisposed to worry about "belief." "O," it seems safe to say, was as worried as anyone in Concord about the religious alignment of his town, a fact reflected by the contents of a letter that hews much more closely to Protestant doctrine than to denominational politics. More important, "O's" primary concern, occurring well before transcendentalism's mid-1830s dawn, was to put a stop to the promiscuous mixing of believers and nonbelievers that he felt certain was then happening in his midst. While it is true that the 1826 "controversy" in Concord dealt with the various shades of Christian belief, rather than the prospect that flesh-and-blood infidels had entered into the fold, the preoccupations that "O" makes manifest in this matter lend a clarifying context to the later assertion by the Unitarian theologian Andrews Norton that transcendentalism represented but "the latest form of infidelity." From a New England insider's point of view, transcendentalism really did entail the most recent iteration of a variegated set of vexed religious questions (pertaining to such issues as works, faith, self, society, and the like) that had long since insinuated themselves into the region. Transcendentalism's arrival in Concord was, in this respect, a kind of homecoming.

Also at home in Concord was the family of Henry David Thoreau. The Thoreaus were not immune to their town's history of religious ruptures. Three of the author's aunts joined the breakaway faction that moved to secede from the First Church in 1826. Thoreau's mother would follow them shortly thereafter, albeit with great reservations. Cynthia Thoreau, like her husband, John, leaned liberal in her religion, and so we can only speculate as to why she was momentarily drawn to the Trinitarians, who by 1827 had raised their own meetinghouse and settled a new minister, the Reverend Daniel Southmayd. Robert Gross suggests that it was the relatively tepid faith of the Reverend Ezra Ripley (a graduate of Harvard College, class of 1776), whose spiritual rigor some of the members of the First Parish where he presided must have felt was diminishing over time.[8] Ripley, for example, had so loosened the requirements for admission to his church that aspirants were no longer asked to testify to having experienced God's saving grace; nor were they expected to make a public confession of their sins. Under Ripley's watch, a simple profession of Christian faith, combined with a stated resolve to lead a moral life, would suffice for inclusion in a church that Concord's Unitarian pastor hoped could accommodate each and every inhabitant in town. One of that town's early historians, John Shepard Keyes, praised Ripley for his mollifying position, which in Keyes's view had gone a long way toward preventing the rancor that otherwise might have attended the breaking up of the local single parish system.[9] Yet not even Ripley would be able to mend all of Concord's fences. As Gross again relates, rather than "producing a peaceful community of saints," the new Trinitarian congregation had "bred constant conflict," as the secessionists took to finding frequent fault with the Reverend Southmayd. One of their number, Joseph C. Green, was aggrieved enough to launch an attack on the church and its minister in the pages of a Boston religious periodical. He was tried and formally excommunicated for his pains—a believer to the bitter end, one surmises, albeit no longer a Trinitarian of good standing in Concord. Cynthia Thoreau's religious fate was far less dramatic by comparison. At the dining room table of the boardinghouse she operated with her family in Concord, she apparently held such frank conversations with her sometime pastor, the Reverend Southmayd—he and his wife boarded with the Thoreaus for a short term after their arrival from Vermont—that she could strengthen her spiritual resolve without any additional deliberation in the Calvinist wilderness. Back to the Unitarian First Parish she returned in short order, sparing herself the further continuance along the "diverging paths" that had resulted from Concord's denominational split.[10]

But the religious questions that divided Concord at large were not so easily laid to rest. Five years earlier, the writer for another local weekly had posed this query at the outset of his regular column, "Moral and Religious," "Which of the ten commandments does a man break, by following his own convictions in religion?"[11] His question proved rhetorical, while still providing a gloss on the degree to which spiritual probing was all but inescapable in Concord. Nearly when- and wherever a person turned, there were religious "controversies" to be resolved. Amid the conflict between Unitarians and Trinitarians, for instance, the *Yeoman's Gazette* adhered to editorial protocols that could only have increased local frictions, the disinterest of the estimable "O" notwithstanding. Just one week after "O's" letter appeared, the paper ran an illustrative parable on the argument from design, under the exacerbating title "The Atheist and the Artificial Globe." The following month it ceded much of its front-page space to a well-timed advertisement for tracts published by the American Unitarian Association. Among the offerings for sale were such titles as *One Hundred Scriptural Arguments for the Unitarian Faith, Unitarian's Answer,* and the triumphant *Causes of the Progress of Liberal Christianity.* Come December 2, 1826, the *Yeoman's Gazette* would be announcing the dedication of "the new Meeting-house lately erected in this town," a quiet acknowledgment of the Trinitarians' decision to establish a church of their own. Just one week later, the *Gazette* returned to its querulous ways with a couple of short articles such as "Young Children at Church" (unwelcome, the writer is sure) and "Miseries at Church" (all of which are attributable to "being annoyed" by one's neighbors). This back-and-forth pattern of appeasement followed by incitement would become a hallmark of the religious life in Concord prior to transcendentalism's emergence on the scene in a few years' time. In the interim, the *Gazette* continued its unholy pairing of disparate newspaper articles. Rounding out the year, readers met with the innocuous "Religion a Solace to the Afflicted," only to encounter in the days before and after Christmas two bold-faced "Anecdotes" (the first on the "shameful" negligence of "the *Lord's* day," the second on what the author names "real religion") by one "Rev. Dr. Lathrop." It was the uncommon resident of Concord who could have found peace in such a community (spiritual, as much as discursive) as that which the *Gazette* had figured in newsprint.[12]

The next decades brought little change in this regard. Religion in Concord over the course of the 1830s and 1840s—the time of transcendentalism's regional ascendance—remained unstable ground, even for someone as rooted (in his person, and in his place) as Henry David Thoreau. As we might predict, the local press continued to reflect Concord's erratic religious fixations, although the *Yeoman's Gazette* was not the only paper in town. Complementing the *Gazette*'s conflicted coverage of the sacred and profane—the paper managed to squeeze within the same page 11 column in late January 1829, a devotional "Hymn" by the Unitarian minister (and future Harvard president) Edward Everett and a fantastic tale of the undead, "The Vampyre," by the English romantic writer Lord Byron—other area weeklies likewise registered the state of spiritual uncertainty in Concord. A paper like the *Concord Freeman*, for example, which one scholar describes as "a hodgepodge of sophistication and provinciality," apparently saw nothing out of sorts in alternating, during the latter half of 1837, between posting journalistic tributes such as "Ministers in Old Times" and offering "A Hint to the Opponents of Materialism and Infidelity." Another local paper, the *Republican*, operated within this same conflicted tradition. It proceeded to publish the poem "Elijah's Interview with God" ("On Horeb's rock the Prophet stood; / The Lord before him past.") on January 15, 1841, after having already saluted subscribers at the New Year with this reprint, "From the *Dial*. Religion." As the effective Whig paper in town, the *Republican* combined national political and local news (including reports on the Massachusetts legislature and agricultural notices) with fiction, poetry, and, of course, religion. This four-page tabloid's masthead indicated that the paper was headquartered in the "Office Over Eaton's Furniture Room, On the Mill Dam," but such a quaint disclosure should not belie that the paper was au courant with the latest trends in religious thought. The *Dial* from which the *Republican* had drawn its "Religion" article just so happened to be the official periodical organ of the transcendentalists. And the unattributed author from whom, in this instance, the *Republican* had borrowed its content was Theodore Parker. As it turns out, what the *Republican* called "Religion" was, in fact, an excerpt from a sermon that the reform-minded Unitarian minister and leading transcendentalist Parker had composed in June 1840. Parker delivered his sermon, "A Lesson for the Day; or, The Christianity of Christ, of the Church, and of Society," on some six occasions in the Boston area over the course of the ensuing months, before placing a revised and expanded version of the same in the October 1840 issue of the *Dial*. Whether the editors of the *Republican* were aware (or better yet cared) of "Religion's" provenance is unclear. What we do know is that the passages from "A Lesson for the Day"—as the *Dial* version of Parker's sermon was titled—to be distributed from the "Office Over Eaton's Furniture Room" contained a message for Concord that surely would have proved stirring. In Parker's view, the institutional formations of the church had ceased to meet the spiritual needs of the people. Church practices were no longer relevant to culture, or what we might call the practice of everyday life. Parker stated his case as follows, in lines meant to arrest the attention of anyone who was ready to receive them:

> The mass of men care little for Christianity; were it not so, the sins of the forum and the market-place, committed in a single month, would make the land rock to its centre. Men think of religion at church, on the Sabbath; they make sacrifices, often great sacrifices, to support public worship, and attend it most sedulously, these men and women. But here the matter ends. Religion does not come into their soul; does not show itself in housekeeping and trading. It does not shine out of the windows of morning and evening, and speak to them at every turn. . . . If good for anything, it [religion] is good to live by. It is a small thing to die religiously; a devil could do that; but to live divine is man's work. ("From the Dial. Religion.")

Two weeks later, the *Republican* would insert into its columns a brief reminder for an upcoming Monday-evening meeting of the Young Men's Association, where participants were to discuss the question, "Is the doctrine of a final judgment taught in the Bible?" In the aftermath of what Parker had written, such abstracted inquiries might have seemed still more jarring than even the religious oscillations to which the people of Concord had grown accustomed.[13]

Meanwhile, there was "hard" news to report as well. If the public discussion of religion in Concord was ongoing, so, too, did social developments at the grassroots keep pace with what was being reported in the press and delivered from the pulpit. One of the lessons to be learned from antebellum Concord is that "religion" was inclusive of all of these developments. As Theodore Parker had written, it was well and fine that "Men" should "think of religion at church, on the Sabbath." But, he continued, unless religion could "show itself in housekeeping and trading," in the unfancied turnover of people's everyday lives, then the religious spirit could not be said to have sunk into the "soul" of New England. Local infighting among the likes of Unitarians, Trinitarians, and "Nothingarians"—this last being one of the latest options available to a citizenry freed, in 1833, from the state of Massachusetts's Standing Order for a single established religion—was one thing.[14] Putting religion into *practice* was another.

Much of Concord exerted itself to justify the truism that Parker had codified when he wrote that religion "is good to live by." To each his own, however, was increasingly the rule by which the complex basis for being that's implied by any given religious life found expression. Cynthia Thoreau recognized as much when she wavered back and forth between Concord's Protestant dividing lines, which, since disestablishment, had come to encompass Methodist and Universalist camps as well. But there were, to Parker's point, more tangible signs of religion to account for in Concord. The first U.S. society dedicated to improving Sabbath observance was formed in 1814 in Middlesex County, Massachusetts, the administrative seat of which was Concord. All of which might sound like an additional instance of religion as an abstraction, until we consider the practical ramifications that attached to Sabbatarianism. With the U.S. Congress having sanctioned the Sunday transportation of mail in 1810, the Sabbatarian movement became a leading example of what one historian describes as "the federal government's intervention in the everyday life of ordinary Americans."[15] Suffice it to say that religion in Concord was not all disharmony. The ever-evolving temper of the town ensured there were happier spiritual strains, as when the Concord Harmonic Society formed in or about 1800 with the aim of improving the quality and availability of sacred music. A Juvenile Library was organized in 1827, too, as a resource for the Sabbath schools associated with Concord's Christian denominations. Added to this were the assortment of auxiliary societies—Missionary, Tract, and Temperance, to name just a few—that graced much of New England and the greater United States in this period. To the extent that institutional life was supportive of religious life, Concord's Lyceum (founded in 1828) and Debating Society (founded earlier, in 1822, only to merge with the Lyceum at a later date) are also deserving of mention. If nothing else, the local Lyceum kept the religious pot stirred, as the

Wednesday-evening lecture series that composed this civic institution during the cold winter months enlisted speakers and topics that had a direct bearing on spiritual questions in which townspeople maintained a keen interest.[16]

Not all of Concord's religious life was institutional; nor was everyone so interested in the religion on offer at a Lyceum, which, despite being a forum for the open interrogation of ideas, was perhaps a less than ideal venue for anyone who, inside a moderately sized community, would be so bold as to pose a serious challenge to religious convention. Robert Fuller does well to remind us that "it is not sufficient for beliefs or practices to function like a religion for us to consider them spiritual." In Fuller's view, derived from the American psychologist William James, spirituality consists of "attitudes, ideas, lifestyles, and specific practices based upon a conviction (1) that the visible world is part of a more spiritual universe from which it draws its chief significance, and (2) that union or harmonious relation with this 'spiritual more' is our true end."[17] According to these terms, Concord beyond the Lyceum, the Sabbath, and the Protestant church house and its attendant societies abounded with the "spiritual eclecticism" that Fuller says has characterized Americans' "churched and unchurched religiosity . . . since the nation's beginnings."[18] Concord's first official historian, Lemuel Shattuck, records 383 people as having been admitted to the First Parish in full communion under the watch of the Reverend Ripley. A total of 449 "owned the covenant," as was said of nonmembers who made a statement of faith; a healthy 1,541 were baptized, one of them being Henry David Thoreau.[19] Yet the town's spiritual life was not limited to such orthodox locations and occasions as these. There was a *kind* of religion in the syncretic rites of Freemasonry, for example, the prevalence of which fraternity in Concord led one professing Unitarian from nearby Framingham to lodge a complaint, by letter, with the editor of the *Yeoman's Gazette* that decried the Masonic "institution" as "*Deistical,* because it is so—and because it is in direct opposition to Unitarianism, which, according to my impression, is true Christianity." There was, moreover, an earthy, lyrical religion in a poem by William B. Gallagher, "Harvest Hymn," which the *Concord Freeman* published on Friday, November 20, 1840. One also suspects that Barney Dolan, an Irish boy from the neighboring mill town of Lowell, was up to something religious—maybe "*ir*religious" is the apt word, since, by the generous terms afforded by Fuller's "eclecticism," religion and irreligion could more or less amount to the same thing—when he was arrested for "disturbing" public worship at his local Baptist church. Even the Sabbath breakers and so-called blasphemers of Middlesex County held some claim to being religious in their way. Neither offender was as common in these parts by the 1830s and 1840s as he once had been in the previous century, but the *practices* in which each engaged were "spiritual" in the sense of implicating him in formal religious communities from which, by virtue of the opposition he'd offered to the establishment, signaled that he would prefer to be excluded. Exclusion within this context might count as inclusion by association, so that Concord would appear to have offered something (or nothing, according to one's tastes) religious for everyone.[20]

These lapses in traditional religious observance are worth highlighting, for they speak to the range of demonstrations in behavior by which townspeople contributed to the formation of a variety of cultures of faith in Concord. For many of these cultures, the barriers of entry were lower than they had been in years past. For others, the hypothetical penalties for inclusion and exclusion alike either no longer signified or had largely diminished. The case of Sabbath breaking is instructive in this regard.[21] Rather than adopt their own legal classification scheme for the adjudication of crime, the peoples of Massachusetts during the revolutionary era emulated the legal code of the influential English jurist William Blackstone. Among the categories of crimes that Blackstone recognized were offenses against government, offenses against public justice, offenses against public trade and health, homicide, offenses against the person, offenses against habitations and other private property, and offenses against God and religion. In the years between 1760 and 1774, most of the recorded crimes in Middlesex County in the Superior and General Sessions Courts occurred within this last category, offenses against God and religion. Of the 370 total prosecutions in this period, 210 were for fornication, a crime that was legally deemed offensive not because it often saddled towns with having to provide support for illegitimate children, but because it was viewed as contrary to God's will. More important for our purposes are the 27 prosecutions from these same years for violations of the Sabbath. Such violations in Middlesex County continued at a rate of about 2 per year until the mid-1780s, after which time these "crimes" saw a sharp drop-off in Concord. As a related publication appearing in 1816 stated, "For many years previous to 1814, the Laws of the State against profanations of the Sabbath, had fallen into general neglect. . . . Thousands of violations occurred every year, with scarcely a single instance of punishment.'" William E. Nelson attributes this change to what he posits was "a general relaxation of social customs" that would have had obvious consequences for Concord.[22]

Whether "relaxation" was also a religion is a question perhaps better addressed by the area's alleged blasphemers. To this day, section 36 of the legal code for the General Court of the Commonwealth of Massachusetts defines blasphemy (in circular terms) as resulting when someone "wilfully [sic] blasphemes the holy name of God by denying, cursing or contumeliously reproaching God, his creation, government or final judging of the world, or by cursing or contumeliously reproaching Jesus Christ or the Holy Ghost, or by cursing or contumeliously reproaching or exposing to contempt and ridicule, the holy word of God contained in the holy scriptures."[23] The landmark Boston trial (and retrials) of the American evangelist and theologian Abner Kneeland in the 1830s would have been a benchmark in these matters at that time across New England. The paper of public record in Concord, the *Yeoman's Gazette*, dedicated multiple columns of coverage over the years to ensure that locals were kept informed of the fate of the last man in the United States to be imprisoned on charges of blasphemy, the result of Kneeland's publishing, on December 20, 1833, "an obscene and blasphemous libel" in the freethinking periodical that he edited, the *Boston Investigator*. The anonymous writer of the *Gazette*'s first report on the Kneeland trial identified the defendant by his association with the "infidel publication" that he headed, perhaps a suggestion of where the "yeomen" of Concord stood in relation to these matters. But mostly the *Gazette* refrained from providing commentary in its coverage of Kneeland, a decision that might have been indicative of the array of positions its readers held on the notorious "blasphemer." The seeming paradox of a republic that protected the religious liberties of its citizens while prosecuting them for blasphemy was not lost on contemporaries, especially in a state that had abandoned the practice of administering tests of faith to public officeholders as early as 1821. Yet when we consider that Samuel Parker, the state prosecutor who brought Kneeland to trial in 1834, referred during court proceedings to other apparently recent trials for blasphemy in Massachusetts in Bristol and Middlesex Counties, we should probably hesitate before we conclude that the blasphemy law was a "dead letter" and "obsolete," as Kneeland had claimed. In the final analysis, the arena that counts most for observing the active religious practices of Concord is neither the judicial court system nor even the court of public opinion. What counts is the arena of culture, where all practices, including religion, recommend themselves to our attention to the extent that they are performed, repeated, contested, and somehow still believed in by the actors for whom they serve as a repository of meaning.[24]

No place was ever more meaningful for Henry David Thoreau than Concord. It inspired a body of writing that intersected with the author's religion, and understandably so, in light of the fact that Thoreau's firsthand attachment to the day-to-day experiences of Concord was at once physical, emotional, spiritual, and artistic. With a population of 2,249 by the year 1850, the town remained small enough for Thoreau to become steeped in its ecology and known to its inhabitants, yet bustling enough to begin to wear the impersonal face of a thriving modern center of trade, commerce, and light industry only nineteen miles west of New England's metropolis, Boston. Concord might have preceded Thoreau historically; the town had been incorporated all the way back in 1635 by a group of English settlers who set great store by this inland area of low-lying marshes. But the two of them—Thoreau the person and Concord the place—grew up together, as the years of Thoreau's maturation coincided with Concord's transformation into a regional hub for business, county government, and the Middlesex judiciary. Robert Gross remarks that "relentless changes" had "reshaped the contours of everyday life" in Concord at the halfway stage of the nineteenth century. This is accurate inasmuch as the "fluid" town of long-term residents and itinerants that enfolded Thoreau as he initiated his literary calling represented a volatile combination of "dazzling opportunities" and "disturbing uncertainties." Less convincing is Gross's related claim that Thoreau met with such exigencies of modernity as Concord had offered him with a life "rich only in renunciations."[25] For many of the families, farmers, and proud freeholders of Concord, the natural reaction to the disruptions that were impacting their town may well have been encapsulated by the title of a popular song reprinted in the *Yeoman's Gazette* on July 14, 1838, the day before Emerson was to deliver his "Divinity School Address" at the Theological School in Cambridge. "Oh! Steal Not Thou My Faith Away" was a plea made as much for the preservation of religion as it was an admission of the seductive appeal of the secular.[26] Thoreau's religion was also to consist of equal parts affirmation and "renunciation." It is a point best made in this critic's own words, from his late essay "Walking" (1862). "I believe in the forest," Thoreau writes, "and in the meadow, and in the night in which the corn grows" (figure 3).[27]

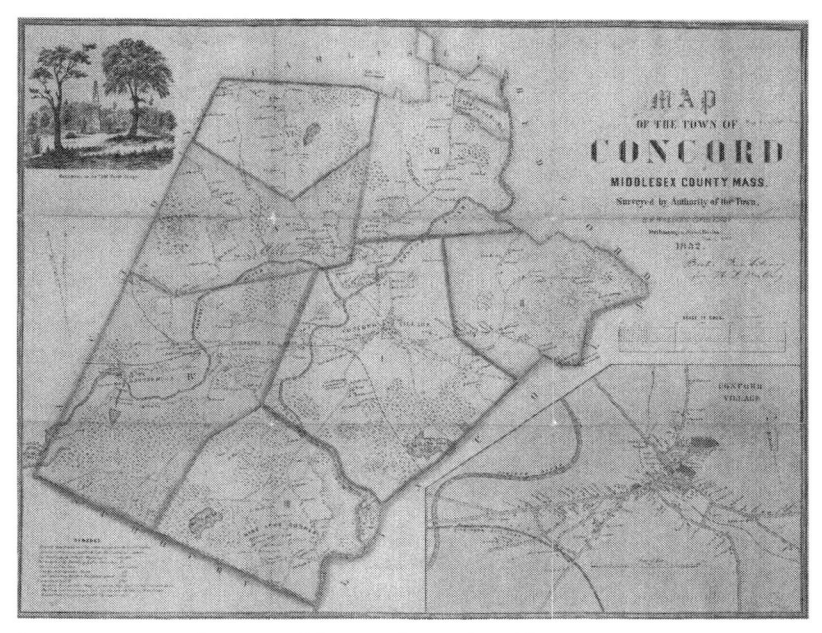

Figure 3. Henry F. Walling, *Map of the Town of Concord, Middlesex County, Mass.* (Boston: H. F. Walling, 1852). Courtesy Concord Free Public Library. Photograph by Kimberly Buchheit.

UNBELIEF IN *A WEEK*

For all his belief, Thoreau began the decade of the 1840s holding firm in the skepticism that was innate with him.[28] This same disposition informed his religion. Wary of conventional churches and creeds, resistant to any form of inherited religious expression that did not emanate from the sanctifying grace of experience, Thoreau was a man very much of his moment, in a town where the collective accord over affairs pertaining to spirit was more apparent than real. Ever the skeptic, Thoreau was also, as his most recent biographer relates, a "spiritual seeker" who resolved at "seeking for the true fountainhead of spiritual truth."[29] He encouraged the rest of us in this effort as well. The urgent tone of so much of the author's writings, which can often be critical and coaxing by turns, suggests that Thoreau regarded his individual pursuit of a transformative encounter with spirit as exemplary in principle, if not a pattern book of religious practice for others to adhere to by the letter.

Concord, at any rate, was no more inclined to follow Thoreau's lead in the practical pursuits of religion than he was prepared to enlist in any one of the orthodox theologies that obtained in his age. "Thoreau cultivates critical readers, not disciples," Joshua Kotin writes, in describing the equivocal patterns of response that Thoreau's audience undergoes when we align ourselves with an author who would have each of us pursue his own course of self-development.[30] Thoreau need not have pressed his point about personal independence as much as he did. Any outward signs of conformity notwithstanding, Concord was already independent when it came to determining its religious practices, and residents were fully capable of finding their way into and out of whichever religious forms proved most fulfilling for them. By the time he published *Walden* in 1854, Thoreau was comfortable enough in casting himself in the role of a religious renegade to take evident satisfaction in playing the spiritual outsider. Meanwhile, in his earlier work, *A Week on the Concord and Merrimack Rivers*, Thoreau strains at being the village "infidel." Or, so he assumes he must do, on the mistaken ground that the critical religious practice he's inherited (an irony of dependency unacknowledged by the radical individualist author) from the region's senior transcendentalists has somehow set him in diametric opposition to his townspeople, a number of whom were as prepared as he was to flout religious convention. Thoreau's aunt Maria held deep misgivings about the contents of her nephew's maiden attempt at book-length publication, writing by letter that parts of *A Week* read "very much like blasphemy."[31] Thoreau's mother and sister Helen concurred in this assessment, as did early reviewers who, like James Russell Lowell, resisted the author's decision—inside a narrative ostensibly recounting an excursion by canoe through two local waterways—to speak freely of the New Testament in the same breath that he extolled the virtues of various world religions. "We were bid to a river-party, not to be preached at," Lowell complained in the anonymous treatment of the book that he submitted to Theodore Parker's *Massachusetts Quarterly Review*. The *New-York Tribune* newspaper editor Horace Greeley nurtured more serious grievances. After announcing Thoreau's "Transcendental" philosophy "a bad specimen of a dubious and dangerous school," he decided that the author's "smartest Pantheistic sentences" and "opinions" of "the Christian Bible" were "calculated to shock and pain many readers, not to speak of those who will be utterly repelled by them."[32] Today, Laura Dassow Walls can say of Thoreau's writing on religion in *A Week* that it is "revolting, a revolt."[33] And, indeed, some of the author's religious commentary in this text does read as rather confrontational at times, as it was no doubt intended to be. Yet in the context of Concord's general spiritual temper in these years, Thoreau was no more a religious revolutionary for the Unitarian establishment to single out for special disfavor than he was an unquestioning observer of the conventional forms of worship that some of his contemporaries had similarly chosen to ignore.

A Week is neither a seasoned personal statement of faith by its creator nor the wholesale critique of "village detractors" whom Robert Milder posits as the instigators behind a book that reads, for him, as the testy response of an author who would set the propensities (religious or otherwise) of Concord straight through an exercise in narration by negation.[34] By the time of his final year at what was then a rather parochial, rough-hewn Harvard, Thoreau had withstood enough of the tired curriculum, regimented classroom methods, and monitory watchfulness of his instructors to perhaps be forgiven if he had blamed the college for stunting his personal growth. He graduated, instead, with modest distinction from a class of some forty-seven seniors, most of them locals, ready to commit to a spiritual "end of life," which Thoreau defined in Emersonian terms in a late undergraduate essay as "the bringing out, or developement [sic], of that which is in man, by contact with the Not Me."[35] Not even the "long gestation" of the 1840s that Daniel Peck says marked the "mourning work" of *A Week*'s drafting was sufficient to bring Thoreau's spiritual "developement" to its completion, however.[36] There is ample reason the New Critics should have discovered a questing metaphor in Thoreau's oeuvre, made manifest by the author's favored contrast between the sacred and the profane.[37] The "spiritual seeker" was still coming into his religion by the time he began to write *A Week* in earnest during his two-year stay at Walden Pond halfway through this decade. Thus, whatever animus Thoreau might have directed against his neighbors for their apparent spiritual narrowness would have been complemented by the honest self-appraisals of a writer who, toward the end of his life, continued to remark that "the very fishes feel the influence (or want of *influence*) of man's religion."[38] Not only does the narrator of *A Week*, who is a close storytelling stand-in for the author, occupy a provisional religious position from which it would be difficult to mount an all-out challenge against his neighbors' supposed spiritual deficiencies. He is far more sympathetic with the popular religious folkways of Concord than has been suggested. In fact, the much-remarked-upon digressions of Thoreau's narrative method are a formal correlative for the religious waywardness that the narrator himself encounters in the persons of *A Week*'s general population of river dwellers.

Robert Thorson states that the Concord River watershed was "the largest, wildest, and most beautiful thing in his [Thoreau's] daily life."[39] And, we should add, the various characters who lined the Merrimack and tributary Concord Rivers—religious "seekers" all of them, on terms sometimes as idiosyncratic as those of the author—provide the colorful cultural *drift* of a text that is content to circumnavigate the diversity of religious practices with which the narrator and his unnamed companion come into contact as they trace (and retrace) their two-way route between Concord, Massachusetts, and their turnaround destination of Concord, New Hampshire. The religious work of *A Week* is as comparative as it is critical. But the basis of Thoreau's comparisons do not reside exclusively or even primarily in the so-called Orient to which his narrator devotes so much of his attention. *A Week* is a comparative work of religion, written by an artist who found a great deal to admire and even emulate in the assorted unorthodoxies that he discovered close to his own home. Thoreau did not compose *A Week* in open rebellion against the religiously divided village of Concord, Massachusetts. He wrote this work in a more accepting spirit of *communion,* attuned to the exigencies of the self's spiritual elaboration amid the captivating strangeness of a society of religious "drifters" not unlike him.

The designated speaker of *A Week*'s opening pages must grow into the more favorable view of Concord's loose religious practices that he comes to hold as his journey develops. He begins his book much like he launches the craft that will carry Thoreau and his brother, John, on their waterborne adventure (a two-week trip in fact, compressed into one for the sake of narration) north to the base of the White Mountains in the late summer of 1839. *A Week* writ large might be a commemorative volume written on behalf of the author's late brother, who died from a tetanus infection in 1842. Yet the early chapters from the work in question—named consecutively after the days of the calendar week, beginning with "Saturday"—are marked by a decided sense of separation, instead of the amity, generosity, and shared conception of community that characterize the narrative as the journey it rehearses lengthens. Readers watch the brothers setting forth from Concord, in the narrator's own words, "floating through the last of these familiar meadows" (21). *A Week* at this moment is suffused with an air of recognition as much as remembrance, as the town that is being left behind still feels close at hand both emotionally and physically. This feeling is short-lived. Soon we see the travelers "gliding out of sight of the village spire," a moment the narrator punctuates with a backward glance that reads as a sigh of relief. "After a pause at Ball's Hill," he states, "the St. Ann's of Concord voyageurs, not to say any prayer for the success of our voyage, but to gather the few berries which were still left on the hills, hanging by very slender threads, we weighed anchor again, and were soon out of sight of our native village" (21–22). Not only does the narrator dispense with the expected fond farewell to his birthplace; he delivers what we can only receive as a parting shot at the metonymic edifice of religion in Concord, the "village spire" that the narrator seems only too happy to have fade from view. Such is the start of *A Week*.

There are nevertheless peoples and practices that exert a strong-enough pull on our narrator to cause him to recast the religions of Concord in a more favorable light. Among the first of the fellow spiritual travelers to soften his critical attitudes toward the town is the "old brown-coated man" from Newcastle, England, who appears in one of the earliest recollections to feature in the book's Concord River passages (24). Thoreau names this personage "the Walton of this stream" (24). The reference is to Izaak Walton, the seventeenth-century English biographer, observant Anglican, and author of *The Compleat Angler* (1653), a pastoral evocation of the joys of fishing that had seen multiple reprintings by Thoreau's day. Whatever the allusive force of this gesture to historical times and faraway places, its power for our purposes derives from how it situates readers in the narrator's here and now. The speaker may remain subject to the lures of retrospection, as he recalls this immigrant arrival from across the Atlantic as "a straight old man . . . who took his way in silence through the meadows, having passed the period of communication with his fellows." But there is no stopping the encroachment of the participial past unto a present occupied by the narrator. Our Englishman might as well be here before us, when we read of "his old experienced coat, hanging long and straight and brown as the yellow-pine bark, glittering with so much smothered sunlight." Most present is this man's religion. Thoreau has the narrator describe a habitual religious practice set "amid the pads and the gray willows" where his Tynesider partakes of a favorite pastime, "fishing in some old country method." The work of remembrance that's performed here transpires much as the fisherman takes to his preferred sport, as a kind of natural resurrection. An entire lifetime's worth of devotion is replayed for us in plein air, as follows:

> I have seen how his coeval fates rewarded him with the yellow perch, and yet I thought his luck was not in proportion to his years; and I have seen when, with slow steps and weighed down with aged thoughts, he disappeared with his fish under his low-roofed house on the skirts of the village. I think nobody else saw him; nobody else remembers him now, for he soon after died, and migrated to new Tyne streams. His fishing was not a sport, nor solely a means of subsistence, but a sort of solemn sacrament and withdrawal from the world, just as the aged read their bibles. (24–25)

In his forthcoming catalog of local river fishes such as the horned pout, or *Pimelodus nebulosus,* the narrator will resort to levity to refocus a discussion that he's raised to such levels of rarefied air as befit his fisherman's "solemn sacrament." We learn, for example, that the above-named fish is "sometimes called Minister, from the peculiar squeaking noise it makes when drawn out of the water" (31). Yet in the overall telling, there is far more dignity than comedy in a man's resorting to outdoor pursuits "just as the aged read their bibles." Indeed, there is sacred ground beneath the "village spire," where common folk have discovered a meaningful basis for devotion in the repetitions of their everyday lives.

Inside the gallery of short biographical profiles that Thoreau draws from time to time in his complete works, there would appear to be little to distinguish his fisherman from a canon of commoners that includes the likes of woodchopper philosophers, unfortunate Irishmen, and agrarian doubting Thomases. As a religious exemplar, however, the former Northumberland outsider whom we meet at the outset of *A Week* is extraordinary in his ordinariness. He worships in ways that are at once his own, even as they are available to anyone who is prepared to act out his daily business with the reverence it is due. The spiritual outlook he epitomizes might not qualify as "blasphemy," as Thoreau's aunt Maria feared. It does postulate as sacred that which traditionalists probably regarded as lying outside the acceptable bounds of religion in mid-nineteenth-century New England. John Broderick has written that the typical action of a Thoreauvian excursion involves a movement "from the mundane known to the transcendent knowable and back again."[40] Something comparable takes place on "Saturday" inside *A Week,* although we should not discount the transcendent potential of our starting point (and ending point) in the "mundane" meeting that transpires in this chapter with an unconventional Englishman at worship. Our fisherman may die in a "low-roofed house on the skirts of the village"; his faith lives in the rudimentary practices that are his answer to devotional literature.

If Thoreau's recognizing as much amounted to an epiphany, his spiritual awakening arrived only after an extended spell of preparation. Thoreau's matriculation at Harvard College in the fall of 1833 proved formative in the development of his religion. Like the other undergraduates of his era, he received a conventional tutorial in Unitarianism over the period of his four years in Cambridge. The course work from his junior and senior years, especially, consisted of the same inoffensive mix of a staid metaphysics, Enlightenment moral philosophy, and the rational theology that had more or less constituted the core religious curriculum at Harvard during the preceding two decades. Years later, after Thoreau's premature death from tuberculosis in 1862, his former Harvard classmate John Weiss would remember him as someone who "went about, like a priest of Buddha who expects to arrive soon at the summit of a life of contemplation, where the divine absorbs the human."[41] Others recalled a more down-to-earth Thoreau on a campus situated alongside the Charles River. As a first-term college freshman, Thoreau never once walked on water; he could boast, however, near-perfect attendance at the required twice-daily chapel and Sabbath services, with the anticipated rise in his compiled absences coming during subsequent semesters.[42] Thoreau tended to toe the line inside the classroom as well. His college essays on such assigned themes as "Use and Objections of Polite Forms," "Taking Opinions on Trust," "Superstition & Skepticism," and "Conformity in Little & Great Things" might have aided his progress in becoming a writer, as they did for a number of his peers, but Thoreau's mild, uninspiring responses to these and similar expository assignments were unexceptionable even by the standards of his day.[43] At the end of Thoreau's tenure at the college, Harvard's president, Josiah Quincy, would inform Emerson that some of his protégé's instructors had found him to be an "indifferent" student since returning from the illness that interrupted his junior year. Yet Quincy left no doubt as to Thoreau's good standing in Cambridge or, for that matter, in Concord. "I appreciate very fully the goodness of his heart and the strictness of his moral principle," Quincy wrote of his young charge, in what we might interpret as a progress report of sorts on the spiritual condition of the artist who, in five years' time, would make his first preliminary attempts at the writing of *A Week*.[44]

Needless to say, the religious education that Thoreau received at Harvard consisted of more than Sunday services with the Reverend Ware, or his readings from William Paley's *Evidences of Christianity*. By the spring of his senior year, he had withdrawn Emerson's *Nature* from the college library, only to return in the early summer to do so again. This master text of transcendental thought opened up religious prospects for Thoreau that would not have been visible to him had he restricted himself to his classroom volumes. Thoreau's immersion in *Nature* (a personal copy of which he soon purchased) also helped prepare him for the friendship he was about to enter into with Emerson himself, the codifier of the "New Views." Still, it was an earlier encounter that occurred not at Harvard but because of Harvard that set Thoreau on his transcendental course. After accepting, during his junior year, a six-week teaching position in Canton, Massachusetts, to help offset his college expenses, Thoreau came under the tutelage of Orestes Brownson, who at that time held the position of the town's Unitarian minister. As had happened with Thoreau, Brownson's attention had been drawn by the new philosophical views from the Continent that were having so great an impact in Unitarian circles.[45] Brownson even began the study of German in order to be able to read the foremost of these philosophies in their original language and extended an invitation to Thoreau to join him in this endeavor. David Robinson says it was here, with Brownson, that Thoreau "first encountered the assumptions about the necessity of spiritual renewal that he would maintain and repeatedly test." For it was in Brownson's conception of spirit that Thoreau came to reckon with the species of transcendentalist he would eventually become, influenced, as he was, by the insistence Brownson made on the indispensable place of the material principle in any modern religion. For Brownson, there was a redemption to be attained in the material world, despite the precedence his own church gave to spirit and spirit alone.[46] It is this extracurricular lesson, among others, that Thoreau carried with him after he left Harvard with his bachelor's degree in 1837. In his future religious practice, the material and spiritual would resolve themselves as mutually sustaining principles. These last might even reappear, say, in the uneventful canoeing expedition of two brothers from Concord, or the dawning realization of the profound that a person came to merely by observing the plodding riverside rituals of an unremarkable old man. For the time being, "this plain countryman," Thoreau, whose religion Bronson Alcott later characterized as being "of the most primitive type," was primed for a review of all such practices, the better to consider the religious potential of each.[47]

Bearing in mind Thoreau's early, if interrupted, preparations to enter into a state of greater spiritual receptiveness, we can return to *A Week* with a renewed appreciation for just how pregnant even his pauses can be. The possibility of religion lurks just about everywhere, or anywhere, as Thoreau suggests when he awakens in his "Sunday" chapter to observe, "The stillness was intense and almost conscious, as if it were a natural Sabbath" (46). Greeting the narrator is a world that bristles with natural spiritualism. "The frogs sat meditating," he says, "all sabbath thoughts, summing up their week, with one eye out on the golden sun, and one toe upon a reed, eying [*sic*] the wondrous universe in which they act their part." There are "fishes," too, which "swam more staid and soberly, as maidens go to church." Our speaker additionally sees "shoals of golden and silver minnows" as they "rose to the surface to behold the heavens, and then sheered off into more sombre aisles" (49). All creation would seem to be alive with an immanent divinity that, on this glorious Concord morning, it has been left to one particular "ecstatic" wayfarer to witness.[48]

At the same time, the narrator reserves some choice words for the traditional rituals of religion in "Sunday." These appear in passages that had likely led the reviewer from the *New-York Tribune* to remark, "Mr. Thoreau's treatment of this subject seems revolting alike to good sense and good taste."[49] If we are to credit Thoreau, regardless, with a "practical Transcendentalism," a "worldly Transcendentalism," or even an "antinomian" and "subversive" spiritualism of pantheistic tendencies, we must account for the stubborn streak of resistance that continued to qualify the obvious pains the author was taking to arrive at a more liberated state of religious acceptance.[50] There are, perhaps, enough sharp barbs strewn in the way of religion throughout "Sunday" to have left Thoreau vulnerable to the charges of "negativity" that had been directed at many of the most vocal transcendentalist critics. Thoreau's contemporary the Concord physician Edward Jarvis accordingly pronounced the author's entire life "a study in negation," with Thoreau himself amounting to no more than "a curious character in local history."[51] Whether such a conclusion is justified depends at least in part on how we react to the antagonism that *A Week*'s narrator nurses for the historical forms of Christianity he has known from his days in Concord. These don't sit well with him. "As we passed under the last bridge over the canal," he writes, "just before reaching the Merrimack, the people coming out of church paused to look at us from above, and apparently, so strong is custom, indulged in some heathenish comparisons; but we were the truest observers of this sunny day" (63). Not content to let this ironic moment pass without further commentary, the narrator proceeds to share his findings from a "singular memorandum" that he encountered in his research in the local archives, among what he describes as "the papers of an old Justice of the Peace and Deacon of the town of Concord." Here he discovers "a relic of an ancient custom," involving two hired men—Jeremiah Richardson and Jonas Parker, "both of Shirley," in Middlesex County—who were held for questioning by local church officials on December 18, 1803, after being caught transporting barrels (at the bidding of their employer) by horse-drawn carriage on the Sabbath. The narrator likens himself and his traveling companion to their scofflaw predecessors, saying, "We were the men that were gliding northward, this Sept. 1st, 1839, with still team, and rigging not the most convenient to carry barrels, unquestioned by any Squire or Church Deacon and ready to bear ourselves out if need were." Then comes the "comparison" that underscores the narrator's attitude toward Sabbath breaking. Referring to a report from "the historian of Dunstable" from "the latter part of the seventeenth century," he conjures up an image of the "cage" that was kept near the region's meetinghouses, as a place to confine "all offenders against the sanctity of the Sabbath." According to the narrator, whose understatement speaks all the more loudly when arranged in juxtaposition with the annals of colonial overzealousness, "Society has relaxed a little from its strictness, one would say, but I presume that there is not less religion than formerly" (63–64).

Thoreau was certainly in a position to know, as he had had more than one brush with Sabbath breaking. On another occasion, as the author related by letter to his aunt Louisa, he had been so bold as to parade one Sunday right past Concord's First Parish with a pine tree that he'd dug up for transplanting, "leaving the church-goers," he said, "gaping and horrified." Thoreau was not about to repent for his behavior, either. "I have been worshipping in my way," he wrote his much-abashed aunt, "and I don't trouble you in your way."[52] Emerson had seen enough such behavior from his young friend to say, "He was a protestant *à l'outrance.*"[53] And, at times, Thoreau does leave one with the impression that he is prepared only to oppose, as he does intermittently in *A Week*. Recalling yet another occasion on which he had been "reproved by a minister who was driving a poor beast to some meeting-house horse-sheds among the hills of New Hampshire, because I was bending my steps to a mountain-top on the Sabbath, instead of a church," Thoreau's narrator assures readers that

"I would have gone farther than he to hear a true word spoken on that or any day." Given the prevailing condition of religion in his New England, however, he had found that "when one enters a village, the church, not only really but from association, is the ugliest looking building in it, because it is the one in which human nature stoops the lowest and is most disgraced." He adds, "If I should ask the minister of Middlesex to let me speak in his pulpit on a Sunday, he would object, because I do not pray as he does, or because I am not ordained. What under the sun are these things?" And, with a final oppositional flourish, he decides, "Really, there is no infidelity, now-a-days, so great as that which prays, and keeps the Sabbath, and rebuilds the churches" (75–76). Standing convention on its head, the speaker in *A Week* would redefine the very meaning of spiritualism, on Sunday or any other day. "By our reckoning," he allows at the start of "Sunday," of what we can only assume was his and his brother's regular weekly practice, "this was the seventh day of the week, and not the first" (63). Much as "the bristling burdock, the sweet-scented catnip, and the humble yarrow planted themselves along his woodland road," Thoreau wrote, they were also "seeking 'freedom to worship God' in their way" (52).

Thoreau would not have to conduct his own search alone. In the winter of 1829, the Massachusetts Senate had recommitted a legislative bill relating to public worship and religious freedom to its standing committee on parishes.[54] On February 14 of that same year, Concord's trusty *Yeoman's Gazette* would follow up this procedural maneuver by the state with a reminder to its subscribers not to confuse freedom of religion with freedom *from* religion, when it published an excerpt from the following work: *The Sum of Religion. Written by Judge Hale, Lord Chief Justice of England, and Was Found in the Closet, amongst His Other Papers after His Decease* (1796). There, the English jurist Hale writes that a man "may be studious to practice every ceremony, even with a scrupulous exactness, or may perhaps, as stubbornly oppose them," and still "he wants the Life of Religion."[55] With or without such counsel, Concord's appointed administrators had done what they could do in their capacity as civic representatives to ensure their community avoided such lapses. In the town's annual report of expenses for the spring of 1837, we find recorded entries for the continuing quarterly payment of $127.25 for the Reverend Ripley's tax-supported salary. We see multiple payments (to multiple persons, in cash allotments or abatements of the local highway tax) made for the supply of cords of wood to this same minister. We run across itemized disbursements to the likes of one Nathan

Hosmer, for setting glass in the meetinghouse and "trimming the pulpit," as well as general maintenance and support fees paid to area residents ($1.78 to Captain Isaac Cutler for shingles and nails for the First Parish Church, $25.00 to Phineas How to underwrite the costs of the Unitarian Sunday School) for keeping the "life" of institutional religion functional and presentable for the people.[56] One suspects the narrator from *A Week* would have had ambivalent feelings about these nickel-and-dime efforts to prop up religion as if it were a chore. After all, Thoreau envisions a religion that is more private than public. He was furthermore alert to a certain mysticism in his religion, the intuitive exercise of which has seen him categorized as everything from "a born supernaturalist" and "spiritual gymnast" to "the greatest and purest Dionysian" in the Americas.[57] At the same time, Thoreau's chief criticism of Christ in "Sunday" was that "he taught mankind but imperfectly how to live; his thoughts were all directed toward another world," when "there are various tough problems yet to solve, and we must make shift to live, betwixt spirit and matter, such a human life as we can" (73–74). There was, in this regard, something almost laudable about a religion that found expression in the upkeep of Concord's First Parish, the lighting of domestic fires, and the sweeping of ministerial chimneys, when much of the local Christian tradition had been committed to being *in* this world without ever being *of* it. Thoreau would take faith out of its institutional framework to ensure that it was planted in such everyday experiences as even the most humble of worshipers could understand. The "life" of his religion was just that, *lived*. To this day, he stands for a faith that reimagines the mundane more than it transcends it. As Thoreau's narrator says in "Sunday," "A healthy man, with steady employment, as wood-chopping at fifty cents a cord, and a camp in the woods, will not be a good subject for Christianity. The New Testament may be a choice book to him on some, but not on all or most of his days" (74).

Come "Monday," what little forward momentum the narrative of *A Week* can be said to possess relents just enough for the book to revert back to a spiritualism that would not have registered with some of Concord's more old-fashioned parishioners, for whom religion inhered in the keeping of a Sabbath that, for Thoreau, was as sacred as any other day of the week. The two brothers, up early, resume their travels upstream in the company of their "countrymen," who, the narrator says, "recruited by their day of rest, were already stirring, and had begun to cross the ferry on the business of the week" (118). At this interval the narrator repeats the proverbial wisdom of the eighteenth-century historian and Congregational clergyman Jeremy Belknap (Harvard College class of 1762), concerning what the former describes as the increasing presence of "new lights" and "free thinking men" within the New England village in the decades before the Revolutionary War. According to Belknap, "the people in general" from his home state of New Hampshire might have been "professors of the Christian religion in some form or other." There were, however, "a sort of wise men who pretend to reject it; but they have not yet been able to substitute a better in its place" (123). Thoreau's narrator demurs at this suggestion, less by explicit objection than by the contrary argument he formulates through illustration. In generic terms, *A Week* is no more a biography of its narrator or his fraternal companion than it is of the river people who populate the volume. The book nevertheless does provide enough of a glance inside the nondescript spiritual practices of these very peoples to constitute an anomalous collection of saints' lives, as told for a modern audience of New Englanders who knew better than Belknap. Despite what this historian might say, there were, indeed, demotic alternatives in and near Concord to the conventional forms of Christianity.

These were as varied as the people who practiced them. In his "Tuesday" chapter, for example, the narrator evokes a chance mountaintop meeting that he had on an earlier excursion with "a very old man, not far from a hundred." "As I stopped by the wayside to gather some raspberries," he recalls, his elderly associate, who was there for a similar purpose, "suddenly stopped, while his cows went on before, and, uncovering his head, prayed aloud in the cool morning air, as if he had forgotten this exercise before, for his daily bread" (208). With the arrival of "Thursday," the narrator's reflections on the classical Roman poet Persius likewise have him translating lines that serve as a metered reminder of the wide province for the religion that he, too, would practice, at elevations at and above sea level: "It is not easy for every one to take murmurs and low / Whispers out of the temples, and live with open vow." "To the virtuous man," our narrator explains, "the universe is the only *sanctum sanctorum,* and the penetralia of the temple are the broad noon of his existence" (310). Even by "Friday," as we read of the narrator's warm recollections of the homespun people who flock to Concord's annual Cattle-Show, we learn of a different kind of congregation than that which assembled for the formal Sabbaths that Thoreau seems only too happy to leave behind him. "I love these sons of earth every mother's son of them," his speaker says, "with their great hearty hearts rushing tumultuously in herds from spectacle to spectacle, as if fearful lest there should not be time between sun and sun to see them all, and the sun does not wait more than in haying-time" (337). Writing by letter on October 8, 1841, to his fellow townsman Elijah Wood, a local farmer and shoemaker whom Concord's selectmen had voted to convene a singing school with two other members from the First Parish in support of the public performance of sacred music, Thoreau made his views on religion quite clear. "Our religion is where our love is," he states. "The strains of a more heroic faith vibrate through the week days and the fields than through the Sabbath and the church."[58] Back inside "Friday," it is this image of his own people rising to worship in humble places that gives the narrator every reason he needs to believe:

> It is worth the while to see the country's people, how they pour into the town, the sober farmer folk, now all agog, their very shirt and coat-collars pointing forward,—collars so broad as if they had put their shirts on wrong end upward, for the fashions always tend to superfluity,—and with an unusual springiness in their gait, jabbering earnestly to one another. The more supple vagabond, too, is sure to appear on the least rumor of such a gathering, and the next day to disappear, and go into his hole like the seventeen-year locust, in an ever-shabby coat, though finer than the farmer's best, yet never dressed; come to see the sport, and have a hand in what is going,—to know "what's the row," if there is any; to be where some men are drunk, some horses race, some cockerels fight; anxious to be shaking props under a table, and above all to see the "striped pig." He especially is the creature of the occasion. He empties both his pockets and his character into the stream, and swims in such a day. He dearly loves the social slush. There is no reserve of soberness in him. (338)

The spiritualism of these "country's people" may be coarse, but it confirms the narrator's contention, from "Monday," that "We can tolerate all philosophies, Atomists, Pneumatologists, Atheists, Theists" (152). That is to say, he recognizes the worth of *all* religions, whether in the form of an esoteric "philosophy" (one with or without God) or any life-affirming practice of sincerity, of "superfluity," since "each takes us up into the serene heavens" (152). "What is 'a man's own religion,'" our narrator had asked during an earlier lull in his journey, "which is so much better than another's?" (140). Here we have our answer. By the termination of his travels, not only is Thoreau's voyager prepared to have the people of Concord vote with their feet, free from "reserve," but he wants them to worship that way as well.

For his part, Thoreau withdrew from Concord's First Parish in 1841, a more than symbolic gesture in a state where, by law, and the allowances made for disestablishment notwithstanding, citizens were still considered members of their parish church unless they submitted a formal motion of resignation (figure 4).[59] Not all of his neighbors would have shared Thoreau's reasons for leaving the church to which he belonged by birthright, but he was by no means alone in taking this step. There were other denominations to join in Concord by that late date. And there were religions taking shape outside of the orthodox parameters of worship in which neither the fundamental tenets nor the much-disputed finer points of belief were to be institutionally determined. One of Thoreau's earliest biographers, Franklin Sanborn (Harvard College class of 1855), remembered the response he received from his boardinghouse landlord when, as a new arrival in Concord, he inquired "how many religious societies there were in town." In a journal entry from 1857, Thoreau recorded the answer that was afforded Sanborn. By the landlord's count, "there were three,—the Unitarian, the Orthodox, and the Walden Pond Society," the last of these being an explicit recognition of the religious imperatives behind Thoreau's spiritual experiments on the outskirts of town.[60] Thoreau, we know, would begin work on the first drafts of what became *Walden* while in residence at his cabin at the aforementioned Pond. This is also where he took important strides in writing *A Week*. A question of his own that he poses in the "Sunday" chapter from that book might have served as a fitting response to Sanborn's query, regarding "religious societies." "There are various, nay, incredible faiths," the narrator asks; "why should we be alarmed at any of them?" (66).

THE TRIALS OF WORSHIP IN *WALDEN*

The work of religion in Concord during the first half of the nineteenth century was as far-reaching as it was fractious, such that Thoreau could memorialize his town's condition of chronic spiritual complaint with a book, *Walden*, that in part renders as personal and private such acts of popular religious deliberation as the rest of Concord was content to carry on in public. Raymond Adams writes that Thoreau's two-year experiment in purposeful living beside the shores of Concord's Walden Pond from July 4, 1845, to September 6, 1847, marked a passage of "spiritual adjustment" for an author who sought "the society of himself" to better "come to grips with problems of his own faith."[61] Less acknowledged by Adams and others is the extent to which Thoreau's attempt at "adjustment," which he codified in the pages of his most acclaimed publication, was symptomatic

Figure 4. *Third Meeting House in Concord,* ca. 1841. Attributed to John R. Wesson, painting on wood. Courtesy of the Concord Museum, www.concordmuseum.org.

of his entire community's affinity for meeting its religion head-on, in one or another of the ongoing religious "controversies" that gripped Concord in these years. *Walden* as a spiritual literary project belongs to these peoples at least as much as it does to its author, that "damned rascal," Henry David Thoreau.[62]

In an address he delivered at the Greenacre retreat in Eliot, Maine, on the occasion of "Concord Day" in 1906, Franklin Sanborn announced that Thoreau "looked on religion as the business or attribute of all men, and not the monopoly of any single race or profession."[63] Precious little of this "business" carried the same air of ineffable transcendence as characterized Thoreau's most deep-seated spiritual experiences. *Walden*'s author, we should remember, is the same writer who, in his journal, defined religion as "that which is never spoken."[64] But when recalled to the society that was the constant companion of his more storied solitude, Thoreau freely acknowledged—indeed, insisted—

that religion consisted of such run-of-the-mill matters as touched anyone and everyone in Concord, whether they would be touched or not. "How vigilant we are! determined not to live by faith if we can avoid it," Thoreau writes in the initial pages of *Walden* (11). Yet the reason for *Walden*'s very being is that neither Thoreau nor anyone else in Concord could have "avoided" religion even if he had wanted to, for the simple fact that everyday life in and around Concord was not only implicated in but also constitutive of religion. The speaker of *Walden* concedes as much in the opening remarks he reserves for "my townsmen" (3). These read as a spirited response to Concord's unofficial inquest into what he calls "my mode of life" out at Walden, where, it seems, the question that's been occupying Thoreau is much the same as that which has bedeviled the residents of Concord (3). Sure, these last would like to know what's been stirring out at Walden Pond and whether they might regard the neighbor who's moved there as some kind of crank. But what they'd really like an answer to is precisely what Thoreau has proposed to show in the book he's composed for the occasion of testifying to just how wide open a field religion is. Given that we "have settled down on earth," Thoreau writes, "and forgotten heaven," it remains to be seen if we might "of necessity rise to a higher and more ethereal life" (37, 40). The question around which *Walden* revolves, then, may begin with the unlikeliest of preachers, preaching.[65] What drives at the heart of that question, however, is *Walden*'s fresh examination of the diversity of "life" practices that common experience would dictate we admit as religious.

Thoreau's contemporaries signaled their readiness to conceive of religion in this more expansive way in word as well as deed. For the otherwise philosophically minded contributors and editors of the *Radical* periodical, the religious life was *lived*.[66] The author of the opening piece from this Boston monthly magazine "devoted to religion" said of his subject, in September 1865, "The word Religion has, we believe, a broader significance than the Christian world has been accustomed to allow for it." He continued, "We shall not, therefore, accept the limitations so commonly recognized. Instead of considering religion as a single, separate department of life, we hope to reveal its legitimate right to consecrate all departments; to be in fact inseparable from all of real life or character in man, and that with no reference to time or place."[67] Such views were not exclusive to the surviving ranks of the region's transcendentalist liberals, who had gravitated toward the *Radical* in the aftermath of their rift with the more conservative members of the American Unitarian Association in 1867.

There was also a "consecrated" life to be had in the routine comings and goings of such ordinary places as Concord, a life that ended up forming the basis for a searching discussion of what the religion of the town would look like. The First Parish naturally played its expected part in these proceedings. Church members debated (often in separate committees organized for the purpose) and voted on everything from the place and frequency of regular prayer meetings to such devotional matters as which selection of psalms and hymns to use for church service, whether and where the recipients of communion would stand for the administration of this sacrament, and the make of the plates to be reserved for such an occasion.[68] The Committee on Psalms & Hymns might have tasked itself with identifying "sentiments" on which "all christians" could agree—the committee's chairman, Thomas Hubbard, maintained in a report from June 1, 1828, that "unanimity is of great importance in a religious society"—but this position, as articulated, failed to account for what the rest of Concord was "doing" when it came to religion. As we have seen in *A Week*, what much of Concord was *not* doing was participating in conventional religion. Well into the 1820s the First Parish was beset by "brothers" (there is no evidence from the period of "sisters" in this regard) who, the Reverend Ripley wrote, had "neglected publick [sic] worship & special ordinances." Those so charged did not include the "poor" families and "adult individuals" who Ripley said were "destitute of the Bible." Nor did it count what Concord's junior pastor H. B. Goodwin described in 1832 as the users and abusers of "ardent spirits as a common drink." For the time being, the ranking officials of the First Parish were prepared to leave the town's tipplers to the supporters of the Middlesex Temperance Society, newly instituted in 1829. Rather, by "neglect" Ripley meant the Sabbath breaker who, since the turn of the century, had in Ripley's own words "appropriated the sabbath to secular business." The pastor was prepared to "reclaim" some of these lost souls and duly convened a committee that, on at least two occasions in the mid-1820s, recommended the offending parties "be viewed & treated as brethren in regular standing."[69]

Offenders from outside the fold of the First Parish were not so fortunate. They were often subject to legal punishment for their violations, notwithstanding the claims of a state report that the Sabbath laws (like the Sabbath breakers themselves) "had fallen into general neglect."[70] Issued in 1816, the *Remarks on the Existing State of the Laws of Massachusetts, Respecting Violations of the Sabbath* made clear that "profanations of the Sabbath" were viewed as a problem throughout the Commonwealth (3). Predictably, legislators from both houses of the state government had charged the requisite "committee" with finding a way to enforce Massachusetts's prohibition on "all actions and practices which may disturb the worship and instruction of others" (4). Ironically, this effort had been hampered in the past by the inability of legal officers to conduct any work on the Sabbath, the day when such infractions as the following practices would, by necessity, have happened: "On all our large roads, every Sabbath witnesses numerous and rapidly increasing violations of the laws, with hardly an endeavour to repress them. Droves of cattle and loads of produce for market, carts and waggons [sic] returning with goods to the country, and pleasure carriages, throng the roads. The business of life goes on; no man regards the Sabbath unless he chuses [sic]; and what will be the end? Where will a single year leave this Commonwealth?" (11–12). Ever at the forefront of these matters, Concord resorted at this time, before the onset of church disestablishment, to having such of the First Parish's "tythingmen" [sic] as Samuel Hoar (Harvard College class of 1802, and soon to be a prominent state attorney) perform what agents of the courts could not. Reporting directly to Middlesex County's justice of the peace, these church-affiliated officials like Hoar kept close watch on Concord on Sundays, and every other day, in a concerted effort to regulate the reported rise in trespasses against religion. The town's criminal court records from the 1810s and 1820s accordingly reveal at least six instances of people (a number of them "labourers," both residents and nonresidents of Concord) who "did utter & swear" a "profane oath." Said profanity usually consisted of as simple a statement as, "'I swear by God' etc. etc.," for which an offender would pay—in lieu of serving three days in jail—a fine of one dollar, in addition to the three dollars in court fees he incurred to cover the costs of his own prosecution.[71] Just as frequent was the charge made, in the language of one "tythingman's" recorded complaint, against those accused of "being a thoughtless and irreligious person . . . inattentive to the duties and benefits of the Lord's Day." There are at least eight such instances of Sabbath breaking in the county for the same period as before, with an identical cumulative fine of four dollars as was levied on those irreverent locals of loose tongue.[72] Our inclination today is probably to regard as innocuous what were, for the most part, cases of Sunday highway travel made "not of necessity or charity." But as the state's published *Remarks* had indicated, the greater worry was the fact of the offense itself rather than the exact flavor of offensiveness. If, as these *Remarks* forecast, "the business of life goes on; [and] no man regards the Sabbath unless he chuses," then the stipulations of orthodoxy could be construed as optional, which is to say elective. That, in turn, left religion vulnerable to an inexorable diminishment over time. Fewer and fewer people would give (and receive) less and less to a spiritual life that could all too easily be cast aside while "the business of life goes on."

The alternative that Thoreau proposes in *Walden* is to reconceive of our everyday "business" in the religious terms that our writer from the *Radical* observed, come one late summer's Sunday, in the masses of men and women assembled on leafy Boston Common. These he characterizes as "unconscious worshipers." Whether "refreshing themselves in the quiet presence of Nature," "resting from the week-day's work," or, by extension, even in performing the very "work" by which they made their way in the world, the *Radical*'s religionists worshiped not by their attendance at any church; they worshiped by virtue of engaging in such practices as had earned the unfortunates of Greater Concord a stiff penalty for Sabbath breaking.[73] Upon the request of the worshiper, and with a vote of confirmation by the entire congregation, the First Parish regularly released and received Christians of good standing so that they could join some church of their choosing, perhaps including Concord's own Unitarian establishment. The name for this process was "dismission." In *Walden*, Thoreau contends for something that is at once more and less "radical" than a simple swapping of church memberships. He isn't advocating for some mildly progressive religious dispensation, either, in which a walk in the park might be construed as a form of "worship." If Thoreau is not, as he says, addressing "those who find their encouragement and inspiration in precisely the present condition of things," he is, in fact, speaking to any reader who is prepared, like himself, to locate his religion in the act of what he calls "faithfully minding my business" (*Walden*, 16, 18). What that "business" was meant less in the author's final reckoning than the "minding." What mattered was the "faith" with which one's "business" was performed.

Thoreau had at his disposal a reliable precedent for such a faith, although he characteristically applied the Protestant notion of "good works" in ways in which even the forward-thinking Arminians among his townsmen had never dreamed. *Walden*'s first chapter, appropriately titled "Economy," draws on the Unitarian concept of what Leonard Neufeldt names "*homo oeconomicus*." By this spiritual doctrine the Unitarians of Thoreau's day understood the moral life that was associated with an enterprising self-culture not as a sign of the religious life but *as* the religious life.[74] Thoreau similarly extended this doctrine well beyond its traditional metaphorical limits. Where he parted ways with the members of his family's First Parish was in his insistence that redemption could be had in even the most elemental instances of what he called doing his "duty faithfully" (18). The speaker that figures in the introductory pages of *Walden* is thus a man on a mission, in the several connotations of that word. He has, first, pressing "business" to attend to and writes to alert his neighbors to the religion that awaits them in the daily transactions that make up their pedestrian lives. There is more than an ironic meaning behind the cutting remark that Thoreau makes early in *Walden:* "Talk of a divinity in man!" (4). Thoreau means these words literally, too. And he would have us pause to reflect on "how godlike, how immortal," is man in his "common mode of living," the "chief end" of which, he says, "to use the words of the catechism," is to attain to "the true necessaries and means of life" (7–8). This is not to say Thoreau's *mission* was strictly (or even superficially) material. It was decidedly spiritual and carried implications for wherever a man might travel at home or abroad. In lines from "Economy" that the author initially delivered as a lecture before his town's Lyceum, he leaves no doubt that his enterprise in moving to Walden Pond has been a religious one all along. Indeed, his resettlement is rooted—"for the root is faith," he says—not only in the historical example of Concord's Puritan forbears, those nonseparatist Protestants who left England for the prospect of establishing a *purer* strain of their faith in the New World (64).[75] The author's project is staked in the here and now and is meant to resonate with "a certain class of unbelievers" who would deny the religious import of their own "deeds" on this earth (64, 7). Thoreau delivers his good news as follows:

> I would fain say something, not so much concerning the Chinese and Sandwich Islanders as you who read these pages, who are said to live in New England; something about your condition, especially your outward condition or circumstances in this world, in this town, what it is, whether it is necessary that it be as bad as it is, whether it cannot be improved as well as not. I have travelled a good deal in Concord; and everywhere, in shops, and offices, and fields, the inhabitants have appeared to me to be doing penance in a thousand remarkable ways. (4)

That "we belong to the community" Thoreau is certain (46). That we in this "community" (of Concord or some other "New England" town) have missed the religious significance of our respective callings "in shops, and offices, and fields" he is equally prepared to accept on faith. And "if a man has faith," he says, he need not "be doing penance" for the practices by which he sustains himself. Rather, "he will cooperate with equal faith everywhere; if he has not faith, he will continue to live like the rest of the world, whatever company he is joined to" (71–72).

As a critic of conventional religion, Thoreau decided that "our hymn-books resound with a melodious cursing of God and enduring Him forever" (78). Or, as he explained a claim that only confirmed for one appreciative "freethinker" from the late nineteenth century the writer's reputation for being "a complete and thoroughgoing Infidel," "There is nowhere recorded a simple and irrepressible satisfaction with the gift of life, any memorable praise of God" (78).[76] Yet with much of "Economy," Thoreau affirms more than he denies the spiritual life he believed to be at hand for anyone disposed to partake of a religion with a difference. As another near contemporary of Thoreau's wrote, "All is positive in this writer."[77] And, as Laura Dassow Walls reminds us, the "profoundly religious" purpose that drew Thoreau to Walden Pond in the first place was in no way depreciated by the fact that his simply being there was, for so many of Concord's townspeople, a stimulus to a community-wide conversation on where and how to live.[78] What keeps us from appreciating the religion we are living, Thoreau suggests, is the elusive conversion experience that must come but once in the lifetime of any Christian who should receive God's grace. The religion of *Walden* inheres in the recognition that grace is only and always offered freely, provided we conduct ourselves here below, in our daily undertakings, "in the same proportion" as we would in "the heavens above" (15).

Catherine Albanese says of transcendentalism that "it began in disenchantment."[79] We could say the same of *Walden,* where Thoreau can't help but observe of the people of Concord "what mean and sneaking lives many of you live" (6). But in casting his eye across the length and breadth of his town, Thoreau additionally discovers the potential for the sacred wherever he turns. By "day or night" he catches sight of "the teamster on the highway, wending to market" (7). At repeated intervals he sees "Squire Make-a-stir," living out his own special "destiny" (7). There are ready examples of "the preacher, and the merchant, and the farmer," too, each contributing his share to what the author calls "the business for America" (46, 62). In light of the pervasive "division of labor" that he decries as a detriment to our capacity for spiritual wholeness, Thoreau regrets that much of the work that occurs within his antebellum world of emerging industries and monetized exchanges is misguided, if not entirely wasted (46). As he states elsewhere, however, of his own conscientious experiments in husbandry in "The Bean-Field" chapter, where the author makes a demonstrative show of the crop he sows for edifying consumption, he also trusted in the human ability to cultivate such spiritually freighted virtues "as sincerity, truth, simplicity, faith, innocence, and the like" (163–64). Accepting, as he does, the "dictionary" definition of "sacrament" as the "outward and visible sign of an inward and spiritual grace," Thoreau did not just regard the everyday face of Concord as what Leslie Perrin Wilson calls "a means of access to broader consciousness" (69).[80] *Transcendence* as such was tautological for Thoreau, in the sense that there was nothing left for him (or anyone else, should they share his sensibilities) to "transcend."

In some respects, the trajectory of *Walden* recalls that of Emerson's *Nature*. The book's movement is from the natural and material underpinnings of *this* world, epitomized by a chapter title like "Economy," to the elevated existence to which conventional religion has conditioned us to aspire, a state Thoreau pays explicit tribute to in a subsequent chapter, "Higher Laws." Then again, we might opt for a less orthodox reading instead, one that reverses the trajectory of a religion that carries us further and further away from the plain dealings that occur outside the hours of ecstasy. This would require that we take the author of *Walden* at his word as he continually recalls our attention to all that's sacred beneath our feet. He accomplishes such a reminder in his performance of the humdrum "business" of life, by which he's learned to center himself, spiritually. Religion is *happening* as Thoreau constructs the cabin where he takes up what becomes his now legendary residence. There's belief circulating through his hallowed practice of bathing in his pristine pond. "That was a religious exercise," he says, "and one of the best things which I did" (88). Thoreau worships while baking his daily loaf of Indian rye. He comes to rapturous consciousness while angling for the fishes whose animal flesh he scruples to eat. With all of these "sacramental" pastimes, the author offers proof positive that "God himself culminates in the present moment, and will never be more divine in the lapse of all the ages" (97).

The takeaway of *Walden*'s organic interpretation of transcendence is that none of us need search for religion any further than the here and now, should we be so "heterodox"—the preferred term in the decades after Thoreau's passing—as to initiate life-sustaining experiments of our own.[81] This was, one could argue, the author's response to the recurrent disagreements over religion that were endemic to his Concord. He does not side with the Sabbath breakers, necessarily, in forgoing what was supposed to have been the holiest of days. He bids us to keep faith in simpler ways, on any given day.

Thoreau's willingness to perform the proverbial part of the village atheist nevertheless had consequences for the framing of his character. Leigh Eric Schmidt cites an 1808 review of the British clergyman and poet George Crabbe's collected *Poems* as the earliest recorded instance of the phrase "village atheist." In his lyric "The Parish Register," Crabbe renders an unflattering portrayal of the local "rustic Infidel," who lays claim to none of the nostalgic charm that this literary stock figure of a defiant, aggressive nonconformity would come to possess in the United States by the end of the nineteenth century. From its inception, the so-called village infidel was, rather, a stark reminder of the difficult history of religious divisions (from early modern times running up to and through the rise of Enlightenment deism, romanticism, and beyond) that had kept towns like Thoreau's own Concord in a state of constant internecine disagreement.[82] The Massachusetts poet and printer Nathaniel Bolton made his bid to rewrite that history with a rebuttal, set to forty-five stanzas of verse, of one of the age's most notorious freethinkers. Bolton's "A Poem: On Infidelity" (1808) begins as follows:

> TOM PAINES there are,
> Here and elsewhere:
> In English and French nation;
> Toms do arise,
> And do despise:
> All written revelation.[83]

In his much-cited eulogy of Thoreau from 1862, Emerson would remind the people of Concord that his departed friend was no Tom Paine.[84] He "was a person of a rare, tender, and absolute religion, a person incapable of any profanation, by act or by thought." As Emerson remembered, "Thoreau was sincerity itself, and might fortify the convictions of prophets in the ethical laws by his holy living. It was an affirmative experience which refused to be set aside."[85] John Weiss shared in this sentiment and said of the author of *Walden*, "No writer of the present day is more religious; that is to say, no one more profoundly penetrated with the redeeming power of simple integrity, and the spiritualizing effect of a personal consciousness of God."[86] Even Edward Horton, in his selection "Love of Nature," from the volume *Noble Lives and Noble Deeds: A Series of Lessons for Sunday Schools* (1893), had perspective enough to distill from Thoreau a message—as Horton writes, "that one can find the greatest revelations at home and through the ordinary channels"—that bore the institutional sanction of area Unitarianism.[87] But for those who had lived right alongside Thoreau through the thick of his at times ungraceful self-discoveries, the "affirmative" religion to which the writer gave voice could be casually construed as an assault on the spiritual beliefs they held dear. Compared to his experience in Concord, Thoreau's college days in Cambridge could be said to have been "whitewashed," when we consider that the student senior who authored an essay in which he argued that "to reject *Religion* is the first step toward moral excellence" somehow emerged from Harvard with his reputation for Unitarian orthodoxy intact.[88] Back in his native Concord, Thoreau was bound to endure a greater scrutiny into his religious dispositions. And he did, at a time when, from about 1842 forward, he had begun to reevaluate the meaning of belief. Robert Gross pointedly understates the legacy of that formative period in the writer's religious life when he concludes, "Thoreau does not fit easily in the genealogy of New England piety from Edwards to Emerson."[89] Or, as Robert Richardson neatly summarizes, Concord may never have "repudiated" the patron saint of its most famous pond for his seeming infidelities, but the town "has maintained a running quarrel with Thoreau from that day to this."[90]

The paradox of reading *Walden*—and of the religion it practices—is that this holiest of books presupposes a falling away from faith, since we meet the narrator at a moment in the beginning of his account, inside "Economy," when his religion is as closely staked to the *practiced* standards of spiritual being he favors as his narrative will ever allow. To be sure, the audience of *Walden* is not privy to all of the narrator's experience, spiritual or otherwise. At the very least, and as with *A Week,* we are missing a good portion of the raw materials, since with both books the author has halved his account of a prolonged experience for the sake of compressing his story line. What's lost as a result is a cumulative sense of how practices that are repeated in the course of everyday living endow a "practical" transcendentalism.[91] As a religion, the transcendentalism that Thoreau carried with him depended on acts of repetition that his readers are not always in a position to see. Still, whatever exceptions he might have taken to Concord's conventional forms of faith, and whatever temporal and structural liberties Thoreau might have taken with his writing (and with his worship), the author was as committed as anyone in town to fostering a robust spiritual life. It was the means as much as the ends of religion as it was practiced in Concord that elicited from Thoreau his distinctive adversarial response.

Less easily reconciled to the reading of *Walden* that's proposed here is the Emersonian premise of the book that was mentioned before. The narrative that gathers strength in this work in the chapters that come after "Economy" contain their fair share of practices set out on instructive display; these double as sacraments for the worshiper who performs them and as homilies for the reader who receives them. But even though we are granted access to the earthly ways in which the speaker achieves communion day by day, as occurs in such chapters as "Where I Lived and What I Lived For," "Reading," "Baker Farm," and "The Pond in Winter," we remain tied to a narrative path that's strewn with seasonal metaphors for spirit, allusive patterns that depend on the scriptures of Eastern mysticism, and myriad signposts of natural religious image and symbol redirecting us toward what the author, in his "Conclusion," describes as a "faith in a resurrection and immortality" (333). Neither Emerson nor Thoreau had an exclusively Western or Eastern religion in mind as he composed the work (early in the literary career of the one, midway through that of the other) that would communicate what was perhaps his most rounded statement on belief. Yet both writers, in both instances, reverted in certain respects to a teleological "plot" that saw them edging away, respectively, in *Nature* and *Walden* from this world to a next world of "higher" religious rewards. In the case of Thoreau, however, even this seeming reversion—a reverse conversion—back to the orthodox norms from which the author has otherwise distanced himself represents a concession of sorts to religious convention. The quarrelsome contrarian has in fact signed on to a compromise, inasmuch as he's assimilated enough of the Christian language of a hoped-for ascension to heaven as to make his everyday transcendentalism seem almost commensurate with the religion of his First Parish. In a cognate reading of *Walden*, Robert Milder credits the first of the multiple drafts of this work with a "contrapuntal form," which is Milder's formula for explaining the book's "movement from critique to prospect and back again."[92] The present reading relies on a similar cyclical "movement," between the here and now of "business" and the *there* and *then* of "Higher Laws." What makes *Walden* a work, in Thoreau's words, of religious "*Extra vagance!*" is its enthusiastic willingness to interpret "movement" as stasis (324). Spiritually, Thoreau suggests, we are who we are as a direct result of where we are today, what we do now, and how we do it. The author's religious mission was finally to this world in the present tense, and this world only.

With that said, much of the author's subsequent life and writings would pitch his religion in the most planetary of terms. Already by the late 1840s, Thoreau was beginning to reconcile his reading in natural history with the core of the religion he'd received from the likes of Emerson. "Now he hungered for a wider view of the universe," Walls explains, "inscribed not in the leaves of dusty books but in the strata of the planet itself."[93] Over the course of the next decade or so, the author thus made good on his pledge in *A Week* to commit himself to a closer knowledge of what he called "heaven's topography" (70). A good portion of this work—which amounts to a religious exercise, if there ever were one—would remain unpublished in Thoreau's lifetime. But whether he were tracing the regional dispersion of plant seeds, monitoring the water levels of his much-loved Concord River, or tracking seasonal change with the data-filled lists and charts he named his "Kalendar," Thoreau lived out his remaining years in worshipful observance of the religious principle that he articulated in his journal. "With all your science," he asked, "can you tell how it is—& whence it is, that light comes into the soul?"[94] The body of Thoreau's naturalist writings are an affirmative response to this question, which was hardly rhetorical. If God's presence was everywhere, always, and freed from a conventional segregation inside the "holy" day of Sunday, then the immersive environment of the Concord that no one knew better than Thoreau represented all the deep time and planetary space a modern spiritual mind such as his could ever need.[95]

CHAPTER 3

Transcendental Women "Losing" Their Religion

> . . . a consciousness so deep & broad—that reverence . . . could not enter into it.
>
> —Elizabeth Peabody, transcript of Margaret Fuller's Boston Conversations, First Series, 1839–40

There were a number of different ways for a person or practice to pass as transcendental in New England in the nineteenth century. In chapter 1 of this study, Emerson, as he so often does, serves as the representative instance of a religious radicalism that, as it began to attract the attentions of a younger generation of educated Christians in the region, elicited a strong-enough response from the local Unitarian establishment to give rise to orthodox fears of a massive onset of "unbelief." For those with a vested interest in defending the hard-earned religious assumptions of Unitarianism, the beliefs of the followers of a so-called transcendental school were anything but and led to charges of outright heresy against nonconformists. For Emerson and others who were drawn to the "New Views," transcendentalism instead represented a positive alternative to what they felt were the spiritual deficiencies of liberal Protestantism. Those who affiliated with this loose group of religious critics qualified in their own minds as neither pretending Christians nor infidels; indeed, they believed they'd broken original ground for belief.

In Thoreau the practical implications of transcendentalism's challenge to religious convention took shape as a host of sacramental practices. However strange these seemed to Thoreau's neighbors, they imparted to their author a decidedly spiritual dimension to everyday life in modern times. This was an era, we are frequently told, that contemporaries experienced as one of increasing secularism. But as we learned in chapter 2, to practice such a defiant brand of transcendentalism as Thoreau did was to be far more spiritual than secular, even by the contested standards of that day.

What the examples of Emerson and Thoreau show is that there was more than one way to lead a religious life in the nineteenth century, even if that life had taken shape around a set of beliefs, and practices, that conservatives were unwilling to recognize as legitimate expressions of faith. What Emerson and Thoreau further show is that a person could identify as transcendental without wholly enlisting in the full range of particular religious inclinations with which any given transcendentalist was associated. To the extent, then, that the transcendental label represented no more of a definitive category than did a problematic term like "believer," the underlying purpose of this study has been twofold. First, this book provides a revisionist account of how transcendentalism complicated the too easy contemporary distinction between belief and unbelief. Central to our discussion in this regard is the critical examination to which we've subjected religious criticism itself, while simultaneously recognizing that no such examination can occur outside the institutional seat where so much of the religious controversy that concerns us occurred, Harvard College. Second, this book tries as well to provide an expanded framework for thinking about when, where, and how transcendentalism reared its controversial head. Contrary to what the examples we've so far seen might suggest, transcendentalism was no more an all-or-nothing expression of one's individual religious outlook than it was an identifiable badge of (dis)honor to be pinned on anyone who should ask such spiritual questions as those to which the "New Views" demanded answers.

With this present chapter, we would add to those questions a historical one of note: What are we to make of transcendental *women's* involvement with irreligion? In response we will revisit the contributions of such noteworthy figures as Margaret Fuller and Elizabeth Peabody to a conversation on atheism, skepticism, and other apparent indicators of religious "unbelief" that commentators have for the most part reserved for men. The two women just mentioned were in fact directly involved in these conversations, and the early portions of this chapter detail the nature of that involvement, as it expressed itself in thought, word, and deed.

There are additional stories to tell about transcendental women in this period. If "transcendental" was a name that certain female members of the area's cultural and intellectual elite carried proudly, others among the region's "ordinary" women would have borne it with reticence at best. Many of the women who appear in these pages were the bearers of traditional burdens that precluded their taking part in transcendentalism's most oppositional strains of expression. That the religious perspectives they'd inherited at birth often formed a portion of those burdens did not mean they were ready to abandon the faiths in which they had been raised. It was not the lot of these women to have ministries to resign or congregations to radicalize. They couldn't repair to some college or wooded retreat to make a flagrant display of such lapses—whether of judgment, behavior, or religious observance—as might have revealed any spiritual misgivings they had. They did not and could not, in short, escape the restrictions that the historical conventions of gender had placed on them. Yet still they encountered the ideas and practices of transcendentalism on whatever terms their circumstances allowed, and in turn they worked through such ramifications as these encounters carried for their religions. These women qualify as transcendental not because they counted themselves among the "like-minded." Rather, they believed and behaved transcendentally because they adapted the ideas, attitudes, and practices of the New Views to such lives as they were already living. And in doing so, they met what was perhaps an unspoken requirement of any truly transcendental expression in these years. That is to say, they surpassed the accepted standards of even their own faiths, and so shared in a contemporary criticism of religion that was redefining the very meaning of belief.

The women of nineteenth-century New England were, in short, as equally implicated as men in the religious controversies over infidelity. This may seem obvious in our own day. But both contemporary and historical accounts (not all of them composed by male writers) of American transcendentalism have by and large minimized women's involvement in such agonized aspects of the moment as made it the "religious demonstration" that Perry Miller said it was. It has been customary, to begin, to associate transcendental women's religious tendencies with some variety of Emersonian optimism, or else to set these same women's spiritual expressions under a sentimental banner that is meant to signal a special feminine capacity for feeling. Even the second-generation transcendentalist and women's rights activist Caroline Healy Dall would emphasize the *emotional* investments that women made in transcendentalism, as if the minds of these sister travelers could not follow where their hearts had led them. In a lecture she delivered in May 1895 in Washington, D.C., before the

Society for Philosophical Enquiry, Dall defined transcendentalism in sexless terms as "the assertion of the inalienable worth of man, and of the immanence of the Divine in the Human."[1] At the same time, she limited the dominion in which the women who were amenable to the "movement" could exercise their commitments by bookending transcendentalism as a centuries-spanning phenomenon of antinomian proportions. The "history" that Dall proposed begins with the seventeenth-century Puritan Anne Hutchinson, whose insistence on "exaltation" and "enthusiasm" in the name of religion our speaker says "was very attractive to women" (5–7). At the other end of Dall's long narrative arc stands the nineteenth-century writer and reformer Margaret Fuller, whose framing of truth (religious or otherwise) and knowledge acquisition is, like Hutchinson's, seen as being personal, intuitive, and peculiarly feminine rather than impersonal, empirical, and emblematically male.[2] Dall accordingly might write women back into transcendentalism's main story line, but the manner in which she pegs her description of this "distinct system" to such women as can manage "an extravagant demand on human nature" undermines her own claims for inclusiveness (23–24). Her gendered categories have also had a foreshadowing effect for subsequent commentators.

In his influential anthology from 1950, *The Transcendentalists,* Miller similarly combines an accommodating appreciation for the wide province of what he names "the Divine" with a delimiting recycling of the concept of "separate spheres." He thereby restricts the kinds of "religious demonstrations" (to repeat the historian's famous formulation) in which the transcendental women of his retelling are allowed to participate. Charles Capper explains that Miller's decision to pair a blanket term like "demonstrations" with a neutral label like "religious" was no coincidence; his doing so informed the multifaceted conception of religion on which he believed antebellum transcendentalism depended.[3] Yet this decision also diluted, on the one hand, transcendentalism's strong religious content by suggesting that the variety of behaviors in which such "enthusiasts" as Fuller and others of her reformist cohort engaged were as politically implicated as they were spiritually motivated. Although there is no denying that transcendentalism's cultural manifestations were many, it is also the case that a religion that encompasses any and every imaginable "demonstration"—from abolition and women's rights to school reform, political economy, and dietary change—ceases to be strictly "religious." Miller's broad-mindedness was in this respect potentially at cross-purposes with his larger project of returning religion to the center of our historical understanding of transcendentalism. On the other hand, Miller might have been an "ironist," as Capper says in acknowledgment of the way his predecessor characteristically highlights such unintended consequences as attended the undertakings and ideas of his historical actors (21). But Miller was also an existentialist, and his view (philosophical no less than methodological) of history necessarily entailed conflict and "struggle," thus pitting real past peoples against what Capper describes as their "own darker selves" (21). Miller's heroic view of history clearly did not preclude for him the radical subjective strivings of the transcendentalists, whose romantic aspirations for a religion equipped for the exigencies of modernity aligned nicely with his views on the larger trajectory of historical change. Such historical contests as Miller describes were nevertheless not for the faint of heart. Indeed, "heart" as such had little to do with Miller's reading of history. His history is a strenuous contest of the mind, the rugged possession of which was by no means the exclusive preserve of men but admitted few women in his analysis. Those women who do appear in Miller's histories, like Fuller, were sometimes accorded "masculine" attributes—a gendered pattern of compensation that began in this formidable intellectual's own day, only to continue into ours—that presumably would have better equipped them to fight the good fights that concerned them.[4] That many of these battles were religious signified little. In fact, the heated exchanges that ensued in the aftermath of such disputes as Emerson's "Divinity School Address" would only have confirmed for Miller the "proper" place of women in a debate that touched on such weighty matters as the sources of spiritual authority and the individual resources of strength required for sustaining belief, or a lack thereof.

That the most recent revisionist work on transcendentalism should have served, in part, to bracket women inside a "separate" historical sphere is an irony that Miller himself would have appreciated. In their important edited collection, *Toward a Female Genealogy of Transcendentalism* (2014), Jana L. Argersinger and Phyllis Cole have provided, in their own words, a timely "gendered study of Transcendentalism."[5] Much as Miller's anthology made religion the key in our attempts to unlock the meanings of transcendentalism's diverse cultural expressions, Argersinger and Cole have invited scholars from an array of academic disciplines to demonstrate the extent to which the "newness" was a product of the contributions made by the women of the nineteenth century. In making this assertion, however, the editors of the volume in question have advanced what could be received as an essentializing claim for the qualitative *difference* of transcendental women's expectations, dispositions, and needs. Like many a transcendental man, the editors' women were, as they write, seeking "alternative communities of literacy, spiritual seeking, and ethical commitment" (10). But their subjects are also credited, "as women of vision," with "substantially different perspectives" than those of their male counterparts (17). Such a reading can hardly be described as controversial, when we consider the extent to which the personal and social lives of women in the period were inhibited by those usages and conventions against which transcendentalism itself would offer both practical and principled resistance. Yet one of the unintended consequences of interpreting this interval in history as being substantially "different" for women is that it breathes new life into some one or more of the gendered stereotypes that this *Genealogy* is meant to dispel. From the perspective of a Margaret Fuller, for example, the spectacle afforded by as well-meaning a woman as Emerson's aunt—the self-educated Mary Moody Emerson, who figures prominently in one of *Genealogy*'s early chapters—taking steps to acquaint herself with the German-inflected metaphysics that her firsthand encounters with transcendentalism entailed amounted to little more than a "hasty attempt at skimming from the deeps of theosophy."[6] Among the aims of this present chapter is to contradict just such stereotypes as these. Despite our better intentions, we have tended to make such assumptions as inform Fuller's bias against the dilettante female philosopher (which, it should be noted, Mary Moody Emerson was decidedly not) an unspoken justification for attending so closely to the *secular* bases of antebellum women's involvement in transcendental reform.[7] Otherwise, when we do treat transcendental women's religious tendencies, we proceed as if they were in possession of a generic brand of "spiritualism"—the term was in general circulation by the early 1840s, before it became associated with spirit tappers and mediums—that bore little, if any, relation to the meticulously considered faiths of men. This trend in the scholarship, which has generally been *a*religious rather than *ir*religious, has come at the expense of our ascertaining whether, why, and how many of the era's women were as prepared as any of the men to swim in such "depths" as they would have waded into by pausing to reflect on the bases of their religious beliefs. For every Margaret Fuller, there was a laywoman struggling mightily with ideas that shook her religious bearings. Each and all of these women were as eager as any transcendental man to find and redefine religion on their own terms. They were prepared to do so, moreover, with or without the formal higher learning that Fuller, under normal circumstances, would have maintained was unnecessary to fully fathom a faith.

It's against these traditions (one scholarly, one spiritual) that we will set about reexamining the relation between transcendentalism, early American feminism, and unbelief. Within the historical context of New England transcendentalism, and against a critical tradition that has given comparatively little attention to transcendental women's *religious* orientations, we want to gauge the extent to which feminism and infidelity were mutually reinforcing in the nineteenth century. The title for this chapter, "Transcendental Women 'Losing' Their Religion," should not suggest that the women who gravitated toward the "New Views" necessarily sacrificed their faiths to do so. To be sure, some of these women were drawn to transcendentalism for just the opposite reason: as an opportunity to renew their faith, rather than to relinquish whichever religion they'd previously known. For other women, the coming into consciousness that transcendentalism encouraged would indeed help to undermine their faiths, at least on the orthodox terms on which they had received them. But, as we have also seen, the "negative" rejection of one religious dispensation might also entail its "positive" replacement by another, so that belief and unbelief became relative positions in an ongoing process of personal spiritual realignment. In the end, transcendentalism would no more induce a woman's slipping into a state of being "without" religion than it had done for men. Often what it did do was to sanction women's existing inclinations for spiritual self-examination. Not only did the female "genealogy" of transcendentalism subtend, then, the "antinomian" imperative that Caroline Healy Dall would later assign to that fervid Puritan Anne Hutchinson, but it was also continuous with the impetus behind the Protestant Reformation, that historic coming *into* religion in which Hutchinson had played her storied part. All of which is to say that if any or many transcendental women qualified as unbelievers, then they were unbelievers of a distinctive stamp. What is beyond question is that they grappled with the complications of their faith, much as they did with those of faithlessness.

It must be stressed at the outset of this chapter, finally, that we have not forsaken our earlier commitment to studying the *lived* conditions of antebellum religion. Our emphasis remains with religious practices as opposed to theological quandaries, even of the more dramatic kind that might have warranted inclusion in one of Miller's collision-driven histories. That being said, the religious practice that most interests us here is the very conversation of ideas—some of them "big," others "small"—that transcendentalism's women initiated as they came to terms with their faiths. Among the more conspicuous of these conversations were the series of subscription lectures that Margaret Fuller conducted in Boston between 1839 and 1844. Fuller's "Conversations," as they were then known, brought together women (and, for a brief time, a selection of men) for the purpose of fostering what Phyllis Cole describes as the "individual's inner potential for spiritual and intellectual unfolding."[8] These occasions have long factored into many of the histories of early American feminism, and rightly so, inasmuch as Fuller's Conversations represent a turning point in the United States in such uses of the freedom of assembly as would help to establish an important precedent in the midcentury push for women's rights. Fuller's Conversations, furthermore, would attract some of the higher-profile women intellectuals of the day, and so amount for our purposes, as they did for contemporaries, to a compelling display of the human "potential" into which transcendentalism was supposed to tap, irrespective of a person's gender. Notwithstanding the attention they have received, however, and in spite of the patently spiritual purposes of gatherings that broadcast a manifest interest in religion, education, and women's position in American society, Fuller's Conversations have remained for the most part separate (and implicitly unequal) from the host of running religious controversies that, in many respects, were synonymous in the mid-nineteenth-century mind with transcendentalism.[9] Discussions of faith and infidelity were as much a part of Fuller's Conversations as they were of the public debates over what transcendentalism portended for traditional Protestant attitudes toward miracles, scripture, and an intuitive apprehension of the divine. We will return the Conversations to their formative place in these larger conversations, for they permitted more than a hundred different women (most of them from New England, and not a few of them recognized public figures in their own right) to contribute to the development of a discourse on unbelief, a discourse that would have taken on a markedly different shape without them.

Much of the religious talk that Fuller facilitated among women has been lost to posterity; such is the ephemeral nature of conversation.[10] Many more of the region's women, Fuller included, committed their conversations—on family, faith, and feminism, among other related topics—to writing, thereby leaving behind them a record of their active participation in a broader discussion on "the latest form of infidelity." In the case of such leading transcendentalists as Fuller and Elizabeth Palmer Peabody, who hosted many of Fuller's Conversations at her bookstore at 13 West Street in Boston, the channels afforded by print publication were an available option for the wider circulation of their religious ideas. Fuller's landmark essay from 1843, "The Great Lawsuit. Man *versus* Men. Woman *versus* Women," as well as her published travel narrative from the following year, *Summer on the Lakes, in 1843*, represent two such instances of the author's public statements on religion, even if readers in our own day have downplayed the religious aspects of these texts.[11] Peabody, too, would publish an assortment of explicitly religious articles in a few of Boston's Unitarian periodicals. But whereas Fuller's statements on faith were somewhat fuzzy, Peabody's were largely ignored by a readership that, despite its affiliation with what was widely considered a "feminized church," stopped short at this time of granting women the authority that attached to the pulpit or its close proxy, the devoted following that accrued to a writer who enjoyed a favorable reception in the religious press. For the many more women to whom reliable access to even these limited print channels was denied, the regular upkeep of correspondence, journals, and diaries not only became their preferred mediums of communication, but also qualified as just such a religious "practice" as has been described elsewhere in this book. Such women as we will meet may have been prevented from taking on such "higher" labors as they perhaps felt were more in keeping with their abilities and inclinations. But when these women were not going through what many of them regarded as the unthinking motions of domesticity, they were often keeping religious counsel. This they might do by themselves, as when they were prompted by even a casual transcendental encounter to pour out the stream of their private spiritual thoughts into commonplace books and the various chronicles they kept of their religious lives. Or these same women could also circulate such writings among family members and friends, in this way promoting a practice of reflective exchange with other women from the very home space that had otherwise kept their religious adventures in check. It was not a prerequisite, regardless, that women's writings make their way into print if their authors were to earn the right to speak freely of such subjects as unbelief. There is a large archive of manuscript writings by women that suggests otherwise. In fact, and as we will see, the sex that was supposed to have had much to say (or, better yet, to *feel*) on such matters as sympathy, piety, and feminine "purity" was engaged in a rigorous written conversation on infidelity as well. It is high time we take a closer look at these underappreciated writings, and we will.

The commitment that some women made to what Kathleen Lawrence calls "aesthetic Transcendentalism" might seem a more conventionally gendered religious outlet by comparison. As Lawrence and others have demonstrated, there was a historical group of transcendental women that resorted to the plastic arts in order to further their own "intellectual, spiritual, and emotional growth."[12] The visual arts enjoyed special favor among these women. This was perhaps to be expected, given that many of them had had their artistic eyes opened by such traditional feminine avocations as sketching and watercoloring. But the transcendentalists' attachment to art exceeded the superficial exposure, or "finishing," to which many women were subjected at one or another of the female academies that operated in these years. That such pillars of transcendentalism as Margaret Fuller and Elizabeth Peabody gave serious countenance to aesthetics in the course of their respective romantic developments should not overshadow the fact that a number of women who had been reared on liberal Protestantism were becoming increasingly receptive to regarding "Art" as a corollary to their religious experience.

At the same time, the popular acclaim that several transcendental women, including Sarah Freeman Clarke and Caroline Sturgis, achieved with their paintings and drawings speaks to the potential that any appreciation of art (whether for art's sake or not) had for diverting the religious ends for which such works had ostensibly been created. Spiritualism and aestheticism were by no means antithetical, as the sacramental trappings of many a world religion would attest. There is an unrealized sense, however, in the aesthetic sensibilities of certain transcendental women that, under the influence of more permissive cultural conditions, Art might have become for them less a complement for religion than it was a substitute for the spiritual urges that not even a reformed faith could satisfy. This is not to say that aestheticism and atheism were inextricably linked, an interpretation that has gained some credence among students of nineteenth-century modernity in the West.[13] Yet we can say that transcendentalism's aesthetic connotations appear to have resonated more with women than they did with men. Nor were these women's devotions to Art always as compatible with their religion as they might have supposed. It was not seldom the case that transcendental women rethought their attitudes toward art and faith in tandem, with the result being that they were quite likely to find themselves holding onto notions of belief that left them further afield from orthodoxy than they had been before.

None of which should surprise us. Transcendental women might have been "different" from men in the sense that there were alternate religious avenues open to them at the historical period in which they lived. But their pursuit of such roads as were less traveled made them more than the victims of circumstance. Some were plagued by spiritual doubts the remedies for which were no more self-evident for them than they had been for the male subscribers to the New Views. Others were drawn to transcendentalism by the exciting spiritual possibilities it promised. In the end, however they arrived at their destinations, the women among the "like-minded" were involved in personal journeys of great significance to themselves and the wider religious culture, and they were unafraid to follow a spiritual path merely because it was fractious.

TALKING TRANSCENDENTALISM

Among the twenty-five or so women to attend the second session of Margaret Fuller's Boston Conversations, the initial series for which ran from November 1839 until May 1840, was Eliza Susan Morton Quincy, wife of Harvard's then president, Josiah Quincy. The general response to these as well as Fuller's forthcoming Conversations would prove favorable, as only a few of the women who'd paid the ten-dollar fee for a twelve- or thirteen-week package of bracing self-development would find themselves too intimidated (by the inimitable Fuller, as well as the unfamiliarity of the occasion) or too put off by the offered content to participate as much as they would have liked. "Mrs. Quincy," for her part, and to use the honorific title by which Harvard's de facto first lady was known, was less than convinced by the substance of these first gatherings, which had brought her east from her home in Cambridge. The elder Eliza Quincy (she bore a daughter by that same name in 1798) might have previously had a grandson enrolled in the transcendentalist educator Bronson Alcott's progressive Temple School, also in Boston. But Quincy was no progressive. "Her character and views were feminine and retired," the editor of Quincy's memoirs writes, and she was a liberal Christian in whom "the great questions of religious faith had early touched and excited her sensitive and reflective mind."[14] Quincy's presence alone confirms that not all of Fuller's collaborators in the Conversations—Fuller preferred to think of herself more as a facilitator than an instructor—carried what Charles Capper calls "radical credentials."[15] Indeed, her appearance in the domestic parlor of what would become, by that

July, Elizabeth Peabody's clearinghouse for the imported literatures of the New Views helps to dispel the Conversations' area reputation as "a kind of infidel association," where, Fuller's friend Sarah Clarke reported to her brother James, "several noted transcendentalists were engaged."[16]

If Quincy was not a woman to associate with rumored "infidels," she was also not the kind of upstanding Protestant to refrain from voicing her objections to Fuller's having selected a course in Greek mythology as the centerpiece for her opening Conversations. In Fuller's estimation, as we gather from Elizabeth Peabody's transcription of these early meetings, the Conversations' emphasis from the outset on what others might have considered a "pagan" literature held the advantage of being "serious without being solemn, without excluding every mode of intellectual action."[17] Not only did Quincy resist what Fuller, in Peabody's rephrasing, billed as an invitation for her women to get "playful as well as deep" (204), but, according to the unofficial record kept of that second meeting, Quincy also "expressed a doubt of these fables ever having been of serious import to the minds of the enlightened Greeks—& a feeling that they were gross & harmful superstitions" (204). Mrs. Quincy's objections were, in short, ones the transcendentalist Fuller had heard before. On her side, Quincy "expressed wonder & some horror at the thought of *Christians* enjoying *Heathen* Greeks"; on hers, Fuller spoke with admiration for the "idealization of the universal sentiments of religion," of which she believed the ancient Greeks to be the epitome (204). That Fuller would continue with her mythological survey—she turned her attention in subsequent Conversations to such subjects as Cupid and Psyche, Minerva and Vulcan—while inviting participants to draw parallels between Greek and Hebrew "fables" suggests she was not about to be deterred by the establishment standards of any emissary from Harvard (207). Fuller would, in fact, risk nothing more in these meetings than what many of the other women from among her core of loyal subscribers were already venturing on their own. For a fair number of these women, the majority of whom included close friends of Fuller's who held ties to the "movement," the years of transcendentalism's ascendance marked an appropriate time for questioning the religious conventions that they had been taught from their childhoods forward to accept as gospel truth. For others, including both young and unattached acolytes of Fuller's, as well as a group of older women who were either married to or in some way related to a prominent male reformer, these Conversations were but one of several venues in midcentury New England where such searching questions as they entertained could be posed with relative impunity. Here, religion was not so much assumed as it was interrogated, in accordance with the transcendental mandate of what Wesley Mott and David Robinson call "a theology of self-culture."[18]

The "theological" underpinnings of Fuller's Conversations amounted to more than an empty figure for what might have otherwise seemed a vaguely spiritual enterprise. Attendees came prepared to talk about religion in both direct and indirect ways. Fuller met these expectations with Conversations that addressed such religious questions as "faith" and "reverence," while proceeding with her overall agenda in accordance with the transcendental imperative for informed yet spontaneous discussion by minds communing in pursuit of "higher laws."[19] A Conversation normally began in the late morning on a weekday, with some two dozen women convening at eleven o'clock or noon for about two hours' worth of focused discussion. In lieu of any assigned reading, the women were introduced to the day's topic by Fuller, who, after outlining the principles to be placed under investigation, solicited questions and commentary from her participants. Such talking points as germinated during this warming-up phase were to derive naturally from the short essays that the women wrote (then later read aloud) ahead of most gatherings. Fuller's purpose throughout was twofold and remained the same for the entire four years in which she offered her Conversations. First, she wanted her women to use these occasions to step outside their accustomed "spheres," however separate they might be. Second, she encouraged those in attendance—not a few of whom commuted from such outlying towns as Brookline, Cambridge, and Concord—to learn to think for themselves, even in the face of as forceful a personality as Fuller's. Many of the women would make immediate use of this last faculty, availing themselves of the full complement of such of Boston's evening lecture series as appealed to their inner beings.[20] However else they disposed of their time in the city, the regular members of Fuller's audiences were never less than challenged by such religious querying as she solicited.

The original conversationalists responded to Fuller's promptings along the divided lines that have already been indicated. Together with the odd Calvinist who attended early on, the conservative Unitarians who came carrying views on the order of the aforementioned Mrs. Quincy's either ceased to express what Elizabeth Peabody called their "cavils" or else elected not to continue to assemble.[21] Others, like Sarah Hodges, the seventeen-year-old daughter of a

Unitarian minister in Cambridge, did their sincere best to rise to the level of spiritual insight to which Fuller had urged her subscribers. On the one hand, and as she related in a letter to her friend Esther Mack, Hodges (who was also receiving private tutorials in German from Fuller) would complain that the Conversations left her feeling "sometimes . . . as if I would rather not have doubts and difficulties suggested to me which I have not yet met with in my experience of life; and as if a simple faith in the words of Jesus were better than, even better without, all philosophy and reasoning of mortal men." On the other hand, and as Hodges would acknowledge in a show of the resolve to which Fuller had inspired her, she conveyed to her correspondent the lesson that informed the very spirit of the Conversations: that it was incumbent on each individual to work herself into, or out of, such a religious position as suited her. "The right way is to have the former firmly," Hodges wrote in reference to her "faith," "and by it to judge the truth of the latter," meaning "all philosophy and reasoning of mortal men."[22] And "mortal" women, she might have added.

As much as Fuller refrained from imposing—in her person, or her pedagogy—her own religious outlook on her charges, she could not help but bring her beliefs on belief to the Conversations she'd started. Fuller's feelings about faith were characteristically open from early in her self-development. Her friend James Freeman Clarke remembered, "Margaret, like every really earnest and deep nature, felt the necessity of a religious faith as the foundation of character" (*MMF,* 1:135). Such a "foundation" as Fuller articulated was anything but a rock of orthodoxy. Already, at the age of nineteen, she could write to another friend who'd asked about her religion, "I have determined not to form settled opinions at present." Rather, Fuller assured her correspondent, she did not "need a positive religion, a visible refuge, a protection." She would make do with what she called her "two articles of belief." "I believe in Eternal Progression," Fuller stated, and "I believe in a God, a Beauty and Perfection to which I am to strive all my life for assimilation." Not for her the "Tangible promises!" and "Well defined hopes!" of what Fuller named "the religion of Revelation" (1:135–36). By March 1834, while she was working as a schoolteacher in Providence, Fuller would admit, "I meet with infidels very often" and harbor "distressing sceptical notions of my own." This period in Fuller's religious unfolding would in fact lead her, as she wrote in her journal, "to examine thoroughly, as far as my time and abilities will permit, the evidences of the Christian Religion" (1:151). But, for the most part, Fuller stood firm by her insistence on leaving the religious door slightly ajar on the prospect that her spiritual self would only ever be expanding. "My soul is intent on this life," Fuller maintained, "and I think of religion as its rule" (1:135–36). That "rule" described a circuitous route that Fuller, by her own admission, recognized as requiring her to be "travelling" along "a thorny road" toward the "truly religious mind" that she, the good transcendentalist, identified with an "inward life" (1:194–95). Such a life would always need further exploring.[23]

Believer that she was, after her own fashion, Fuller was also prepared to offer an unprejudiced assessment of the spiritual claims of unbelief. She had found the "sceptical notions" that dogged her to be "distressing," we know. But because "her creed was, at once, very broad and very short"—that's how the New York newspaper editor Horace Greeley recalled the "profoundly religious" Fuller— she was willing to contemplate the possibility that irreligion might lead her (or anyone else) to the inner reserves of self-knowledge for which she was striving (*MMF,* 2:158). That infidelity should have entered into her Conversations, at a later date, was thus almost to be expected. In describing the city of Boston in these years, the local man of letters Thomas Wentworth Higginson would conjure up an image of "upheaval," saying that the "eighty-two pestilent heresies" with which the colonial Commonwealth of Massachusetts had been confronted at the time of the English Civil War paled in comparison to such "blasphemy" as had become the order of the day in Fuller's antebellum prime.[24] Fuller's giving heed to infidelity was more than a reflection of her general cultural conditions, however, Higginson's hyperbolic remarks on Boston notwithstanding. It was a product of her commitment to consciousness, her thoroughgoing investigations of which she was unwilling to accept as either preordained or exclusive of views that she personally did not hold.

Fuller's sixth Conversation, from her first year's series, suggests just how far she and her subscribers were prepared to go in stripping conventional religion of its usual protections. Not the least of these was belief's default status as the accepted spiritual condition for the region. At this particular meeting, as at others before and after, Fuller and her attendees stopped well short of equating being with believing. They reprised, instead, a classical discussion that set whatever residual liberal Christian assumptions the women had brought with them within a thoughtfully provocative, free-associative context that exempted no subject from scrutiny. In the meeting at hand, this meant Fuller's asking each woman for a definition of Wisdom—as embodied in the mythological figure of Minerva, with whom Fuller identified—only for her to abruptly change course (in response to a remark from her audience) and next ask the class for a separate definition of Beauty. At this point religion enters into the picture, as the women, with alacrity, one by one offer to define Beauty on terms that *transcend* the discussion's starting point at "Minerva & Vulcan." The transcript of this Conversation reads as follows: "Caroline Sturgis said it [Beauty] was the *attractive* power—the *central* unifying power—Maryann Jackson who had already remarked that beauty was always Sublime—said it was the *Infinite apprehended* under the *fewest conditions possible*. Anna Shaw said (before) that it was the *Infinite revealed in the finite*—to which Miss Fuller objected as a definition because it did not discriminate beauty from truth & love—Mrs. Geo. Ripley said it was the *aspect of the all*. it was the *mode* in which truth appeared—(these were not precisely her words)" ("Conversations," 208). Now that the Conversation had been framed within the more familiar religious parameters of the "finite" and "Infinite," we hear that "the distinction between the sublime & beautiful was touched upon" in turn, at which stage "Miss Fuller expressed the hope that she should rise above the sublime." That "Mrs. Ellen Hooper" (née Ellen Sturgis, a New England poet and transcendentalist of some distinction) should say that "she did not wish to do this—nor could she conceive of ever being in a state when there would not be an infinite above us"—suggests there was more at stake in these exchanges than the enlargement of Fuller's classroom method, with its romantic repurposing of Socratic give-and-take. By hook or crook the women of this sixth Conversation had instigated a frank and fully committed inquiry into religion. They did so, it should be emphasized, without any apparent fear of raising the red flag of heresy:

> Miss Fuller said that she could conceive of a state of being so harmonious with the divine order, that there would be no strain upon the soul such as is made by what we call the sublime. Mrs. Hooper thought that this would be to be God.—Miss Fuller admitted that it would be to be divine—& that she hoped—as long as we were conscious of the sublime we must have a painful sense of the inadequacy of our nature—Her idea of heaven was that we should get above this painful sense.—that the inadequacy would be no longer felt—that there would be no above or below—& the soul would enter into the divine happiness. ("Conversations," 209)

What Fuller proposes in this passage is nothing short of a spiritual reordering of cosmic consequence. Bracing for the day when "there would be no above or below," she more than hints at what "it would be to be divine." As we hear from Elizabeth Peabody's report, "Miss Fuller said she did not say *when*—she did not make the date of it the hour of death—but, that in the possibilities of her being was the loss of all imperfection—& the attainment of a divine nature, was the faith that reconciled her to this human nature—as the pedestal of that divine nature" (209). Fuller's "faith," in other words, relayed to her women the message of personal spiritual empowerment that Emerson had announced with wanton confidence in *Nature*.[25] Not only would Fuller bridge the traditional gap between the "finite" and "Infinite," but she would also have her women see that a frank discussion of faith could well be the means to their discovering a personal divinity that no orthodox church in New England would recognize.

WRITING A FEMININE INFIDELITY

In "Letter IX" of her *Letters from New York,* the Medford, Massachusetts–born abolitionist and transcendentalist Lydia Maria Child would write that "the education of circumstances" had taught her "to look calmly on all forms of religious opinion—not with the indifference, or the scorn, of unbelief; but with a friendly wish to discover everywhere the great central ideas common to all religious souls, though often re-appearing in the strangest disguises, and lisping or jabbering in the most untranslatable tones."[26] Child had been present in Boston for that memorable sixth installment in the first series of Margaret Fuller's Conversations. She had even offered her opinion then and there that Wisdom was "the union of the affections & understanding," the faint traces of which definition reappeared in her later characterization of transcendentalism, from April 1844, as "the doctrine of perpetual revelation, heard in the quietude of the soul" ("Conversations," 208). By her own admission, Child, like Fuller, preferred "to look at truth as universal, not merely in its particular relations" ("Letter IX," 67). So, too, did this preference apply to her conception of religion. Like Fuller, with her wide-open "idea of heaven," Child owned up to her "tendency to *generalize*" in matters of faith ("Letter IX," 67). This did not mean that she forgave the uninitiated for concluding, as she complained in "Letter XIII" from the second installment of her popular *New York* series, that "the minds so classified" as *transcendentalists* "are incongruous individuals, without any creed."[27] It did not sit well with Child that the name *transcendentalist* "is in fact applied to everything new, strange, and unaccountable." Her complaints were not without a touch of smiling irony, however. Child, recognizing the predicament of anyone unversed in the "New Views" trying to decipher them, wrote, "If a man is nonconformist to established creeds and opinions, and expresses his dissent in a manner ever so slightly peculiar, he is called a transcendentalist" ("Letter XIII," *Second Series*, 125).

That Child should have added irony to her "nonconformity" was not as out of keeping with the tone of women's involvement in the New Views as we might suppose. The women of transcendentalism did not shrink from approaching what they revered with irreverence. This was very much the case when it came to their attitudes toward religion. From "the general laugh" that ensued at the eighteenth of Fuller's debut Conversations, when "All spoke of men & women as equally souls—none seemed to regard men as animals & women as plants" ("Conversations," 217), to Louisa May Alcott's send-up portrayal of the motives behind the transcendentalist Fruitlands community in her story "Transcendental Wild Oats" (1873), many of the women associated with this episode in the religion of New England evinced what one observer calls a "satiro-comedic element" in their expression.[28] Whatever they did or did not believe, these women did not always have to take their spiritual selves too seriously.

As satisfying as the alternative tonal register of transcendental levity might have been for some, the communications medium of print set women in an even better position to enter into the alternative religious conversations that transcendentalism made possible. It was not that talk was cheap. Print publication, rather, lent women an air of authority that was otherwise denied them in an age when they were ineligible for admission to a school like Harvard and prohibited, by Saint Paul's dictum in the New Testament, from speaking in church. There were, of course, exceptions to women's exclusion in the middle decades of the nineteenth century from the male-dominated arenas of public speaking and writing. Abolitionist lecturers like the Grimké sisters, as well as the Quaker "prophetess" Lucy Stone, drew much public notice for their rousing speeches in this period. In bidding for full church membership, moreover, female parishioners regularly delivered some form of a tried and tested conversion narrative to their congregations, as they testified to having received God's saving grace. But, as Sandra Gustafson explains, both of these oral modes of communication—prophecy and the conversion narrative—depended on sentimental "rhetorics" that "carried the weight of the Lord's masculine authority." Women evangelists in this era were "female vessels for a masculine deity." Thus, they were hindered by the restrictions on women's "voice" that had been in place, historically, for more than two centuries.[29] If, by comparison, women appeared to have a freer rein in the domain of sentimental writing, the piety they practiced within this "dense and contentious" arena of "public avowals of religious belief" was, Claudia Stokes has shown, riven by the "sectarian affirmations" and "renunciations" of what was, effectively, a rough-and-tumble Methodist discourse that "implicitly" arranged them in "opposition to other competing religious groups." Not all sentimental writers were Methodists, of course. Such women writers as traded in sentiment were nevertheless influenced by a discursive mode that Stokes says was far from determined by the "decorum, conventionalism, and deferential obedience that have so often been attributed to literary sentimentalism." Indeed, it was not uncommon for sentimental writers to cast their perceived spiritual rivals as "heretical," so strenuously did they oppose those with competing religious beliefs.[30] Neither channel, then, spoken or written, was all that a transcendental woman who hoped to speak to a broader audience about her religion might have desired.

Some of them did write, regardless, with the effect of leveling such religious differences as they chose to address in their work. Unlike the "contentious" Methodist sentimentalists whom Stokes identifies as denominationally driven (4), these transcendentalists subscribed to an egalitarian ethos less for the sake of converting their readers to any particular religious feeling than to convince them of something that was perhaps still more heterodox: of the need, as Child would say, "to look calmly on all forms of religious opinion." The idea behind much of the transcendental women's writing is that any given religious "form," even irreligion, is an ideal vehicle of individual worship, to the extent that it satisfies the spiritual requirements of the person or the people who embraced it. Where the transcendentalists passed from being ecumenical to "heretical" was in the wide berth they gave unbelief. This was more than a question of religious tolerance; it was a question of redefining faith on entirely new terms.

Those terms were "secular" to the extent that secularism in modern America has amounted to a proliferation of religious possibilities rather than an absence of, or unresponsiveness to, religious faith.[31] José Casanova is careful to distinguish this spiritual state of the American nation from what exists in Europe. Secularism in the United States, he contends, has operated "to multiply to the nth degree the myriad options of belief rather than those of unbelief."[32] Grant Shreve elaborates this interpretation for the antebellum United States, explaining that the multiplier effect that a contemporary crisis in religious authority had on spiritual choice in the United States was produced not, as in Europe, "out of a dialectic of belief/unbelief where orthodoxy and atheism are its two poles." American secularism was instead "generated out of the unavoidable encounter with multiple ways of believing." The resulting religious field "of so many conflicting belief positions" may have produced, Shreve says, a "phenomenological fragility" among believers.[33] But it also helped foster, even in the vicinity of Unitarian Boston, enough of a disruption to religious convention as to afford the women of transcendentalism a role in the conversation on religion. Among the contributions they made to this conversation was to offer a fresh examination of unbelief, a religious option that certain commentators past and present had dismissed out of hand.

For much of the long nineteenth century, unbelief did in fact qualify as one of the "many conflicting belief positions" that inform Shreve's reading of religion in the United States. The women who had access to print in these years were among the reasons this was so. By rights the North Atlantic controversy on infidelity should have been neither as long-standing nor as rancorous as it was had unbelief really been unavailable to Americans as a religious alternative. Yet especially in New England, unbelief was, at the very least, inescapable reading material, at once the stuff of formal doctrinal inquiry and literal front-page news in such publications (and there were many of them) as afforded space within their pages to religious topics. Lending credence to Conrad Edick Wright's claim that infidelity emerged as a "serious threat" in America after the revolution—Harvard's eventual president John T. Kirkland thought enough of this threat to warn the college chapter of Phi Beta Kappa against it in 1798—Hannah More, in 1811, swore her readers away from "entertaining" either "some secret infidelity" or the religious "indifference" she named "practical infidelity."[34] The Polish-born Jewish suffragist, abolitionist, and freethinker Ernestine Rose went so far as to mount what she titled "A Defense of Atheism." "If I have no faith in your religion," she alerted readers of the *Boston Investigator* days before the start of the U.S. Civil War, "I have faith, unbounded, unshaken faith in the principles of right, of justice, and humanity."[35] The poet and hymnist Eliza Clapp articulated women's interrogative posture toward belief succinctly in 1845, in her book *Studies in Religion*. On behalf of women everywhere who had a searching, assertive interest in "spirit," Clapp wrote, "We are full of questions," and "We are all askers of them." The most pressing of these questions was this: "How shall we find out what we believe?"[36]

It was the women of transcendentalism, Clapp included, who most contributed to shaping what became a feminist conversation on unbelief. These women followed the lead of Elizabeth Peabody in this regard, for it was Peabody, as much as anyone, man or woman, who established the transcendentalists' exploratory standard for all matters of religion. As an intellectual counterweight to Margaret Fuller, Peabody was raised to inquire, without reservation, into the most complex spiritual questions. By the age of thirteen she had begun a lifelong correspondence with the liberal Unitarian minister William Ellery Channing. This was the same age at which the then Salem, Massachusetts–based Peabody crossed over "into heresy," Phyllis Cole says, the result of reading what Peabody called the eighteenth-century English theologian Nathaniel Lardner's "Socinian book" on "the Logos," an experience that this precocious teenager described as "like taking hold of hot coals to touch."[37] Having next had her first formative encounter with the writings of Samuel Taylor Coleridge, in the latter's short-lived English journal *Friend*, Peabody was exposed to the transcendental emphasis on spiritual intuition some five years before Emerson. On the strength of such evidentiary claims as this has Peabody been called "the first transcendentalist."[38] And Peabody, it must be said, was very much aware of the enormity of her situation. In a letter she wrote to the transcendental reformer Orestes Brownson in 1840, she took reflexive note of the "little historical fact [that] there in the bosom of Unitarianism, an unlearned girl, with only the help of those principles of philosophizing she gathered from the perusal of Coleridge's friend & . . . relying simply on her own poetical apprehension, as a principle of exegesis, should have seen just what is here expressed, concerning the socialism of true Religion & the divinity of Christ."[39] But as much as Peabody considered herself, in her own words, "a student of controversial divinity"—she said this out of a feeling of fellowship with the Christian men of the Harvard Divinity School, where she was unwelcome on an equal footing—she was not above looking for religion outside the normal corridors of the college, the church, and the private study.[40] She was convinced, rather, that women's common experiences must mold their religious interpretations. So, in her letters, Peabody took pains to personalize transcendental ideas in ways that would let them be understood by those of her female correspondents who were less learned than she was. She adopted a similar rhetorical strategy in her pedagogical writings (Peabody is credited with having started the first English-language kindergarten in the United States) as well, emphasizing such transcendental principles as she felt would have practical applications for the women who were charged with the development of individual selves in that traditional sphere of feminine influence, the elementary school classroom.[41] Following her own accelerated passage into spiritual self-possession, Peabody would write in her diary, "Now that I had found my own mind and its powers, the testimony of men was of comparatively little consequence to me."[42] She was nevertheless not content to rest knowingly in her own discoveries and worked hard to make sure that the tools of transcendentalism's religious questioning were as available to male students of divinity as they were to the women of domesticity, whose household lives must not have always seemed as if they were implicated in what passed on high.

Anyone looking for an easy introduction to such religious concepts as Peabody had at her command would have had to look elsewhere than her published writings. Channing, her mentor, advised Peabody that "you in your schoolroom, can . . . preach Christ more effectually, perhaps, than the minister in his pulpit!" (*Reminiscences*, 126). And to some extent this proved true, given the self-effacing reserve that Peabody demonstrated in the work she prepared for print.[43] What this work lacked in authorial voice it made up for in religious vision, however, as Peabody remained consistent in the articles she sent to press in extolling such creative, revelatory powers as she, like Emerson, believed were to be found within any given individual. As Peabody wrote by letter to her friend Eliza Guild in 1838, amid the fallout from Emerson's "Divinity School Address," it had come as some comfort to the pioneering Peabody "that this heresy does not belong to his mind alone."[44] Yet despite her sympathies with the religion of the person who, for all intents and purposes, was transcendentalism's public face, Peabody would remain more wedded to the example of personal self-renunciation imaged in Christ than was perhaps typical among the "like-minded." She would, in fact, trace with her work an alternate variety of the infidelity with which Emerson stood accused. More than that, Peabody would level her own charge against Emerson, but on different grounds than those that Andrews Norton occupied. In 1834, over the course of three successive issues of the Unitarian *Christian Examiner*—a journal edited at the time by Norton, who was also then serving as the Harvard Dexter Professor of Sacred Literature—Peabody offered a series of different vantages on the "Spirit of the Hebrew Scriptures," to use the running title of her submissions. By the last of these (Norton cut Peabody off after only three of a planned six installments, not wanting to commit to running the forty thousand words constituting the whole), Peabody had adopted what might be described as rather permissive views on infidelity. In a circumambient statement titled "Public Worship" that combines higher criticism of the Old Testament with some forward-looking reflections on "the antediluvian traditions," Peabody, who was no apologist for what she styled "the Patriarchal religion," sets what she must have felt were reasonable limits to what she or anyone else could regard as belief.[45] "In the days of the first revelation," she writes, "and even in the days of Moses, there were no skeptics from philosophical speculation. The infidel of that day, was only one practically; overwhelmed by physical passions, or thoughtless of God through the multiplicity of momentary impressions" ("Hebrew Scriptures," 3:84). Or, as Peabody established in the second of her essays, "Spirit," "Moses was . . . not writing to a people skeptical from philosophical speculation, but only skeptical, if they ever were so, from stupidity and sensuality" ("Hebrew Scriptures," 2:309). Given the company she kept, Peabody was unlikely to meet with such skepticism as she construes here. Even if she did, she seems prepared to account for an infidelity that she can only imagine as a "momentary" bout of such "thoughtless" response as usually greeted an overabundance of "impressions."

What Peabody regarded as the "egotism" of Emerson was another matter altogether. More than twenty years after the publication of the first half of her "Hebrew Scriptures" series, Peabody would update her position on "skepticism" with a pair of articles that address atheism by name. The two pieces ran concurrently in different journals in September 1858.[46] In the first of these, "The Atheism of Yesterday," the author picks up where she had left off almost two and a half decades before. Positing the virtual impossibility of being "without" religion, Peabody goes on to say that atheism as it was practiced in the past "was always a denial, and a denial presupposes an affirmation." At the same time, without ever conceding that the once suspect supporters of the "New Views" were *against* a theistic understanding of religion, Peabody, in a statement that goes some way toward countering all those earlier attempts to cast transcendentalism as a "negative" faith, maintains that "the denial of a God presupposes the existence in man of some faculty anterior to reflection, which may apprehend Infinite Being" (227). As for the atheism of her own present day, Peabody was not so forgiving. In "Egotheism, the Atheism of To-day," Peabody all but names the impassioned individualist Emerson as the "negative" representative of such a "faith" as "stagnates in the mere affirmation of the spiritual, [when] men deify their own conceptions" (243, 245). In a famous rapturous passage from *Nature,* Emerson had assured his readers that "all mean egotism vanishes" in such moments of transcendence as he himself achieved in crossing a bare winter common.[47] Peabody argued instead in her "Hebrew Scriptures" for an opposing "social principle" of "sympathy," by which all of us would always be "engaging" our "feelings for others" (1:188). In Peabody's eyes, "faith commits suicide" in Emerson's religion, as must be the case whenever that "which denies other self-consciousness to God than our own subjective consciousness" takes root. "Man proves but a melancholy God," Peabody writes. And though the "Egotheist" was, from her perspective, "not without a degree of religious instinct," he practiced that "transient form" of faith that Peabody, after Norton, names "this 'latest form of infidelity,' as the understanding has rather blindly denominated it" ("Egotheism," 245). Peabody did not discount "Egotheism" because it was atheism. Her conception of religion did not even require a belief in a divinity per se; what Peabody called "spiritual activity" was inclusive enough to admit any manifest "*principle* of acting *from* the love, *in* the wisdom, *with* the power of God" (242). What Peabody objected to was the Egotheist's "worshipping ME" (252). For inasmuch as this ominously Emersonian figure "sees that nothing man says or does is so great as himself, the sayer and doer," he upset the potential for such a faith as was shared by transcendental women from Peabody to Child to Fuller: a belief in the widest possible margin for belief.

If Peabody was the first female transcendentalist to address infidelity, she was not the last. Margaret Fuller would have her say on irreligion, too. Like Peabody, Fuller made use of her access to print publication for this purpose, similarly resorting to both professional journal and book formats for her work. Unlike Peabody, Fuller wrote less as a theologian than as a modern incarnation of the romantic religionist, with the comparable result of raising the ceiling on faith in ways that were proscribed by convention. From an orthodox perspective, Fuller's transgressions were at least twofold. There was, first, the special religious position she envisioned for women. Toward the end of the century, a group of prominent female reformers would recall that Fuller's loose associate, the transcendentalist Theodore Parker, regarded her "as a critic, rather than a creator or seer."[48] Privately, Fuller aspired to so much more, projecting herself (and, by implication, any woman who might follow her example) instead as a "poetic priestess, sibylline, dwelling in the cave, or amid the Libyan sands" (*MMF,* 1:299). In fulfilling this role, Fuller refrained from openly challenging women's historical subordination to a church structure that had effectively silenced them, but she did, in her writings, promote what has been called a "gender-inflected millennialism" at "the intersection of . . . liberal religion and feminist reform."[49] Her second offense, as far as conservative Christians would have been concerned, was to commit a softening of the stance against infidelity, even as she assessed the challenges that had lately beset faith in her century. Unbelief was real for Fuller. Yet she deemed it far less of a threat than the collective farce she felt a nation of religious hypocrites had made of faith.

Such hopes as Fuller had for women's religion she discussed at length in her essay "The Great Lawsuit. Man *versus* Men. Woman *versus* Women."[50] By 1845 Fuller had expanded this piece into a full-length book, the feminist milestone *Woman in the Nineteenth Century*. For the time being, she broadcast her thoughts in the *Dial*. This was the same journal that she edited from 1840 to 1842 and from which her friend the "Christian transcendentalist" Frederic Henry Hedge had kept a politic distance, declining by letter to Fuller in 1840 to contribute work of his own out of fear of being branded "an atheist in disguise."[51] Fuller obviously had no such fears; nor did she consider her views on women's religion to be even remotely heretical. "The Great Lawsuit" reads, rather, as a meditation by Fuller on the equality of the sexes, couched in the transcendental language of spiritual immanence that the speaker she appoints to the task equates with a personal coming into consciousness. The legal metaphor of Fuller's title notwithstanding, her subject with this manifesto is first and last religion. Arguing broadly for a human "inheritance" that we have not yet received in full, Fuller for the most part pitches her remarks on a prophetic plane, where she claims for men and women alike a "divine instinct" that will enable us to "interpret the open secret of love passing into life" (2–3). The key to Fuller's spiritualism is "faith," not so much in an "All-Creating" and "All-Sustaining" God, but the Emersonian God that Fuller accepts as residing inside each and every one of us (3). For Fuller, the "soul" that is in command of itself is equipped for more than a "telescopic peep at the heavens"; it is the means by which mortal man, and woman, has access to "the highest ideal man can form of his own capabilities" and "which he is destined to attain" (1, 4). Fuller is furthermore keen to emphasize, on the one hand, that hers is "a positive appeal from the heart, instead of a critical declaration what man shall not do" (5). She advocates for no *negative* religion. She is equally careful to articulate, on the other hand, that the twin themes of "The Great Lawsuit"—transcendentalism and feminism—are not contradictory. As she writes, "An improvement in the daughters will best aid the reformation of the sons of this age" (7).

Fuller does acknowledge the "skepticism" with which her remarks will be greeted by the average reader, who "wants faith and love," she says, "because he is not yet himself an elevated being" (18). She is bothered less, however, by a "decrepit skepticism" than she is the insincerity that she sees in a supposed "promised land" where "everything has been done that inherited depravity could, to hinder the promise of heaven from its fulfilment" (4, 7). Fuller cannot and does not defend how Americans have greeted such religion as they might have encountered. But she writes as if they could not have done otherwise, given the backwardness of the era in which they lived. Compared to Fuller's experience of unpretending earnestness while coming of age in New England— as a girl of fifteen she spent her afternoons thrilled to be reciting Greek at the Cambridge Port Private Grammar School and as a young woman in her midtwenties exulted in the intellectual companionship of such acquaintances as the Harvard professors Edward T. Channing and Cornelius C. Felton—the mass of Americans was spiritually impoverished. Fuller felt the effects of this difference in the availability of spiritual resources, as well as the will to utilize them. And as a result, she writes, she could only watch as "the name of the Prince of Peace has been profaned by all kinds of injustice towards the Gentile whom he said he came to save" (7). It was, for Fuller, the peddlers in "cant" and "hypocrisy"—"these word-Catos, word-Christs," she calls them—who had the run of "this country" and who perpetrated "the meanest of crimes" in what she calls a religion of "the market-place" (7–9, 13). Still, hers was not a fallen world. Fuller might have been ready to allow "the worldling . . . his sneer here as about the services of religion," namely, that "the churches can always be filled with women" (38). But, as was the case with Peabody, she can almost not believe in unbelief, when there remains so much to believe in out from under the normal auspices of convention.

Whatever her feelings about belief, Fuller remained certain there were enough *believers* to counteract the "sneering skepticism" that she admits was a "sign" of the times. More important, she writes from the conviction that such "puffed" displays of empty piety as filled "the wind of declamation, on moral and religious subjects," would be righted by women, who were poised to restore religion to a better state (18, 9). "The especial genius of woman," Fuller writes, "I believe to be electrical in movement, intuitive in function, spiritual in tendency" (43). In other words, rather than argue that women be afforded a public role in administering and disseminating religion, she accepts on faith that women are creatures *of* faith and are thus suited for taking the lead in the romantic maximalist effort for a self-affirming spiritualism that recognizes no distinctions of gender. The final plea of "The Great Lawsuit" is for what Fuller calls spiritual "free-agency" (12). She would have women, and men, depend solely on themselves in their religious lives. That religion was already in each of our "souls" Fuller accepts on trust. That those "souls" needed stirring was her professed reason for writing. If others were inclined to approach the work of consciousness raising as a "critical" endeavor, as an assault on a pervasive skepticism, for Fuller it was only ever an affirmative undertaking.[52] She wrote "The Great Lawsuit" as one woman's prayer for sincerity, at a moment when many of her contemporaries were distracted by what they were prepared to recognize only as blasphemy.

Spent by her exertions in bringing "The Great Lawsuit" to press, Fuller sought a different perspective on life, letters, and religion by the spring of 1843. She longed for a journey to Europe, the seat of so many of the "New Views" with which she had familiarized herself over the course of the preceding decade. With no such trip in the offing, she welcomed the opportunity to accompany her friend James Freeman Clarke and his sister, the Conversations alumnus Sarah, on an extended tour of the American West. The logistics of the trip were as varied as Fuller could have wanted, given that she wished to break free from her everyday routines. By turns, the friends traveled much of the way by train and steamboat, trading these modes of transport for carriage and foot when circumstances required. The four-month journey was equally a change of scenery for Fuller; her itinerary described a circular journey around the Great Lakes. The group set forth from Niagara Falls, heading as far north as Mackinac Island and Sault Ste. Marie, in Michigan. To the west, they reached a farthest point at Milwaukee; to the south, they ranged as far as Pawpaw, Illinois, before heading home by way of Buffalo, New York. The published account that Fuller produced of her travels bore the title *Summer on the Lakes, in 1843* (1844). This was no misnomer, as the friends did in fact spend a good amount of time on the waters of said lakes. Mostly they spent their time on land, however, getting to know the diverse cultures of the towns and villages of Wisconsin and Illinois. Fuller was back in Boston on September 19, 1843. With her were the notes she'd use as the basis for the book that she planned to write over the ensuing months. What Fuller also took away from her travels was a sense for what Susan Belasco Smith calls "the true spirit that animates daily life" out West.[53] Much of that spirit was *spiritual* and of such comparative strangeness as many of her readers in the East could only imagine.

If *Summer on the Lakes* reads as a mixture of genres—Fuller combines in this work the elements of everything from European and American travel narrative to autobiography, social commentary, and transcendental meditation—it adheres as closely to religion in its images and themes as does "The Great Lawsuit." It would be more accurate to say that if "The Great Lawsuit" can be somewhat elliptical in confronting irreligion, then *Summer on the Lakes* is candid to the point of being caustic. The object of the author's most biting remarks are not the ragged "infidels" we might expect a member of the coastal elite to discover at the western outposts of "civilization." Fuller reserves her greatest scorn for the self-deceiving "believers" from among her own peers: eastern in origin, western in orientation, and Christian by tradition. Early in her journey, aboard a steamboat launched from Buffalo, Fuller's narrator (her trip in fact begins in late spring, during the second week of June) is careful to observe that "the people on the boat were almost all New Englanders, seeking their fortunes" (12). "They had brought with them their habits of calculation, their cautious manners, their love of polemics," our narrator, a close double for Fuller, continues (12). And what the people she observes most enjoy is religious disputation, of which subject Fuller speaks as follows:

> It wearied me, too, to hear Trinity and Unity discussed in the poor, narrow doctrinal way on these free waters; but that will soon cease, there is not time for this clash of opinions in the West, where the clash of material interests is so noisy. They will need the spirit of religion more than ever to guide them, but will find less time than before for its doctrine. This change was to me, who am tired of the war of words on these subjects, and believe it only sows the wind to reap the whirlwind, refreshing, but I argue nothing from it; there is nothing real in the freedom of thought at the West, it is from the position of men's lives, not the state of their minds. (12–13)

However else Fuller might have felt about her countrymen, she makes it known from the beginning of her book that the "narrow doctrinal way" they were pursuing out West would bring them no closer to "the spirit of religion" they'd need "to guide them" in their new settlements. As far as she was concerned, neither would "the clash of material interests" they must eventually allow to replace their religion prove any more of a spiritual compass, "so noisy" was the course they had chosen to follow. Lost as they must have been, in consequence, in a "whirlwind" expanse where religion was more than a metaphor, these peoples of the speaker's native New England region represent the very reasons a believer of Fuller's liberal persuasion came to transcendentalism in the first place. Having grown "wearied" of the debates over "Trinity and Unity," she, like the rest, sought a new faith in order to be "free."

For the author of *Summer on the Lakes,* that search was ongoing. It had, in fact, carried her well clear of such respectable sanctuaries as the Harvard College Library, where Fuller, during the interval she allotted as the preparation phase for her book over the first half of 1844, became the first woman to enjoy research privileges.[54] In the meantime, in the midst of her travels to the West, Fuller found religion in places well beyond the eastern drawing rooms that she had, temporarily, left behind. Four days out from Buffalo, during a landing along the white-pebbled beaches of the Manitou islands, the author passes through scenes of "mushroom growth" that betray the recent white settlers' "rudeness of conquest." Promising "not [to] be so obliging as to confound ugliness with beauty, discord with harmony," Fuller goes on to say that she can "trust by reverent faith to woo the mighty meaning of the scene, perhaps to foresee the law by which a new order, a new poetry is to be evoked from this chaos." In fact, "our visit was so far for a religious purpose," Fuller's narrator declares, "that one of our party went to inquire the fate of some Unitarian tracts left among the woodcutters a year or two before" (18–19). But it is at a later stop in Mackinaw, in the northern tip of Michigan's lower peninsula, that Fuller arrests readers' attention with a consideration of religious difference: not between man and woman but between the Native Americans and what her speaker calls the "civilized or Christianized" newcomers to this area (143). Stopping short in her reflections, Fuller's narrator states, "I have not wished to write sentimentally about the Indians, however moved by the thought of their wrongs and speedy extinction" (143). True to her word, she speaks of "the conflicts which sprang from the collision of the two races," the result, from her point of view, of the colonizers' having "felt themselves justified by their superior civilization and religious ideas" (143). The narrator's own feelings are markedly different from those of her "civilized" predecessors. She makes this much evident in the following paean to a native faith:

> The Indian is steady to that simple creed, which forms the basis of all this mythology; that there is a God, and a life beyond this; a right and wrong which each man can see, betwixt which each man should choose; that good

> brings with it its reward and vice its punishment. Their moral code, if not refined as that of civilized nations, is clear and noble in the stress laid upon truth and fidelity. And all unprejudiced observers bear testimony that the Indians, until broken from their old anchorage by intercourse with the whites, who offer them, instead, a religion of which they furnish neither interpretation nor example, were singularly virtuous, if virtue be allowed to consist in a man's acting up to his own ideas of right. (128)

Drawing much of her information on the local Indians from "Old Adair," which is to say James Adair, an Indian trader who wrote *History of the American Indians* in 1775, the narrator grants that this observer's forty years of dealings with the nearby tribes to the south enabled him to do "great justice to their religious aspiration" in his reporting (128). As a people, we're told, the Native Americans of Adair's description are "clear and noble in the stress laid upon truth and fidelity." Adair himself suffers in the implied comparison, as *Summer on the Lakes*'s speaker indicates with a passage that applies as much to her counterpart's writing technique as it does to his religion: "An infidel; he says, is, in their language, 'one who has shaken hands with the accursed speech'; a religious man, 'one who has shaken hands with the beloved speech.' If this be a correct definition, we could wish Adair more religious" (128).[55] Upending the normal order of religious valuation—with the "noble" Native cutting an honorable figure of "truth and fidelity" in relation to the "accursed speech" of the "infidel" intruder—the narrator of *Summer on the Lakes* suggests just how far beyond the pale of religious convention she is prepared to travel.

The author, Fuller, has something other than ethnography on her mind as she writes the above lines from well outside the confines of domestic tradition. A woman in the wilderness, she claims to have located a far more reliable refuge for her faith here, on the edge of "civilized" life, than anything she has so far discovered in the comfort zone of her commonwealth. *Summer on the Lakes* bears a close resemblance to "The Great Lawsuit" in this respect. In both of these religious statements, the ideal believer—a woman in the one case, an Indian in the other—takes the narrative shape of an ideal belief. That belief is represented, respectively, as an embodiment of either the gendered or the ethnic opposite of such failings of white male religious privilege as have been handed down to the Americans of the nineteenth century from the cradle of New England. There are, to say the least, a heterogeneous variety of different forms that faith can take in Fuller's writings. If these were considered out of bounds according to the usual expectations of her day, then Fuller, like the other transcendental women of her century, was not averse to blazing a new trail of belief.

A STUDY IN IRRELIGIOUS RECEPTION

In their coauthored study "Transcendentalism in Print," Ronald J. Zboray and Mary Saracino Zboray have discovered what they describe as a "hunger for multifarious religious reading matter" among New Englanders generally in the six decades before the U.S. Civil War.[56] The related appetite for transcendental ideas in the region was similarly strong, Zboray and Zboray confirm. And as the oral tradition behind Margaret Fuller's Conversations makes clear, there were various conduits by which transcendentalism could be disseminated and debated. Among the most important channels for transcendentalism's spread was print, whether of original transcendental material or else its redaction in periodical reviews and pamphlet formats. The coauthors show that the region's women readers included a reliable, if not uncritical, audience for these printed expressions of transcendentalism. At the same time, they demonstrate that "common readers," as they call them, "self-consciously incorporated transcendentalism in print into their everyday lives" (360). Thus, it turns out that women were not unknown to read to one another from transcendental texts in the most pedestrian of spaces, from the bustling factory floors that were "manned" by the female operatives of New England's textile mills to the therapeutic water-cure establishments frequented by members of the middle and upper classes. Of all the spaces where transcendentalism could depend on a thoughtful (if not always hospitable) reception, however, none was more reliable than the family domicile. It was the "feminine" sphere of the antebellum home where women often met the transcendental challenge to their religion head-on, since it was in the comparative sanctuary of the domestic setting where women were free not only to receive but to respond to such tangible artifacts of the New Views as had been placed before the reading public by an assortment of writers, printers, and publishers. As Ronald J. Zboray and Mary Saracino Zboray write, transcendental texts in this way "became entrenched in the everyday" (360).

There was nothing "common" about any of this. Although women's reception of transcendental ideas—as conveyed either in print or in some other expressive medium—might have facilitated what seemed to be familiar interpersonal exchanges in recognizable settings, the collective feminine encounter with what were, in the period, the outer bounds of liberal religion in New England was sometimes a hazardous affair. Quite simply, a woman's reception of transcendentalism could still bring her to the brink of what many contemporaries regarded as irreligion. Precisely because the varieties of religious belief at midcentury were so many, a woman's meeting with transcendentalism in the semiprivate space of the home could be less of a remedy for a person's (or a people's) outstanding spiritual complaints than it was another inducement to the questioning of one's faith. Any religious test that a woman underwent as a result of her "everyday" reception of transcendentalism no more qualified as "common" for being self-administered than it did for being part and parcel of her ordinary routine. Indeed, no matter when, where, or how it occurred, a woman's meeting with transcendentalism frequently represented a high-stakes moment in her spiritual life. In the end, the range of spoken, written, and contemplated responses such meetings generated were not unknown to carry the resident domestic questioner well beyond the relative sacred space that was religious convention in the nineteenth century.

What's noteworthy, to begin, about laywomen's participation in the "movement" is the extent to which they set the terms of their transcendental reception. During his annual summer retreat to the resort town of Newport, Rhode Island, the eminent Unitarian minister William Ellery Channing might have "lamented" with nineteen-year-old Hannah Lowell Jackson that "a lady's time is unavoidably in the present state of society frittered away." Yet Channing also "seemed to think that we," meaning young women like Hannah, and as Jackson recorded Channing's remarks in her diary, "must each one for herself make a stand against it & say that we will have some time to read & think alone."[57] By all accounts, the region's women were, in fact, very much given to independent reading and thinking; if they were not necessarily doing so "alone," they did maintain informal conversations with each other (and themselves) through correspondence, private journal entries, and commonplace practices that folded transcendentalism into an ongoing examination of their personal religious orientations. As would be expected, women's schooling prompted some of these reflections. This was the natural result of formative minds coming into contact with religious ideas that must have seemed as fresh and exciting as they were dangerous and taboo. For example, in the journal she kept at Elizabeth Sedgwick's Lenox Academy for girls in the Berkshire Mountains of western Massachusetts, a young Isabel Morgan could pay tribute in her journal in the summer of 1845 to the "beautiful writings" of the transcendentalist Theodore Parker, which "Mrs. Sedgwick" had apparently read out loud with approval to her charges. But in a separate entry just one day later, Morgan would record her notes from a subsequent school lecture called "Systems of Necessity" that addressed such "false principles" as attached to "pantheism, mysticism, skepticism, and those that deny the freedom of the will."[58] Whether in school or out, a woman who had entertained "skepticism" even as an academic exercise was not always to be dictated to in her religious preferences. At the very least, and as the cases of other women in the area suggest, the effort required to reconcile any unfamiliar spiritual "ism" with one's professed religion entailed just the kind of self-directed thought that Channing had thought it necessary to recommend to Hannah Jackson's generation. His concerns were redundant in this regard. Women had already accepted the transcendental challenge, and they were working through its implications both with and without the tutelage of spiritual leaders and teachers. In the words of the daughter-in-law of Concord's Reverend Ezra Ripley, a minister's wife who otherwise professed to "acquiesce in God's election," there was a "spiritual guidance" to be had "in strict accordance with the laws of the mind." And neither man nor woman needed to commit such an "aberration" as to "become transcendental," this same Sarah Ripley wrote by letter from the mill town of Waltham, in order to validate one's "own way of looking at truth."[59]

Apart from the comparative autonomy that women enjoyed in their thinking about religion, what further distinguished the feminine reception of transcendentalism was the degree to which the "movement's" passage to and through liberal religion appears to have encouraged the taking of a range of liberties that once would have been unthinkable. Much as Fuller's Conversations had helped to loosen women's tongues, the "everyday" discussions of religion that transcendentalism elicited freed the hands, minds, and hearts of women who were disposed to acknowledge having strayed from the straight-and-narrow conventions of their faith. Martha Lawrence Prescott was one such woman, and her example is as representative of any of those provided of how someone of a conventional New England upbringing could, as a result of her indirect exposure to transcendentalism, evince habits of religious self-examination that exceeded even the norms of her native Protestantism. "The more I study it the more I doubt." That's how an eighteen-year-old Prescott confided to her diary in the spring of 1836 that her readings in the materialist philosophy of

John Locke—the reaction to whose work marked a point of departure from Unitarianism for many a transcendentalist—had left her feeling vulnerable to the Enlightenment giant's "lengthy & subtile speculations." Prescott first encountered Locke's thought in her course work at the Concord Academy, the same school from which the future author of *Walden* had already graduated and would soon return to teach between the years 1838 and 1841. Not only did the writings of the English philosopher "make the brain ache to think of," as Prescott wrote, but "Locke's doctrines," she'd heard said of a figure to whom the romantic transcendentalists of her generation had raised objections of their own, "evidently lead to infidelity & indeed were the foundation of the Voltaire system in France."[60]

On the whole, Prescott's outlook on life would prove "more spiritual than material," in the words Leslie Perrin Wilson uses to describe one conscientious Unitarian who became a valued member of Ezra Ripley's First Parish Church.[61] Still, amid the many notes of religious discord that were being struck by Prescott's townspeople—her family had only recently moved to a house on Concord's Monument Street in 1833—this sometime classmate of Thoreau's sister Sophia remained ever watchful of her private religious impulses at a time when such matters could not be taken for granted. "Hope I shall find something before long which will free me from my skepticism," she confessed, "else I must not think at all" (April 5, Wilson, 128). It was in this way that Prescott fell into a pattern of nursing "speculations" that were intended as a kind of counterweight to Locke's. These punctuated a life that was otherwise fairly typical for a girl of Prescott's age, place, and social station among Concord's comparatively learned and increasingly leisured middle classes. On any given day, Martha, on the brink of womanhood, could be found being fitted for dresses, paying social visits with her mother to the homes of neighbors, making repeated resolutions "to be more agreeable to others," courting "sympathy" from family and friends, and coming to question whether the "housework" to which she was being introduced (and "which I do abominate," she was careful to record) was any less burdensome than what she had read in the impossible Locke (April 5 and 23, 128, 133; May 12, 139). "Woman was made for something higher than a cook, a drudge," she wrote, "& yet how many spend their lives in nothing else?" (May 12, 139). Meanwhile, whether she was completing her assigned reading for school, attending lectures at the local lyceum, or participating in such extracurricular activities as were afforded by the Concord Academic Debating Society, Prescott enacted her part in what was more and more a familiar ritual for many of the young women of New England, who had come of age, spiritually speaking, at the moment of transcendentalism's emergence in the region as a religious alternative to the orthodoxy that had informed their upbringing.

Prescott was no transcendentalist. She was a volunteer of several years' standing as a Sunday-school teacher for her parish. She left ample space inside her diary to defend the "strict observances" of her religion (April 12, 130). Somehow she construed the demeanor of at least one Unitarian defector, the local celebrity Ralph Waldo Emerson, as "dignified & Christian" (May 15, 141), this coming just four months before the September publication of the author's groundbreaking book, *Nature*. And, perhaps consoling herself for the impasse she'd reached with Locke, Prescott reasoned as well that the high price paid by "the most worldly & irreligious men" for their superior educations was that they were also, in her mind, the most eligible to be counted as "infidels & atheists" (May 8, 137). "I am certain," she decided, with a phrase taken from Luke 10:42, "that without religion there is no permanent happiness. There is a craving which nothing earthly can satisfy, a consciousness of the vanity of our pleasures. . . . It is indeed 'the one thing needful'" (May 15, 114).[62] Prescott's protestations to the contrary, it was not, however, "the most worldly & irreligious men" alone who were at risk of turning "infidels & atheists" in these years. The very "skepticism" conceded by this adopted daughter of Concord—the religious "doubt" that resulted from her brush with such reading materials as would have been standard fare for her male peers at Harvard—suggests that even those women who resisted turning fully transcendental occupied a place in a religious culture that the "New Views" had already changed.

The women of that culture were changing, too. Prior to her marriage to the Harvard-educated writer and lawyer Richard Henry Dana Jr., Sarah Watson, of Springfield, Massachusetts, had already stated by the fall of 1833 a strong preference in her diary for what she named the "liberal" ministrations of the Reverend William B. O. Peabody to those of the other ministers who presided from time to time over her local Unitarian church. While Peabody invited his parishioners to take pride from their neighbors' having supposedly branded them "heretics, merely because they are not a set of blind bigots," a Mr. Hawes had somehow found nothing inconsistent in railing against "unorthodoxy" after having opened a recent service by asking his congregation, "What is religion?" For such apparent effrontery, Sarah had little tolerance. She had still less for the tired sermonizing of her senior pastor, the Reverend Dr. Osgood, who on one Sunday had caused her to testify that she "came home without having received one idea." When it came to "ideas," rather, she had a number of additional options at her disposal. She could resort to the prayerful urgings toward the "cultivation of all our powers" made by another visiting minister, Horace Bushnell. Or else she might take the advice of a corresponding friend and read the chapter "Natural Supernaturalism" from Thomas Carlyle's "greatly decried" book *Sartor Resartus* (1833–34)—translation, the tailor, retailored—the "seriocomic novel of ideas" that Dean Grodzins says anticipated transcendentalism with its account of the struggles of a German professor of "Allerley-Wissenschaft" to resist the "Everlasting No" of skepticism with the "Everlasting Yes" of a reconstituted faith.[63]

The religious negotiations of women like Sarah Watson amounted to more than a flirtation with infidelity. They were a homespun instance of women responding to the spiritual mandate that transcendentalism had brought home to them: as Thomas Carlyle might have said, to find a faith that "fit." This transcendental imperative was more easily talked about than accomplished, many women realized. As Catherine Robbins, of Northampton, wrote in her diary in October 1836, it was, in fact, surprising that "undisciplined people" such as herself "have not settled into a state of indifference and a stoical unconcern as to what does happen," considering the "resistance" they were all but required to offer "to the untoward circumstances and unexpected evils of every day."[64] In Robbins's words, a person didn't need to make "pretensions to transcendentalism" to recognize that one's coming into (or out of) religion could never quite prepare her for the "new scenes and new subjects" to which a woman in these years was subjected. Nor did she need to agonize over the vicissitudes of what Robbins called "the present and the sensible" world (February 12, 1837). If nothing else, her attendance, say, at the transcendentalist Emerson's lectures ("Still is there a sacredness and reverence mingled with my admiration of him," Robbins wrote, "though his principles are all familiar to me") had given her reason enough to believe in a "life" that she would otherwise characterize as "one long exercise of patience and faith" (February 27, 1838; October 22, 1836).[65]

Not all women were as decorous as Robbins in giving expression to their religious sentiments, such as they were. Over in Cambridge, Louisa Lee Waterhouse, wife of the Harvard physician Benjamin Waterhouse, was more inclined to bury Emerson than to praise him. She marked her completion of Howard

Malcolm's book *Travels in South-Eastern Asia* (1839) with a satiric remark made in April 1840 that can only have been intended as a rebuttal to the interfaith position staked out by the Concord sage. After recording in her diary that she had taken an abundance of notes on "Buddhism in my own words," she crossed out these comments only to replace them with "No one wants to know Buddhism."[66] For her part, Sarah Smith (Cox) Browne, of Salem, in between her running tallies for such household expenses as gingerbread, potatoes, utility bills, and rent, would admit by letter to her husband in June 1855 that "in childhood" she had "played with the 'History of the Devil,' yet I came out, intuitively, on the liberal side."[67] The offhand quality of such remarks as these accounted for the style as much as the substance of many women's thoughts on religion. That is to say, religion was something they *lived* with from day to day, and what might strike the modern ear as carrying a note of flippancy was in fact a testament, in the way of tone, to just how ingrained a habit the worrying over religion was during the transcendental decades of the 1830s, 1840s, and 1850s. Thus, there is nothing especially remarkable in the former mill girl turned Norton, Massachusetts, educator Lucy Larcom's writing, in April 1855, that she did quite "like" the "hominy fed" transcendentalist "Hennery" David Thoreau, "since I can read Walden." "He's a curiosity, any way [*sic*]," Larcom would add, despite her "doubt whether, in the nature of things, the world can become philosophic enough to appreciate philosophers."[68] Nor was there anything surprising about Larcom's friend the suffragist Harriet Hanson Robinson, rehearsing the punch line in her diary from 1855 to a joke about an alms-giving "gentleman" by the name of "Mr. Jesus Heavenly Sheppard," or in her writing the following year with some credulity of "the table-tipping power" of Larcom's abilities as a medium. "These so-called spiritual communications," Robinson decided, after having witnessed Larcom summon what appeared to be an ice cream–eating "spirit" in her home kitchen, "are singular and some of them are rather striking to an unbeliever."[69] In other words, much as women in these years exercised the right to cross back and forth between belief and "unbelief," they passed just as easily between spiritual and unexceptional realms that, for them, necessarily intersected. However humdrum their lives might have been otherwise, these women seldom relented in the free and open and ongoing evaluations of their own faith.

What the feminine conversation surrounding transcendentalism and other forms of liberal, or even radical, religion had made possible was a cultural environment in which a woman's soul-searching could edge ever closer toward infidelity without drawing any undue attention. We might say that impiety had more or less become mundane, just a routine component of common experience. What transcendentalism made possible, in other words, was a woman like Elisabeth (Dwight) Cabot, and many more like her. Cabot, tellingly, spent one Sunday from September 1859 dividing her time between pursuits that, if they seem incongruous to our minds today, were anything but to hers. After a morning's vacation spent away from Boston at the beach—Cabot makes no mention of her earlier attendance that day at Sabbath services—she could record in her diary that by nightfall she was not only "Reading Emerson and being miserable in consequence," but also tending to the schoolwork of her two daughters, Katy and Nellie, in the midst of deciding how "To walk with Christ" while "Writing a note to Mary and reading Progressive Education."[70] At the very least, this day in the life of a woman who would be so bold as to take seriously the spiritual claims of transcendentalism (she later praised Emerson's "poetical insight" and took pleasure in his writing, "as a heathen might who was unconsciously imbued with the spirit of Christianity, but had never heard of its name") provides a context for what would become the opening entry from Cabot's commonplace book, which she began keeping in 1851.[71] Here we find a handwritten copy of one of the more well-known poems by Margaret Fuller's intimate friend Ellen Sturgis Hooper, beginning, "She stood outside the gate of Heaven and saw them entering in."[72] Still, for every soul who grew weary, as did Cabot, in making her spiritual way in the world, there was a woman such as Louisa (Gilman) Loring, who seems to have drawn inspiration from *not* having a religious end in sight. Prior to entering "extracts" from the Swedish mystic Emanuel Swedenborg's "Divine Providence" into her commonplace book, in September 1832, Loring would inscribe this line from the eighteenth-century German poet and philosopher Georg Philipp Friedrich Freiherr von Hardenberg, better known as Novalis: "Philosophy cannot bake bread, but she can put us in possession of God, freedom, and immortality. Which is the most practical, Philosophy or Economy?"[73] If it was not a question to which those who read Novalis (among whom Loring might count herself) received a ready answer, it was also not a question to which the readers of that era were expecting one, either.

This is not to suggest that every woman in nineteenth-century New England waxed transcendental. For some, "everyday" life was more a matter of remaining vigilant in the face of religious uncertainty than it was an opportune time for the sampling of different spiritualisms. The orthodox response to such threats as were posed by transcendentalism we have already seen; it was little different with women than it was with men. One combative Congregationalist from Framingham, Massachusetts, fresh from reading Matthew Henry's six-volume biblical commentary, *Exposition of the Old and New Testaments* (1706–), would opine in her diary in September 1858 that "we need to know much of the heavenly science to conduct the earthly warfare, 'for we wrestle not with flesh and blood'" (Eph. 6:12).[74] Frances Merritt Quick was this diarist's name, and she'd write, too, of "how grateful is [sic] the gifts of God by Jesus Christ, to have the work of salvation predetermined." Yet there remained for Quick great danger in her day, above all in the "intangible yet soul-destroying tendency to alienation from God."[75] She was prepared to check this "tendency," for as far as Quick was concerned, "Parkerism, spiritualism, Emersonianism—all systems, beautiful systems in the makers' eye," each was a "work" that "God shall try . . . of what cost it is."[76] Women Unitarians' objections to such alternative religions as these could be no less adamant than Quick's, as we'd anticipate from the denomination's more conservative wings. Feroline (Pierce) Fox, wife of the Harvard-educated minister to the First Religious Society of Newburyport, reserved a special disfavor for the same person whom Quick blamed for "Parkerism." To her sister, Mary (Pierce) Poor, Fox would write as follows in August 1842 of Theodore Parker's *A Discourse of Matters Pertaining to Religion*, "I cannot bear his spirit, or rather his want of reverence for things I esteem holy, and though the book may abound in eloquent passages I care not to read them, if Jesus is lightly esteemed and his high mission disregarded."[77] Nor was Mary Poor herself sparing in her own criticisms. She wrote with mild sarcasm to her husband in April 1841 that "there is no harm in 'free discussion,' so the Chardon street [sic] people tell us."[78] Her reference was to Boston's Chardon Street (now New Chardon Street), which, beginning in 1838, was home to the Chardon Street Chapel and its founder, the barnstorming millenarian and Advent Christian Joshua V. Himes. Even the feminist leanings of the transcendental *Dial* journal were incomprehensible to Mary. "All this fuss about equality appears very ridiculous to me," she informed her husband (who was away on a trip to Maine), before going on to recount a recent session of Sunday school she'd led at her church in Brookline.[79]

Like the liberal religionists whom she criticized, Mary practiced a faith that was very much implicated in the rest of what transpired in her life, which consisted of everything from her opinions on female friendship and the equality of the sexes to her reports of the weather, gardening, and the innocent "truths" of children. Whether Mary recognized the reality of her compound existence is irrelevant, at least for our purposes. What counts is that she demanded there be a consistency in the patterns of alliances that her life comprised. When the forms didn't "fit," she, as much as others from her traditionalist milieu, was prepared to take whatever steps she deemed necessary to be able to continue to affect a spiritual complacency that, up until that time, had more than served her purposes. Neither the Quicks nor the Foxes nor the Poors of the antebellum world much cared for the transcendental thrill of improvising one's religion. To a woman, they had already found their faith; with this they'd stand pat.

Such intransigence was indicative more of women's individual tempers than of the times. Better illustrative of the period's religious possibilities were the views of Emerson's aunt Mary Moody Emerson, who in the spring of 1826 would ask her nephew William, "Do you think the professors of xianity so exclusive as to view their friends with altered eyes who dont believe with them?"[80] Women, as Mary demonstrates, had religious room to maneuver, despite the straitened circumstances of their domestic lives. So while a woman like Mary, Calvinist that she was, could write from rural Maine to another of Waldo Emerson's brothers, Charles Chauncy, that "the loose latitudinarianism of some unitarians has opened the way to infidelity," she was receptive enough to the "moment" to make forays, in the 1830s and 1840s, into what she called the philosophical materialism of the "Lockeites & Priestleys," the "transcendental pantheism" of Coleridge and Schleiermacher, and the "ends & orts of Kantism."[81]

Other women shared this receptiveness. Among them was the above-named Sarah Alden Bradford Ripley, in whom Mary Moody Emerson took a particular interest when Sarah was, in her own self-portrayal, a sixteen-year-old "devoted to books and a sick mother." Later in life, Ripley remembered this at first unwanted mentor as being "sharp as a varna" (the Sanskrit word for type, order, or class, as in Brahmin) and having an "insatiable" appetite for "metaphysicks [*sic*]."[82] Yet Sarah would rival the spiritual adventurousness of this busybody religious seeker in her own middle age. By the spring of 1844, she could write to the sometime assistant minister from her town of Waltham of "the reality of the deeper depth in the soul's consciousness, the intuition of the Divine." Indeed, Sarah took what she called an "Epicurean" delight in conversing on such subjects, admitting that she had skipped religious services that Sunday morning after fleeing by horseback to nearby Lincoln "to feel spiritual, because one can enjoy a day 'the bridal of the earth and sky,' by one's self at a window."[83] But it was in her accustomed household setting where Sarah's spirit really came alive. Her description of a family gathering held the Wednesday before the traditional fast day of April 1844 not only depicts the Ripleys as they "prepare," in Sarah's telling, "for the once holy day now become a holiday." Sarah's recounting of these festivities also reveals a woman who wanted anything but to be *settled* in her faith, whatever comfort others might have derived from what Sarah herself would have considered a kind of spiritual lethargy. Sarah sets the scene of her home religion with a description of her plans for the day's meal. The "meat" has been "stuffed," she reports, "and the puddings and cake in the oven." In her real-time rehearsal of the day's unfolding, she meanwhile awaits the arrival of her relations from the surrounding area. There's Uncle George, his "great boots bringing with them no small quantity of Concord soil," plus a touch of the "radicalism" for which that community was known. Sarah's eldest daughter, "Lizzey," "comes freighted from the halls of the great"—that is, the kitchen—bearing the foods for the afternoon's repast. Nor could Sarah forget her son, Ezra, at the time a student at Harvard and who is invoked by his mother as "the sophomore with nonsense from Cambridge." With everyone assembled, Ripley takes stock of her domestic situation with a remark that suggests the nature of the table talk that ensued. With a nod to the Unitarian establishment in Boston, she writes, "Uncle George and Lizzey agree that their souls have no fellowship with Beacon Street."[84] Clearly, Sarah looked elsewhere for her religion as well.

She would have discovered a plurality of religious positions to occupy in such domestic settings as the sentimentalists of her day assumed were a guarantee of spiritual *stability*. True, the Ripleys maintained at least ostensible ties to Protestant orthodoxy, not least from the fact that their home was a destination for the instruction of a number of delinquents from Harvard College who'd been "rusticated." But Sarah, well versed in Latin, Greek, botany, astronomy, chemistry, philosophy, and several modern languages—the result of both her early supervised learning and the self-education she'd overseen ever since—practiced a devotion of perpetual motion. In a letter from late June 1844, she claimed the Latin line *Tempora mutantur et nos mutamur cum illis* (Times change, and we change with them) as a personal motto, even as she adopted a religious outlook that bore more than a passing resemblance to the implied transcendentalism of Uncle George. After relating, by letter, that "I have not been to church today, could not think of sacrificing the day to others," she writes as follows to a friend of the family: "How I feel its [her Latin motto's] truth when I look back to the period when the doings and sayings of the theological school at Cambridge would have been enough to fill my horizon. And now I yawn at the very thought. How well it is that the world is so large, that lichens grow on every tree, that there are toadstools as well as sermons for those that like them."[85] Not unlike Emerson (Sarah's unflattering description of a visiting minister as a "spectral illusion" appears to be a conscious echo of a phrase from the "Divinity School Address"), Sarah was ready for something other than what she called, at the turn of the year in January 1845, the "self-satisfied formalists which swarm in Unitarian pulpits, and not only in those I suppose." As she further explained, "But the form, in which a soul deeply stricken with religious conviction clothes the expression of its faith and love, is an idiosyncrasy, which we cannot always understand unless we understand thoroughly the person who is the subject of it." For a woman such as Sarah Ripley, religion was a "lichen" or a "toadstool," popping up in unexpected places "as sermons for those that like them." A spiritualism that, for others, depended on a certain consistency was defined, for her, by the "idiosyncrasy" of subjectivity and lost nothing as an "expression" of "faith and love" because it was personal and changeable. "I should like to be in the pulpit once," Sarah continued, the better to speak "religion" to "the Boston Pharisees" whom she identifies as the "sleek combed citizens with varnished boots and souls narrower than their purses."[86] For the time being, she believed as only she, Sarah, could believe.

THE AESTHETICS OF FEMININE SKEPTICISM

Such was the spiritual open-mindedness (and -heartedness) of New England's transcendental women that some of them were receptive to a cognate religious form as well: the faith in *forms* that characterized their belief in the soul-revealing potential of the plastic arts. As writers with a desire to explore women's "inward states," transcendentalists like Margaret Fuller and Lydia Maria Child might have resorted in their work to the "intensity of expression" and "floridity of language" that Dorri Beam says characterized popular feminist discourse in the mid-nineteenth century.[87] But it was among the vanguard of transcendentalism's female *visual* artists that the rituals of the creative process itself came to be seen as a more readily translatable way for artists and audiences alike to tap into their inner spiritual reserves. The heightened awareness that draftswomen demonstrated for perspective, line, and composition, among other recognized "formal" aesthetic categories, was accepted as proof that "seeing" could, indeed, be regarded as a kind of believing, when such visual renderings as they were capable of producing (or recognizing) corresponded so naturally with the transcendentalists' general perception of the divinity within. The transcendentalists' appreciation for the visual arts, it should be noted, was not an outcome of their having reverted back to the rational empiricism that constituted a part of their Unitarian heritage. It was a further illustration of the far reach of their subjectivism, which imparted a metaphysical dash of color to how they beheld the physical and social world.

Seeing for these women was also *not* believing, insofar as transcendental aestheticism encroached on traditional areas of piety. Sarah Ann Wider explains that the women of transcendentalism were much given to habits of "attentiveness," a heightened sensory responsiveness that dissolved thinking, feeling, and being into an abiding faith in form.[88] Such a sensibility could well have been regarded as a spiritual imperative, by which the creator and receiver of a work of art managed, Wider says, "to call forth outer form from inner substance" (165). But "attentiveness" might also be viewed as a visual variety of skepticism—and the transcendental aesthete a special kind of infidel—whenever aestheticism replaced spiritualism as an end pursued for itself. Emerson, we know, maintained in *Nature* that "all mean egotism vanishes" at those moments when "the currents of the Universal Being circulate through me." "I become a transparent eye-ball," he wrote. "I am nothing. I see all" (*CW,* 1:10). The Unitarian minister turned writer and landscape painter Christopher Pearse Cranch nevertheless suggested just what such omnivorous sightedness as Emerson described portended for the religionist who was "all" eye. Cranch's famous caricature of the "transparent eyeball" is funny enough as a graphic exaggeration of transcendentalism's inherent tendency toward individualist excess (figure 5). As tongue-in-cheek spiritual commentary, Cranch's drawing is memorable more as an upside-down image of the diminishment of religion. Emerson's "I" may profess to be "nothing." Yet in Cranch's rendering, the transcendental "I" has become everything, a literal giant bestriding the diminutive church with steeple that sits as an afterthought to the near left of the picture's central Emersonian figure.[89]

It was an image that resonated with women like Sarah Freeman Clarke in their search for a visual corollary for the miracle that was their spiritual selves.

Figure 5. The "transparent eye-ball" of Emerson's *Nature*. From Christopher Pearse Cranch, *Illustrations of the New Philosophy*, ca. 1837–1839. MS Am 1506 (4), Houghton Library, Harvard University.

Prior to her attendance at Margaret Fuller's Conversations, Clarke recorded her struggles as an aspiring artist with what she called "the central difficulty of self-culture."[90] Wanting badly to create on canvas, she said by letter to her brother James, such "a true work of art" as Emerson had effected in his lectures, Clarke came to openly regret "that part of self which passes away" in the creative process, even in as unencumbered an undertaking as keeping a journal (February 11, 1838; December 31, 1837–January 1, 1838). "The most interesting inquiry to us is," she continued, "how we can come into possession of our inheritance, which is *truth*." In what she named her "Transcendental Bible," no less a woman than Emerson's wife, Lidian Jackson Emerson, would satirize what she regarded as the "egotistical" transcendental preference for an impersonal God. The transcendentalist, for the Christian Lidian, was one who had rather absurdly resolved both to "ask not" for "a wise Providence over the earth in which you live" and to "care not that a benign Divinity shapes your ends."[91] For Clarke, by contrast, "the universal law of God seems to be," finally, "Use all the truth you have, and you shall have more" (LS, December 31, 1837–January 1, 1838). And so, like the other transcendental women of her acquaintance who'd adopted art as a route to "truth," Clarke sought "more" of the same, becoming a *creator* in the multiple senses of that word. "God" was not dead for Clarke; she never questions that a divine figurehead is the source of "the universal law." Nor, in her correspondence, does she express any doubt that she can "come into" truth's "possession" on her own. She had, in short, no fear of Elizabeth Peabody's "Egotheism," and so her manner of attaining to the meaning she needs thus became something of a mannerism, according to which such attention as she was trained to lavish on life's kaleidoscope of visual detail loomed ever larger in the consciousness that, as a transcendentalist, she assumed was limitless. Whatever appreciable sense there is that religion plays an active, shaping role in her life gets belittled in her visual imaginary as a result. Meanwhile, women who were as formally discriminating as Clarke hinted at what a reconceived understanding of belief as an aesthetic practice might look like, by effectively overdetermining the soul's response to spirit.

The enlargement of art's (and the artist's) self-sustaining spiritual powers emerged in due course as a recurring motif among other transcendental women, who led the way in elaborating the aesthetic dimensions of the "Newness."[92] As was so often the case, Elizabeth Peabody helped orchestrate this aspect of transcendentalism's development. In her capacity as the editor of the short-lived journal *Aesthetic Papers,* the solitary issue of which appeared in May 1849, Peabody underscored in the introduction she authored that "aesthetics" was "neither a theory of the beautiful, nor a philosophy of art, but a component and indivisible part in all human creations which are not mere works of necessity; in other words, which are based on idea, as distinguished from appetite."[93] That "idea" rested on a "deep spiritual basis" and was, as a rule, "religious" (3). "Aesthetics" was furthermore a "watchword" for Peabody, used to "to designate," she said, "that phase in human progress which subordinates the individual to the general, that he may re-appear on a higher plane of individuality" (4). Here again is the transcendental sleight of hand that informed Cranch's ironic, inflated rendering of an ecstatic Emerson as "nothing": Peabody "subordinates" the "individual" to the "general," only for her universal person to "re-appear on a higher plane of individuality" than before. Complaining elsewhere in her *Aesthetic Papers* of "the speculative infidelity of modern times," Peabody in effect proposes a "speculative" aestheticism of her own, one that corresponds with the definition of "*creative* criticism" that the minor transcendental poet and author Samuel Gray Ward (Harvard College class of 1836) offers in a subsequent piece from the same journal.[94] Whether it's *aestheticism, criticism,* or *religion,* Peabody has not only inscribed into her *Aesthetic Papers* a way, in Ward's words, "to see what has taken place in the world under a new point of view" but also supplied a method "to find a point from which facts arrange themselves in a new and unexpected manner, so that circumstances, before isolated, are seen as a part of a new whole" ("Criticism," 12–13). For aesthetic transcendentalists like Peabody and Ward, the world's forms were no more rigidly fixed than was a faith. Ward in fact defined "faith" as "the sum of the convictions of a man, or a nation, in regard to spiritual things," a definition that almost suggests a stable, quantifiable category (19). He goes on to write, however, that "not religion alone, but the whole life of man . . . rests upon faith; in other words, upon a form of truth commensurate to man's progress,—a relative, not an absolute truth" (19). This was hardly an orthodox position. And when we relate Ward's remarks back to how he and Peabody conceived of "aesthetics" as the rearranging pursuit of a "new point of view," we can begin to see just how freely those who held the "New Views" played with the notion of "truth" as "absolute." From their perspective, the distinction between transcendental aestheticism and spiritualism lacked a difference and stipulated that the form a faith takes is more or less formless, since it relies entirely, and improbably, on a subordinated individual's "relative," elevated vantage.

The worldview that accompanied this outlook was more than a theoretical contradiction in terms; it was religion, guided by the light of an internal insight that was meant to be turned outward upon whatever a self could see. As much as any woman transcendentalist, Margaret Fuller put this aesthetic into practice. "What is done here at home in my heart is my religion," she wrote in her journal in September 1842, on a visit to Concord from Cambridge. This was Fuller at her most romantic, inward bound and sensitive to the faintest vibrations of her intuitions. At the same time, in order to be the "faithful skeptic" she wanted to be, Fuller committed herself as well to the necessity "to see, to think, . . . to reject nothing but accept nothing till it is affirmed in the due order of mine own nature."[95] As Robert Habich explains, she accordingly "sought correspondences between art and the inner life" as a way to "confirm" such feelings as sat at the seat of the "home" that was her "heart."[96] Back in Concord the following month, Fuller could thus write on October 27 that "these stern religions are a legitimate growth" (a comment made in response to Sarah Clarke's confession that she "had at one time a tendency toward Calvinism") before sitting down two days later with her longtime friend Cornelius Felton, Eliot Professor of Greek Literature at Harvard, to peruse the engravings from a book recommended to her by Sam Ward, Atanazy Raczyski's three-volume history of German art, *Histoire de l'art moderne en Allemagne* (1836–41). After leafing past what she calls "a few engravings of the old rigid pious class," Fuller finally paused on reaching a reproduction of the "modern" artist Karl Friedrich Lessing's 1832 painting *Le Brigand*, with its noble portrayal of a weary robber and his son seated high above a sweeping, dramatic landscape (figure 6). This picture had much to recommend itself to the Europhile Fuller, who surely appreciated its sympathetic portrayal of common volk. But it was not the picture's content that caused her to stop as she thumbed through the pages of Raczyski. Fuller's attention had been arrested by the image's "form." Her response was as follows: "It is a wild and lovely landscape. In the foreground the Brigand is seated, by his side his young son asleep. He is a man of five and twenty, of a lofty and impassioned style of beauty, his form has the grace and freedom given by a life of reckless daring amid the lonely scenes of nature, but the tragedy of a mistaken lot is seen there too" (Habich, 289). However hard the fate of the two unfortunates whom the artist depicts, Fuller is most taken by the painting's "lofty and impassioned style of beauty." Taking heed of the picture's "lonely scenes" of windswept rocks and forlorn faces, she speaks with veneration of the eponymous "Brigand," whom she says has led a life "of reckless daring." Yet Fuller takes an even greater delight in the picture's heroic *representation* than she does its ostensible hero. It is, for her, the "freedom" with which the artist has manipulated "form" that imparts a touch of what she calls "grace" to the painting.

Peering into "the foreground" of a picture that reads, for Fuller, as a "natural" revelation, we discover that such "grace" as this image figures is ours for the taking, too. The artist, we'll notice, has focused the eyes of his human figures inward and downward. This gesture draws father and son farther away from the firmament above, which the painting's close framing has narrowly cropped. Our eyes follow in a similar direction, as we reflexively monitor, as seers, Lessing's subjects. Fuller would write in her journal, "I belong nowhere. I have pledged myself to nothing. God and the soul and nature are all my creed" (Myerson, "Margaret Fuller's 1842 Journal," 336). That sentiment might have had obvious

Figure 6. Karl Friedrich Lessing, *The Robber and His Child* (1832). Philadelphia Museum of Art, the W. P. Wilstach Collection, bequest of Anna H. Wilstach, W1893–1-65.

origins in the writer's absorption of the thought of her friend Emerson. For our present purposes, it also serves as a rather uncanny summary of the spiritual condition suggested by Lessing's canvas. We're "nowhere," the American author and the German artist would both seem to agree. But our concomitant "pledge," as Fuller suggests, to commit ourselves to "nothing" definitive in the way of worship should be received more as a sign of religion than resignation, since, like the "Brigand," we have at our disposal all the aids to religious reflection that we could ever need. These lay within, not without, and, according to the terms of Fuller's developing aestheticism, were best accessed by the faith in Art that she and others of what Sarah Clarke called their "intellectual coteries" professed.[97]

Those women with the skill and inclination to do so resorted to drawing and paintwork of their own to express their individual spiritualism. Anyone needing a justification for why she should worship within this different medium had only to refer to Theodore Parker, who wrote to a young and unmarried female follower from Chatham, Massachusetts, in 1855, "I do not see how a *religious* woman can accept the grim and dreadful theology which is now taught in the name of Jesus Christ."[98] Fuller's "soul sister" Caroline Sturgis, for her part, produced drawings that circulated among some of the leading transcendentalists, including Emerson. These became aids for a visual reflection on what Kathleen Lawrence names the "passion and mystery" of the transcendentalists' shared sense of the divine (91). The aforementioned Sarah Freeman Clarke was another woman who passed into religion and out of religious convention in her artwork, in her case through the paintings and drawings she produced over the course of several decades. Clarke came to her artistic calling through hallowed transcendental channels. In 1835 she worked for a year without pay as a drawing instructor in Bronson Alcott's now legendary Temple School, where, just one year earlier, she had enrolled her younger brother for a course in what she hoped would be a kind of moral primer. Come the summer of 1838, Clarke served as an observer apprentice under the noted American landscape painter Washington Allston, who, despite being a close friend of Andrews Norton and a favorite among the Harvard Unitarian elite, enjoyed a favorable reputation among many of the transcendentalists. Women, in particular, responded well to the Boston-based Allston's work, not least because of his painted luminous portrayals of maidens who manifested a deep appreciation of music, nature, or their own thoughts.[99] Elizabeth Peabody said of seeing Allston's *Beatrice* at Boston's Athenaeum, in 1826, "I felt in it the power of genius to unfold the soul's treasures to itself" (figure 7), while Clarke, after the Civil War, championed the whole of the well-traveled American's paintings for being "so divine in their expressive repose."[100] Allston was not without his critics. Clarke herself recognized the untenable nature of her position as a self-reliant transcendentalist working under the tutelage of a senior artist. And Fuller, after attending a memorable exhibition of the artist's work in Boston in the summer of 1839,

Figure 7. Washington Allston, *Beatrice* (1819). In this portrait of Beatrice Portinari, the deceased Florentine noblewoman who was memorialized by the Italian poet Dante Alighieri, the American painter is thought to have paid tribute to his devout first wife, Ann Channing. Photograph © 2020, Museum of Fine Arts, Boston.

would write a somewhat unflattering review in the *Dial* that spoke to the vast religious differences that obtained among contemporary aesthetes. Here she took Allston to task for relying so heavily in his subject matter on either scenes from the Old Testament or, still worse from a transcendental perspective, what the writer felt was an antiquated representation of the biblical miracles. As Fuller writes, "a miracle effected by means of a relique, has the disagreeable effect of mummery."[101]

Clarke was guilty of no such lapses in the seven etchings she produced during her trip to the West with Fuller, images that would later reappear as illustrations in the latter's *Summer on the Lakes*. Three of these are taken from the artist's original drawings of Mackinac Island; three more are of the Illinois prairies; a final etching represents an Indian settlement in this last territory. Susan Belasco Smith describes Clarke's productions as "graceful and delicate," adding that "in these Clarke tames and compresses the vast frontier she and Fuller visited" ("Introduction," x). There is also religion in these images, rendered in a transcendental idiom of prodigious subjectivity that restores the contemplative self to the center of creation. Fuller, in her *Dial* review of Allston's exhibition, singled out his landscapes for praise, writing that they represented "Nature and the soul combined; the former freed from slight crudities or blemishes, the latter from its merely human aspect" ("Impressions," 82). Clarke accomplished something comparable in the images she contributed to Fuller's first monograph. To begin, what "grace" there is in Clarke's pictures inheres in something other than a strict verisimilitude. The artist offers stylized views of the landscape and its inhabitants, removing whatever "crudities" Fuller may have detected there with an aesthetic that registers somewhere between joyous whimsy and heavy iconography. Whether she's representing flora, fauna, human figures, or topographical forms, Clarke manages to convey a simultaneous sense of symbolic seriousness and silliness. As in her image *Indian Encampment*, the artist's earth is freighted with meanings that carry lightly, a seeming paradox at which we can only smile (figure 8). What "soul" these pictures project, moreover, is attributable less to anything readers see than to the act, and art, of seeing. Clarke formalizes her perspective on perspective in the person of the watchful Indian whom she seats in the foreground of this illustration. Like the nameless, faceless native who surveys the scene before him (or is it a her?), we settle into an image that's all astir through our steadied—and steady*ing*—reflection on universal motion. Horses gallop. Wind blows. Smoke billows. And we receive it

Figure 8. Sarah Freeman Clarke, *Indian Encampment,* in *Summer on the Lakes, in 1843* (Boston: Charles C. Little and James Brown, 1844). Boston Public Library, Rare Books.

all from a prospect of inner peace, transcendentally attuned, as Fuller suggests, to the fact that we are "combined" to a world that wears more than a "merely human aspect."

Clarke was not afraid to flip the script in visualizing this faith. In her drawing of a different Indian settlement, this one at Mackinaw Beach, the watcher becomes the watched: the Natives gathered to the left of this mirrorlike image peer back directly at the viewer (presumably the artist, Clarke), who's situated beyond the picture's frame (figure 9). Fuller would insist in *Summer on the Lakes* that the "infidel" Native be judged "according to the standard of right and motives prescribed by his religious faith and education," rather than be measured by any such belief system as had been imposed on him by his colonizer. "Looked at by his own standard," she implies, the Native, and not "the white," is "really the superior in enlargement of thought" (143–44). Clarke duly reverses the triumphant "white's" point of view in *Mackinaw Beach,* summoning the European Christian to sit before the subaltern Indian's evaluating gaze for a change. With or without her Native Americans, however, Clarke's graphic representation of Fuller's ethnoreligious proposition functions as her own forthright statement on the unconventional "aspect" of her faith. Even in her hushed depiction *Rolling Prairie of Illinois,* for example, the artist translates her position—on life, religion, and the formal relation between them—from the wide-angled vantage of an eye that is lord of all it comprehends (figure 10).

Figure 9. Sarah Freeman Clarke, *Mackinaw Beach*, in *Summer on the Lakes, in 1843*. Boston Public Library, Rare Books.

Figure 10. Clarke's *Rolling Prairie of Illinois*, in *Summer on the Lakes, in 1843*. Boston Public Library, Rare Books.

Here, inside this image of transcendental rapture, belief would appear to be a visual corollary for infinity. From the "rolling" perspective of Clarke's captured landscape, the seer can believe anything, and everything, she sees, given that she's already taken in a figurative horizon far more sweeping than the literal one that is shown. That is to say, Clarke's drawing confirms what Fuller's book contends, that the most boundless expanse a person can reckon with is one's own self. For Clarke, that reckoning would proceed through art. As she stated the case rhetorically in a question she posed to her brother, "Is it not the characteristic of a true work of art that it takes you captive for the time, and carries you out of yourself, that it may restore you to yourself raised and improved?" (LS, December 31, 1837–January 1, 1838).

Regardless of how the women of transcendentalism would have answered that question, the one that preoccupied so many of them in the nineteenth century was codified in the title of a selection from the collected *Poems* (1856) of the author, educator, and illustrator Lydia L. A. Very, "What Is It to Be Religious?"[102] Very was the sister of the transcendental poet Jones Very (Harvard College class of 1836), who, in August 1837, claimed divine inspiration in a letter to Henry Ware Jr., at the time the professor of "pulpit eloquence and pastoral care" at the Harvard Divinity School.[103] She was also the daughter of a notorious freethinking mother from Salem, Massachusetts, a woman who brazenly denied God's existence. Lydia Very herself occupied a mediate religious position between her brother and mother. She was, as a result, very much aware of how the "New Philosophy" had altered the spiritual landscape of her native New England.[104] Her poem, in fact, more or less reads as a rhymed and metered acknowledgment of what transcendentalism made possible, from a spiritual perspective: an elective affinity between a self and her own spirit. Very's verse, in other words, records a *woman's* choosing between faiths, precisely because she can. One of those faiths is masculine and bears a diction of unappealing modifiers to match. The speaker of Very's poem lets it be known that she (the critical posture the speaker adopts serves as an additional indicator of her gender) prefers not "to love a dim old church," "to raise four prayers a week," or "to rank men by their money's worth." She neither has "a lengthy creed to say" nor wants "by printed forms [to] statedly pray" to any God who'd "scorn a fellow soul . . . while my own spirit is not whole!" Our speaker has another religion in mind, which is ripe for the taking. Indeed, she promises to breed a new belief, said to be "better than forest, bough, or sky" and, as a worshiper's final reward, "seeks immortality!" In her answer to the poem's titular question, then, "What Is It to Be Religious?" the self-sufficing speaker responds not with a "what" but a "who." Her final position on religion is one that women transcendentalists would choose again and again, on the understanding that such choices were a blessing best bestowed by one's own self. In the affirmative words of Very's speaker, "May it be I!" (167–68).

CHAPTER 4
Transcendentalism, Urbanism, and Unbelief

> Nobody can read the newspapers without perceiving that during the last year, at least, religious radicalism has held high carnival in Boston.
>
> —"The Battle of Ideas in Boston," *Christian Register*, June 26, 1869

"Boston Jail—alias *Hades*—alias *Hell*, June 18, 1838."[1] These were the words (there were many more to come) that the Universalist minister turned notorious freethinker Abner Kneeland penned while he sat in Boston's city prison, after some four long years of well-publicized legal travails. The judge who presided over his final appeal to the highest court of Massachusetts had found him guilty of what he called "the propagation of erroneous or heretical doctrines," and Kneeland went on to serve the sixty-day sentence he received with self-dramatizing flair.[2] He may be remembered now as the last person to be jailed in the United States on charges of blasphemy. But Kneeland was equally a source of reliable entertainment at a time when religion—the introspective individualism of a contemporaneous trend in transcendentalism notwithstanding—had increasingly become the stuff of mass consumption. At this interval in the onset of modernity, amid all the noise emanating from a regional preoccupation with "infidelity," the traditional edifications of religion were balanced, for many New Englanders, by what today may seem a countervailing tendency toward amusement. Thus, the public spectacle of Kneeland on trial, like the sensational performance that Kneeland enacted behind bars, underscored just how much a person's faith had come to depend on his willingness to substitute the satisfactions of distraction for the fulfillments of devotion. It was within this context that the self-described "Pantheist" Kneeland, with his loudmouthed refusal to accept such labels as were suggested of him as "deist," "atheist," or "infidel," emerged as a fitting symbol for a religion that could easily pass as just another form of recreation.[3] Or, as Kneeland remarked, in following up on the defense provided him in the press by a self-identifying "Cosmopolite," religion in his day consisted "not in *believing,* but in *doing.* . . . This religion has no reference to another world; but its arts are wholly confined to this life."[4]

And what a life it was. Having converted from Baptism to Universalism in his early twenties, the Gardner, Massachusetts–born minister and evangelist developed strong misgivings about revealed religion, that is to say, a religion that relied on *revelation,* or the disclosing of some form of truth or knowledge by an acknowledged deity. Over time, Kneeland's doubts caused rifts within the churches where he served, and he eventually left the Universalist denomination altogether. Less and less a Christian in his beliefs, Kneeland came to be a freethinker by his own admission. At this stage in his career, he could adduce at least three reasons for his professed skepticism. In his own words, these included "all the discrepancies I found in the gospels," a related notion that the first five books of the Old Testament had been "compiled since the Babylonish captivity," and a general uneasiness with "the internal evidence of the Bible."[5] As he was no longer welcome in most pulpits, Kneeland, by December 1830, finally wound up in Boston, where he founded the *Investigator,* a provocative new journal of free thought. In an advertisement from 1834, Kneeland would tout the paper he edited as "a periodical printed weekly in this city, on a fine super royal sheet." More to the point, his *Investigator* was, "in religion," a forum for "open and fair investigation, opposed to every species of coercion for the dissemination of opinions, and rejecting all theories as erroneous, that will not bear the test of reasonable examination, however strongly they may have entrenched themselves under the barriers of antiquated formulas, arbitrary customs, or a pretended divine revelation."[6]

These were hardly views that would have ingratiated Kneeland with his neighbors. And as his paper drew precisely the kind of notice it solicited, the editor and author of much of the *Investigator*'s columns found himself standing trial on a formal charge of blasphemy. Ever partial to lists, Kneeland compiled another one to account for his troubles. In *An Appeal to Common Sense and the Constitution, in Behalf of the Unlimited Freedom of Public Discussion* (1834), he cited as the source of the state's case against him a "certain number" of the *Investigator,* which was alleged to have "copied" an assertion from Voltaire's *Philosophical Dictionary* that "Jesus Christ was born a eunuch." Again according to Kneeland, the second cause of his accuser's complaint was that, "in another number, the Christian doctrine of prayer is held up to ridicule, by an ironical pity for the Deity, subject to the drudgery of hearing and answering so many various and contradictory positions." The third of his offenses, by Kneeland's count, was that in a later edition of his periodical, he'd taken to "contrasting his doctrine with that of the Universalists" and by doing so "declares his disbelief in a God, (distinct from nature); in Christ, whom he regards as a mere chimera; in miracles, or in a future life" (4). All of which explains his occupying a cell in Boston's city prison at the start of the summer in 1838. Having exhausted the legal appeals process, Kneeland resorted once more to the court of public opinion, which he'd presumed all along to be a higher source of authority than the church or state. In a letter addressed to his peers, he made a forcefully worded plea for what he called "a sincere and honest expression of opinion concerning God and religion." After all, he wrote, his supposed crimes amounted to "no more than what is done every day, and especially every Sunday, by every clergyman in this city" (*Review*, 46).

Kneeland, it should be said, was no more a transcendentalist in his opinions on religion than many of the women whom we encountered in the Massachusetts countryside. Unlike Kneeland, these women were engaged in a deliberation on religion, whereas Kneeland, ostentatiously, was not. In fact, the comparative quiet that distinguished women's questioning of the nature of their faith contrasts markedly with the example of a man who, for a decade or more midway through the nineteenth century, was regarded by many Americans as an enemy of the people due to the brusque freedoms he took with the very notion of belief. Still, in a book, such as this, which samples the varieties of contemporary "unbelief," while arguing for transcendentalism's being heavily implicated in the origins and evolution of the same, it is all but impossible to trace the development of irreligion in the period without acknowledging that Kneeland and his adopted city both played a conspicuous part in further dramatizing what was already dramatic enough: an entire regional culture's close reckoning with religion, at a time when the very principle of worship was widely perceived to be under special duress. However common an occurrence it became, however "rational" the outcome of the Protestant resort to self-examination that it entailed, the spiritual searching that typically accompanied a person's entertaining the thought and practices of transcendentalism could involve a fever of emotions that most converts would have had trouble containing. It was Kneeland's genius to capitalize as much on the style as the substance of such struggles as attended even the most conscientious conformist's confrontations with religious convention; he multiplied and amplified such moments of "truth" as all worshipers underwent for the sake, if not the faith, of a growing audience of interested onlookers, who had surely experienced spiritual trials of their own.

The city of Boston facilitated Kneeland's project in this regard, providing the aggregate population base and integrated civic infrastructure to make his protracted (and self-promotional) standoff against the spiritual norms of his time and place a study in popular cultural overexposure. With its sophisticated networks of print publication and rail distribution, its innumerable performance hall spaces and assembly rooms, and an educated, expanding citizenry that was unafraid to combine its shared commitment to a progressive cause with the occasional indulgence in a cause célèbre, Boston was more than a "Hub" of rigid cultural hierarchies under the joint control of Harvard and a moneyed coterie of local elites. As Martin Green has shown, the vitality and strength of such Boston Brahmin–dominated cultural associations as the Handel & Haydn Society, the Athenæum, the Dante Circle, and a selection of exclusive singing clubs were unique among the nation's cities at midcentury.[7] Indeed, the New York editor of the *Nation,* E. L. Godkin, described the rival metropolis to the north as "the one place in America where wealth and the knowledge of how to use it are apt to coincide."[8] But as much as culture in Boston would be consolidated, and "elevated," under the highbrow stewardship of cultural entrepreneurs, the "arts" as such retained throughout much of the nineteenth century a share of the promiscuous mixing of "high" and "low" that had characterized the city before the war. "When we look at Boston before 1850," Paul Dimaggio maintains, "we see a culture defined by the pulpit, the lectern and a collection of artistic efforts, amateurish by modern standards, in which effort rarely was made to distinguish between art and entertainment, or between culture and commerce."[9] And when we trace the religious controversies that run from Kneeland to Emerson on through a long line of transcendentally inspired instigators up to the end of the century, we similarly find that not only did religion in New England's urban capital qualify as an "entertainment," but even such genteel pastimes as were afforded by a heady public spiritual dispute were likely to be lively enough to draw sizable audiences from across the intersecting spectrums of culture and class.

In a burgeoning commercial city like Manhattan, such innovative popular entertainments as were engineered by the cultural impresario P. T. Barnum were adapted to the peculiar tastes of a people steeped in what one commentator calls "the arts of deception."[10] Hence the exhibits of freaks, fakes, and other assorted oddities that played to appreciative crowds in Barnum's American Museum, on Broadway, beginning in the 1840s. Here in the heart of venture capitalism, the populace was accustomed to a heightened degree of risk, and they were willing to pay for the stimulation that came from taking their chances.[11] Up in the rarefied air of Boston, meanwhile, where "ideas" were still reputed to be taken seriously, residents gravitated toward a different brand of amusement, but one nonetheless informed by such vernacular sensibilities as even the members of the local intelligentsia possessed. Controversies involving religion had long been front-page news in Boston. Thus, the commotion that swirled there around a "blasphemer" such as Kneeland, or an "infidel" such as Emerson, who delivered his "Divinity School Address" not even three and a half weeks after Kneeland's conviction, provided much of what amusement the locals saw fit to allow themselves. These were no sideshow attractions. At a time when much of the greater public remained fixated on such sobering topics as creeds, the historical Jesus, and the critical interpretation of scripture, the hullabaloo surrounding transcendentalism gave rise to perhaps as much of a carnival atmosphere as had surrounded Kneeland's courtroom defense from the mid-1830s. The subsequent debates that transcendentalism elicited on faith in the following decades were not only engaging, then, in an interdenominational way, but also fun, assuming that those who patronized such novel sources of mindful entertainment were interested enough—and many of them were, apparently—in the "New Views" to feel they had a personal stake in the proceedings. Kneeland, with all of his headlines and grandstanding, might not have been a transcendentalist in his core beliefs.[12] But the precedent he set in demonstrating how to make the most of a city's available resources for a freer, franker conversation on religion would allow the "like-minded" to contribute in unexpected (and not always unwitting) ways to the supply of Boston's leisure-time options in the years before, during, and after the U.S. Civil War.

With its "suburban vision" of American society, "transcendentalism," Robert Gross has written, "came to terms with urbanism, embracing the city while evading it at the same time."[13] It is possible to go a step further and claim that the public exhibitions of "unbelief" to which transcendentalism contributed not only ranked for a time as one of the featured entertainments among an assortment of urban diversions in Boston. Transcendentalism also held the attention of many

New Englanders whom we might not normally count among the "movement's" main witnesses. It would probably beg belief to suggest that transcendentalism in New England was ever intended as a wholesale "amusing" of "the million," to paraphrase the title of John Kasson's influential examination of "a new mass culture" in the United States at the turn of the twentieth century.[14] We can nevertheless say that those contemporaries who had even a passing familiarity with the esoteric strains of faith, and faithlessness, that typified the commitments of the "like-minded" partook of enough of the "unquiet" energies that Colin Jager attributes to the local "modernities" of "secularism in the romantic age" to help make transcendental religion surprisingly fit for public consumption.[15]

To be modern, one could argue, is to be amused. To live in the city, one could say, is to never be bored, or at least to retain a residual faith in the prospect that there's always more there for the taking than whatever business as usual is at hand. However much transcendentalism afforded the visitors and residents of Greater Boston a religion equipped for the exigencies of everyday life in the middle decades of the nineteenth century, it also provided, inside a metropolitan setting where the dizzying array of spiritual choices to select from must have seemed endless, a reliable antidote for the ennui that often threatened to beset those who badly wanted, and needed, to believe in something other than the same old orthodoxies. Unitarianism represented but one among the many religious options that Bostonians had at their disposal in these years, given the increasing levels of credence the city afforded such divergent (and, in the eyes of some, outrageous) spiritual expressions as Protestant revivalism, Roman Catholicism, spirit tapping, and the European variant of Christian socialism known locally as "Associationism."[16] In transcendentalism, the city's residents met with a religion that retained just enough of a hint of familiarity to reassure any would-be believer that he had not strayed too far, spiritually speaking, from his accustomed home. What the city's transcendentalists also discovered was a religion that possessed all of the novelty of a full array of available religious alternatives, at a time when "newness" counted.

In what follows, we examine two representative instances of transcendentalism's entertainment value in nineteenth-century Boston, the better to demonstrate how "the latest forms of infidelity" came to function, if not as a fad, then as a popular force for changing the strictures of conventional faith in the area. Both of our chosen case studies serve to illustrate that transcendentalism was disruptive (or subversive, according to its most outspoken critics) more for what the "New Views" were stirring from "below" than for what they were causing to occur from "above," among those who had been schooled in the nuances of the most recent advances in theological and philosophical discourse. In other words, we would do well to examine the popular *medium* of transcendentalism's dissemination—as embodied by the people of Boston themselves—as much or more as we should unpack the *message* of spiritual possibility the "newness" conveyed, if we are to account for the impact that transcendental religion had on the streets of the city where it achieved its greatest currency.

The focus in the first of this chapter's case studies (following up on our intermittent treatment of Kneeland, whom we can regard as a "special" transcendental case) is on a figure we've encountered before, Theodore Parker. Parker's most insightful biographer, Dean Grodzins, justifiably recognizes the different phases of his subject's varied career: the dynamic transcendentalist, the celebrated city preacher, the politically driven reformer and abolitionist. As the urban orientation of the present discussion would indicate, our interest is with the middle-period Parker. It was during this stage in Parker's life that the sometime minister to a sleepy parish in the Boston suburb of West Roxbury transitioned into becoming, by the mid-1850s, pastor to a congregation which, at twenty-five hundred worshipers, was by some measure the capital city's largest. At the time of the founding, in 1845, of Parker's Twenty-Eighth Congregational Society, as his new institutional seat was known, Boston was a place of many amusements. None of these proved more popular than Parker, behind his pulpit. Curiously, the ability of this unpolished, self-effacing minister to draw crowds numbering into the thousands for Sunday-morning services (Parker dispensed with the Sabbath's customary afternoon services) and the occasional midweek lecture relied, in part, on the participatory excitement that surrounded what were sometimes full-blown productions. These featured music, singing, and other dashes of pageantry in combination with the traditional offerings of sermon, prayer, and what Parker insisted, despite his many departures from convention, was a form of "Christian" fellowship. Grodzins is right to emphasize in his biography what he calls Parker's "highly unorthodox," "arch-liberal" theology (*American Heretic,* x–xi). Grodzins is equally attuned not only to "how and why Parker became a heretic," but also to "how heresy worked as a religion for him and others" (x). With this latter question in mind, we can propose here an *urban* interpretation of what lay behind Parker's popular appeal during the years of his ministry in Boston.

As the example of Parker's friend Emerson indicates, the popularity of the preacher turned lay teacher had an important precedent in the lyceum lecturer, whose public performances in this period were no less spiritual for being rendered—in both cases by figures who became iconic—in what was usually regarded as a secular space.[17] Nor should Parker's popularity (and unpretending modesty) be assumed to disentangle too nicely from his notoriety, as the examples of so many transcendentalists before him (on this score we could again include Emerson, Fuller, and Bronson Alcott, who drew fire from many quarters in Boston after word spread of the sexual topics he'd discussed with the children in his Temple School, at the corner of Tremont Street and Temple Place) suggest.[18] What remains to be said of Parker's Twenty-Eighth Congregational Society, however we parse its minister's own popularity, is that it was part and parcel of the city's emergent entertainment industry. Parker's congregation occupied a particular niche in the religious marketplace; it was one that had been cultivated by a number of the other transcendentalists, who were likewise selling an image of belief compounded from elements both spiritual and skeptical. All signs indicate it was a religion that sold well in the city.

Complementing our treatment of Parker is a revisionist reading of the Boston phenomenon that was Francis Ellingwood Abbot. A Unitarian minister turned spokesperson for "free" religion, Abbot had appeared before the public in a number of different capacities—and in a number of different locations, including extended spells in Dover, New Hampshire, and Toledo, Ohio—before returning to the city where he was born and raised in order to pursue his work for the Free Religious Association, which he had cofounded in 1867. Beginning in the late 1860s, and continuing through the first half of the 1870s, Abbot, whose ties to transcendentalism (and Harvard) were many, regularly took to the stage of Boston's Horticultural Hall as a popular fixture of the winter season's lecture cycle. The keynote of Abbot's well-attended talks usually involved some variation on his great theme: the need for a religion that had been not only freed from the burdens of dogmas and creeds, but also replaced by a faith that rested on a more solidly scientific basis. Abbot promoted his views on free religion in the *Index*, the weekly eight-page paper he edited (and mostly wrote) from his provisional base in Toledo. Yet he was known in Boston mostly because of the publicity generated by his keenly anticipated lectures. These were hardly riotous, but the speaker's brash radicalism all but guaranteed a large turnout whenever he was in town. Journalistic lookers-on from the sidelines, meanwhile, from both the mainstream Christian press and the city's pockets of progressive sympathizers, were sure to provide extensive coverage and commentary of the lectures themselves, frequently reprinting some or all of Abbot's "sermons" in their entirety. The editorial debates that ensued were as instrumental in keeping free religion a perennial topic in Boston as anything Abbot did or did not say in his original addresses. What remained consistent between these lectures and their extended afterlives was that they continued an earlier transcendental controversy over unbelief, as locals carried what happened, with or without Abbot's blessing, in Horticultural Hall into a larger arena of public discussion on what constituted religion in a modern age. Clearly, not all of Boston could agree on whether a religion that was "free" warranted inclusion among the traditional faiths they had only ever known. No one seemed to complain, however, that the contesting of this question was such good sport.

ENTERTAINING TRANSCENDENTALISM

From his darkened cell, "No. 13," in what he called the city's "common jail," the convicted blasphemer Abner Kneeland could see that the people of the region would turn out for a little transcendentalism under almost any conditions, even if it meant a trip to the "*Hell*" that he'd described in the "review" he wrote of his trial and conviction. Kneeland conceded that the accommodations he received while incarcerated were "very decent, to be sure, for a prison" (*Review*, 46). He also admitted that, during a brief reprieve, he was transferred away from his spot among the general population of convicts to the comparative comforts of the debtors' prison, where he received a call from a most unexpected visitor. Kneeland recounted this visit as follows, in what seems a sincere (if self-serving) statement on the lengths to which New Englanders would go in those years to offer support to whatever it was they believed:

> Fellow Citizens:—While I was in the debtors' apartment, and before I was returned to this infernal pit, intended only for felons, I was visited by one of the students from Harvard University, who informed me that the circumstances of my imprisonment was [*sic*] felt very much there, particularly among the students; that he, with others, has signed a petition for my pardon; but that he hesitated to do it, because he did not consider that I had been guilty of any crime; but still, he wished to have me liberated, and did not see how it could be done in any other way. . . . He admitted that all the Unitarians were as liable to be prosecuted as I was, admitting that they should be equally bold in publishing their honest sentiments. (53)

That our student from Harvard should have signed a petition on Kneeland's behalf is not in itself extraordinary. The dean of Boston Unitarianism, William Ellery Channing, had cosponsored a widely circulated petition of his own, obtaining for his troubles the signatures of such noted transcendentalists as Emerson, George Ripley, Jones Very, Theodore Parker, John Sullivan Dwight, and Bronson Alcott.[19] Nor is it all that remarkable that Kneeland's cause should have found favor "among the students" at the college, considering, on the one hand, the proximity of Cambridge to Boston and, on the other, the far reach of the media storm that the principal in the case had started four years earlier, with his provocative comments, from 1834, in his *Investigator* newspaper.

What does surprise is Kneeland's revelation about the "respective views" of him and his interlocutor. According to Kneeland, his visitor "no more believed in the divine authority of the Scriptures than I do." What's more, "he said that they were the Infidels who thought that truth could be in danger from what any body could say, write, or publish, or that God, or religion, needed the aid of human laws for its support." Kneeland would "presume" that, in his own words, this unbelieving emissary from Harvard "spoke the sentiments of the students generally." There was much, then, that the two men shared. What they did not hold in common was the Emersonian worldview with which our collegian proceeded to catechize one of the nineteenth century's most forthright atheists. In Kneeland's remembrance of the scene that ensued, he "soon perceived" that our visitor from Harvard "had something to say about abstract truth and consciousness which was as totally unintelligible to me as it would be to talk to a man who was born blind of the beauty of colors." In the eyes of the designated infidel, "he," Harvard, "seemed to be on the same ground, if I understood him, of my friend Brownson, and if there be any truth in such notions, I heartily wish I could understand them; but it is all mystery in a mist to me" (53–54). Kneeland was referring here to his "friend" Orestes Brownson, the transcendental writer and reformer who would convert to Catholicism some seven years after his own arrival in Boston, in 1836. As for the "abstract" talk of "truth and consciousness" that Kneeland found "totally unintelligible," this was unadulterated transcendentalism, from the mouth of a young undergraduate who had apparently been reading more than his assigned course work at the college.

The date of Kneeland's initial letter, from "*Hell*," in this retrospective reflection was a Monday. He dated his follow-up letter to the "fellow citizens" of Boston as Thursday. Either in the interim between those two dates or else predating his opening epistle—Kneeland never says which—he had received his well-wisher from Harvard "in the debtors' apartment," where he was being temporarily held before his return to less comfortable quarters. The entire episode might be apocryphal, of course. Kneeland was anything but sparing in the service of his own cause, and we have no way to verify that the meeting he described ever took place. What we do know is that a popular pocket version of Kneeland traveled at least as well as transcendentalism. For years, newspaper reports from across New England had kept readers abreast of the latest developments in his ongoing trials. And so the prospect of meeting the famous blasphemer in person might have been difficult to resist, especially, if we are to believe Kneeland, he wielded such influence "among the students" in the vicinity. At the same time, Boston had long been a beacon for those who were studying at the college, situated just several miles northwest of the big city. As Andrew Peabody (Harvard College class of 1826) reminisced toward the end of the century, after his retirement from serving as Harvard's Plummer Professor of Christian Morals between the years 1860 and 1881, the "weekly liberty" that was most prized by students in Cambridge during the 1820s was the freedom they received on Saturday evenings to escape the residence requirement that was otherwise in place at the college throughout the week. Despite the nine o'clock curfew that necessitated their being back on campus in the evening, under the threat of "heavy penalty" should they return late, and notwithstanding that students often had to walk the distance to Boston, since the only "public conveyance" to the city in that era was "a two-horse stage-coach, which ran twice a day," Harvard's young scholars appear to have found the lure of Boston all but irresistible.[20]

Those who made the short journey south pursued such pleasures as struck their particular fancy. Recalling his own time in the city, as a pastor at Boston's New South Church toward the close of the previous century, Harvard's President Kirkland remembered the response he gave to a visiting country deacon, who had sought him out for advice on a dispute within his parish involving the "dogma" of "the perseverance of the saints." Kirkland's response to his pastoral colleague, from 1794, would have been as meaningful then as it was fifty or even one hundred years later. "Here in Boston," he replied, "we have no difficulty on that score: what troubles us here is the perseverance of the sinners."[21] There were ostensibly more uplifting attractions on offer in the city as well. In light of the requirement that they spend most of their time on campus, students at Harvard might not have been able to take full advantage of the nightly lecture series that Boston made available, particularly outside of the summer months, when the warmer weather afforded opportunities for outdoor entertainments. But, as Kenneth Walker Cameron observes, "The campus certainly did not ignore Boston intellectual activities, even if student impecuniosity may have kept away all but the avant-garde and those receiving complimentary tickets." Through newspapers, classroom conversations, and the various literary societies to which they belonged, students were able to remain well apprised of what was happening in Boston's lyceums and lecture rooms.[22] Whether they were able to attend a "Sunday Evening Lecture" from Orestes Brownson, say, titled "The Truth of the Christian Religion," or a sixth talk the following year, in 1837, from a series of addresses by Emerson, called "Religion," is hard to ascertain.[23] What we do know is that, as Emerson explained in his journal, the excitement that the "New Views" incited in the city for "societies, systems, or bookstores" was only "whistled at" in the country, just "ten miles out of town." Outside of Boston, in other words, and as Emerson continued, "God & the world return again to mind." Inside the city, we are thus led to conclude, "God" and the more conventional trappings of religion were left at the proverbial door.[24] Catherine Albanese writes that what brought the transcendentalists "to their 'holy experiment' was a disturbing sense of alienation from the accepted verities of Brahmin Boston."[25] That's true. But what kept many of them—and others, who may or may not have been "believers"—coming back to Boston was the sheer exhilaration that must have arisen from the sense that spiritual immanence was somehow attainable in a city where there were a staggering variety of religious radicalisms available.

By the time of Kneeland's imprisonment, in 1838, Boston was the fourth-largest city in the United States (it would climb one place in the rankings by midcentury), in addition to being the nation's rail hub and the center of American publishing. As such, Boston could afford locals and out-of-towners alike more than the shop-front spiritual offerings that had characterized the city in its quainter colonial days. Boston had become a modern metropolis by the time of transcendentalism's first stirrings. And with the transformative sociocultural changes that accompanied this historic shift came the repackaging of religion as an exchangeable commodity, albeit one with the potential to (re)make its owners as *whole*. Whether it was Harvard, Concord, or rural parts of the commonwealth farther removed from the city, what much of the region wanted when it came to Boston was, if not religion, then the consolation of a faith that held out the possibility that life was more than the "mist" of misplaced beliefs that the likes of Abner Kneeland said it was.

A person need not have been one of the "Friends of Universal Reform," to invoke the name of a motley gathering of religionists that met in conference at Boston's Chardon Street chapel on November 18, 1840, if he were to find a spiritual expression to his liking at this time. But the bizarre assemblage to attend this first in a three-part series of so-called Chardon Street Conventions was indicative of the kinds of "religions" that were there for the taking in the city.[26] Over the course of three sermons that he delivered in 1845, James Porter, a Methodist minister from Lynn, Massachusetts, would work, as he said, "to counteract the influence of these men, which threatens immense and unmingled mischief to every good cause, especially to pure religion."[27] It was easy for Porter to lump his enemies (whose individual differences he otherwise acknowledged) together under the title of "Come-outers," on account of their "coming out from all church associations" (3). These peoples weren't just "wanting in spirituality," according to Porter (3). They were guilty of suggesting that "every man is a bible to himself" and that "we have as many scriptures as there are different convictions" (8). Nor, Porter feared, was such perniciousness confined to the convention's annual meetings. It didn't matter if he referenced the "pantheistic and transcendental atheism" of the abolitionist William Lloyd Garrison, the offices of whose *Liberator* newspaper Porter singles out to denounce, or bid us to "cross the street and step into the office of the Investigator, Abner Kneeland's infidel paper" (8–9). The pastor from Lynn had a map of *urban* unbelief already drawn in his head.

Emerson, who reported on the initial Chardon Street Convention in the July 1842 issue of the *Dial,* would take a more forgiving view of a meeting in which he himself had participated. In Emerson's recounting, religion in the city, at least as it had appeared at Chardon Street, seemed ready-made to meet the spiritual appetites of almost anyone, no matter how strange:

> The singularity and latitude of the summons drew together, from all parts of New England and also from the Middle States, men of every shade of opinion from the straitest orthodoxy to the wildest heresy, and many persons whose church was a church of one member only. A great variety of dialect and of costume was noticed; a great deal of confusion, eccentricity and freak

appeared, as well as of zeal and enthusiasm. If the assembly was disorderly, it was picturesque. Madmen, madwomen, men with beards, Dunkers, Muggletonians, Come-outers, Groaners, Agrarians, Seventh-day Baptists, Quakers, Abolitionists, Calvinists, Unitarians and Philosophers,—all came successively to the top, and seized their moment, if not their hour, wherein to chide, or pray, or preach, or protest.[28]

Emerson might write with more than a hint of ironic distancing in this passage, but he nevertheless makes an important point about the veritable free-for-all that the Boston of his description had made of faith. No longer did there seem to be a difference in one's wanting to "pray, or preach, or protest." The "straitest [sic] orthodoxy" and "the wildest heresy" were rubbing shoulders, moreover, and no one seemed to mind. And befitting a city with a reputation for being a place of spiritual exchange, the "religious demonstration" that Perry Miller later made synonymous with transcendentalism here appears to consist of something as negligible, and interchangeable, as the "great variety of dialect and of costume" that characterized a wild roomful of religious reformers. Far from the corridors of theological controversy, we've entered into a religion that Emerson likens to "eccentricity and freak."

Popular oddities in Boston came in a variety of flavors and catered to a heterogeneous audience that, despite the "sacralizing" tendencies of the city's tastemakers, was as indiscriminate as it wanted to be in the pursuit of tolerable entertainments.[29] By the opening decades of the nineteenth century, both Presbyterian and Congregational reformers were touting the use of hymnal music for creating a more devotional atmosphere at church services. As Michael Broyles explains, "Their argument established the idea that music could enrich," even though such claims were limited to church music per se.[30] It was a dyed-in-the-wool transcendentalist, the Harvard-educated John Sullivan Dwight, who led the way in making the case that secular instrumental music could be a religion in its own right. As Dwight informed an assembly of the Harvard Musical Association in August 1841, "*music is all sacred,*" and to appreciate as much was to be able to distill "almost the very essence of prayer."[31] The larger and larger audiences for which amateur and semiprofessional music ensembles performed in the 1830s and 1840s were nevertheless not always reliably discerning. These groups drew (and recruited) members of the working classes to join in occasions that were otherwise increasingly dominated by Boston's arts-reverencing bourgeoisie, who were themselves susceptible to the hackneyed enjoyments of a professionally mounted production like *The Skeptic*. Englishman Henry Russell composed the oratorio for this flamboyant orchestral work, which debuted to great fanfare in Boston in 1837, specifically for the sensation-craving middle-class members of his American following.[32] There were alternative forms of entertainment to be obtained as well, not least from Boston's rollicking theater scene. Its Puritanical history notwithstanding, the city could boast enough stages—a partial list of which includes the Boston Museum and the Boston Theatre, the Adelphi, the Bijou, the Arena, the Globe, the Howard, and the Park, to name only a few— to satisfy an insatiable demand for drama. Indeed, as the century progressed, the dramatic arts would become as inclusive a category of aesthetic expression as the simple hunger for amusements was mixed, with playhouses offering not only traditional literary fare but a full range of miscellaneous entertainments that encompassed everything from minstrel performances and lyceum-style lectures to wax tableaux and traveling galleries of "curiosities." P. T. Barnum himself might even have approved of these last.

In the midst of all of this popular cultural ferment was what we could call the transcendental *event*, "staged" not so much for any attention-grabbing effect as for the radical rethinking of religion it offered the paying customer with his price of admission. This is not to attribute to an Emerson, a Parker, or an Abbot a showman's ethos of hucksterism or mere playacting. The sincerity of transcendentalism's most public performers is not in question. What this chapter proposes is this: that from the perspective of its popular reception, transcendentalism was, in certain respects, indistinguishable from the other entertainments with which it shared literal stage space. For at least a portion of the paying public, in other words, transcendental attractions must have been as much a part of a nascent business in entertainments as they were a milestone, of romantic proportions, in the history of religion in New England. This is not the heretical suggestion it might seem. Rather, it is to stress that transcendentalism's reputation for heresy, for infidelity, was as much the reason it became anathema to some of the citizens of Boston as it was "must-see" entertainment for others.

THE THRILL OF "PARKERISM"

"For all the Athenians and strangers which were there spent their time in nothing else but either to tell or to hear some new thing" (Acts 17:21). This was the biblical text on which the Reverend John Brazer, D.D., based his sermon, from the early 1840s, titled "Morbid Appetite for Excitement." Brazer might have been pastor to Salem's North Church, where he had been installed in 1820. Yet he invoked the Apostle Paul's visit to the fickle historical city of Athens in order to illustrate "a depraved appetite for mental excitement" that he said not only was "endemic to all people, and is reproduced in all ages," but had also reappeared in "modern times and in modern places."[33] Still, however inclusive his vision might have been, however much his professional life revolved around Massachusetts's second city, Salem, Brazer appears to have had the metropolis of Boston in mind when he spoke of the central conflict of modern culture: between the search for "mental excitement," on the one hand, and what he described as "earnest seriousness and enlightened zeal," on the other. Of the latter Brazer writes, "without which there can be no religion that deserves the name" (101–2).

Brazer himself was well schooled in conflict, in addition to holding unwavering opinions on faith. Having graduated at the head of his class at Harvard in 1813, he had served as a tutor there from 1815 until 1817 before his promotion to college professor of Latin, a position he occupied from 1817 until 1820. It was the strict piety of Brazer's classroom management that had contributed to the student uprising on campus in 1818, the memory of which incident did not prevent the soon-to-be-ordained minister from holding a position on Harvard's Board of Overseers from 1829 until the time of his death, in 1846. The student disturbances in Cambridge (those, at least, in which Brazer was immediately implicated) had long receded into the past before the North Church's clergyman became preoccupied by what he felt was the sorry deficit in the collective spiritual attention of his contemporaries. It is nevertheless hard not to hear a hint of academic pedantry in the way the sometime instructor scolds New Englanders for the want of "seriousness" they betray in their endless clamoring for "excitement." Brazer discovers evidence of this "disease" just about everywhere (99). He sees it in the enthusiasm for newspaper writing, in the rise of speculative business practices, in the "migratory" restlessness of "the people," in the growing popularity of "silly and trashy novels and romances," and even in "that rage for political and party excitement which is the primal and all-pervading curse of the country" (99, 101). Most worrying of all, Brazer contends that "a feverish excitement" has begun to characterize religion in the nineteenth century. For him, the "high prerogative" of what he calls "pure faith" is "to regulate and tranquilize the mind" (103). In his own age, he had found instead that the Lord's Day, rather than being "one of rest and peace," is "so crowded with public meetings as to leave little space for the no less important duties of quiet self-communion" (103). Not only that, but the frequent "public meetings" that a place like an unnamed Boston "extended, hour after hour, throughout the week" had so completely cluttered the religious calendar that "the bell which announces them mingles strangely its solemn sounds with the hum of busy life." Wherever Brazer turns, he finds that "ordinary employments are frequently deserted," while "the streets and highways are thronged, at unwonted hours, by those who promote or share the wide-spread excitement" (105). It was enough to leave this minister wondering how to resolve what he insisted was "the great problem presented to rational and enlightened Christians . . . at the present day." For Brazer, the paramount dilemma of religion in the modern city was this, "how to make a worthy and profitable use of any newly-awakened interest on the subject of religion, without yielding to the folly and excess to which it always tends and often leads" (109).

Theodore Parker confronted this question in his Boston ministry during the 1840s and 1850s, albeit not in a way of which Brazer, had he lived, would have approved. Parker's early commitment to the spiritual cause of transcendentalism was reason enough for Brazer or any other abiding member of the denomination to have wanted to distance himself from their Unitarian colleague. With the controversial ordination sermon he'd delivered in South Boston on May 19, 1841, *A Discourse on the Transient and Permanent in Christianity*, combined with the fallout that attended the publication of his first book, *A Discourse of Matters Pertaining to Religion* (1842), Parker had effectively made himself persona non grata in the region's Unitarian community for both the style and the substance of his transcendentalism. This was the result of his having established, first, that he staked his religion on a belief in the infinite spiritual depths of the human soul, as compared to his depreciation of a modern church and an earthly Christ that he regarded as at best finite resources for an "Absolute" Religion. Second, he had signaled to his counterparts at the area's churches that he would need to upset religious convention before he could restore anything like the "quiet self-communion" that Brazer and others of his unsmiling fraternity favored. Parker duly received both his punishment and his reward for his trespasses against orthodoxy. Much to his chagrin, he was excluded from the privilege of ministerial exchange with all but an outcast few of his peers, who were disinclined to associate with a member of their profession whose views had been deemed "heretical." Nor were Parker's writings any longer welcome in the usual

Unitarian reviews, where the denomination articulated its de facto vision of Christianity. That Unitarians were capable of reaching such a consensus (even Harvard was no longer willing to invite the reputed "infidel" back to his alma mater, where he had for several years been examining students at the Divinity School on the ancient languages) was evidence for Parker that they had violated their own rule against requiring of their followers a pledge of allegiance to any official creed. The region's ministers responded by maintaining that they did, in fact, subscribe to an *informal* creed, which asked that all Unitarians accede to a belief in Jesus Christ and the Bible as infallible guides to the faith. Parker's convictions were clearly opposed to this requirement. And so he was more or less left to go it alone as a transcendental dissenter when he was approached, in 1845, by a group of reform-minded Bostonians with an offer to form with them a new church in the city. Not all of these "Friends of Theodore Parker" shared his views on religion. They did agree, as liberal Christians, on his right to be heard. Parker accordingly ministered to his "Friends" on a trial basis over the next year, as he continued to oversee his West Roxbury congregation. He persisted in this interim arrangement until the start of 1846. By then Parker had decided that his future was with Boston's Twenty-Eighth Congregational Society, so called at the pastor's own suggestion. His "society" was to be the twenty-eighth in the city formed in keeping with the "congregational" practice of church governance, whereby each congregation within an affiliated polity assumed control of its own affairs. The relative independence that resulted for the city's different Unitarian congregations could manifest in any number of ways. At the Twenty-Eighth Congregational Society, it meant that Parker would preach what, when, and how he wanted, and with such levels of "excitement" as would have been inconceivable to the likes of Brazer.

Parker was not entirely unprepared for the magnitude of fame that was to follow his appointment with the Twenty-Eighth Congregational Society. The first edition of his initial *Discourse,* named above, had sold out within a week of its appearance as a forty-eight-page pamphlet; an additional three editions would appear by the end of the intervening summer. His pulpit appearances, moreover, were already the stuff of local legend. According to several of the members of the on-again, off-again transcendentalist James Freeman Clarke's Boston congregation, the Church of the Disciples, it was the "stirring words" of Parker's commanding preaching (which they had previously heard at Parker's occasional Thursday-evening sermons in the city, before Boston's Unitarian

Association) that had restored their faith in "the unseen & eternal" and reanimated their "love to God & man."[34] More to point, it was the passionate fire of Parker's perfectionist, Platonic spirituality that had led them to invite Parker to deliver a series of five lectures, titled "Religion," at Boston's Masonic Hall in the fall of 1841, the attendance at which Dean Grodzins says quickly became a "hot ticket."[35] Whatever theological content there was in Parker's pulpit performances—and there was plenty, despite his habit of sometimes declining to draw the doctrine for his sermons from an explicit biblical text—these lacked the showy appeal of a certain strain of evangelicalism, to which the minister's method might otherwise invite comparison.[36] His religion was, in fact, as disarmingly simple as his message was plainspoken; mostly this baldheaded, square-shouldered, and unassuming preacher wanted to reassure his listeners of their ability to live spiritual lives in modern times, and at their own discretion. As for Parker's presence, it was the magnetism of his person, rather than any practiced stage tricks (to which he did not descend) or the sonorous effects of a resounding voice (which he didn't possess), that enabled him to make what Elizabeth Peabody said was "a prodigious impression on people in spite of clerical opposition."[37] The minister's "Friends" were well aware of his winning attributes when they approached him with their offer to preach in 1845. These were only enhanced by Parker's subsequent stay of some fifteen years in a city ministry that, given his unique set of talents and ambitions, he made inimitably his own.

It would take a centrist Unitarian paper like the *Christian Register* several more decades before it recognized "Theatre Preaching" as a legitimate setting, and technique, for the urban sermon.[38] The pastor to the Twenty-Eighth Congregational Society was already an acknowledged master of this mode of performance, having earned special distinction by the early 1840s for never failing to entertain. One reason this should have been so is readily apparent, even today. Whatever else Parker was in his public performances, he took great pains to ensure that he avoided ever being *dull*. Indeed, dullness was not just a sign for Parker of personal fecklessness; it was both a cause and an effect of spiritual disaffection. Not long after he was installed at his church in West Roxbury, for example, Parker had already written and delivered by 1837 a sermon called "Spiritual Deadness," or, as it was known by its alternate title, "Spiritual Indifference." Here he stresses that, although "spiritual indifference . . . is a common fault," the "degraded" result of our "spirituality" being "smothered in the cares & concerns of this life," there was a remedy for this malady within our reach. Parker writes that, rather than have "half the meaning of life . . . lost to him," a worshiper in his day and age could instead come to realize what any transcendentalist had seen firsthand, that religion "grows naturally out of the infinite faculties of man."[39] A person's being able to come to this realization, Parker explained in his journal on May 19, 1851, depended at least in part on forces that he said were constitutional. In Parker's own words, "When causes external or internal excite any particular faculties (or organs) of man, & the effect of its faculty is not presented, there is always . . . waste of the vital fervor of the man!"[40] Yet Parker was not abandoning the would-be religionist to his own hereditary traits. In addition to what he asked his parishioners to do for themselves, he was only ever offering to *minister* to their spiritual needs, to play an active, shaping role in leading them to the spiritual life that resided inside each and every one of them. To this end, and as he recorded in his journal in June 1840, he set about restoring an Athenian brand of "excitement" to a traditional church service that he sensed had grown stale. With such cold comfort as most worshipers found in meeting on Sundays, it was no wonder they'd become spiritually "indifferent" or "dead." Parker describes their predicament as an ordeal of endurance:

> no amusement & recreation on Sunday but must sit hours in the church & hear two sermons on abstract subjects, written in a language peculiar to sermons, filled with sentences taken from an old Hebrew or Greek book—which though produced in the rudest age is appealed to as the infallible canon, the standard of all truth. . . . A sermon delivered in a tone never heard out of the pulpit, by a pale man who knows nothing of real life, except for stolen glances at lying romances, who is never seen in places of amusement, but is restricted to the company of . . . old women of both sexes, or none at all, a man who as the symbol of all this humbugging, is clothed in an antique dress [the black robe and white collar] never seen out of the church, & defunct colleges. This is the entertainment provided for real living men & women, & served up twice a . . . Sabbath from week to week, year out & year in, & the unfortunate man is lucky if he is not forced to . . . [take] [in] three of these feasts in a day.[41]

In place of this "sham" religion, Parker chose to divert and instruct his society in proportionate measure. To do this he gave "amusement" the deference it was due, with Sunday-morning meetings that were to become a popular cultural institution in Boston up until the time of the minister's passing, in 1860. In a letter to the society's Standing Committee, from October 1847, Parker protested that he was "not much of a business-man."[42] He had already proved, however, that he was a consummate professional in the production of religious services that commanded widespread appeal. One of Parker's parishioners, the transcendental reformer and writer Julia Ward Howe, reminisced later that she had long looked to Boston as a place "rather eager to entertain a novelty," and in the society she was able "to enter reasonably into the functions and amusements of general society, and at the same time to profit by the new resources of intellectual life which opened out before me."[43] Howe's status-conscious "society friends shook their heads," she relates, out of worry about what she was "trying to find at Parker's meeting" (150). It was "not atheism," Howe explains, "but a theism" (150). Just as important, it was a form of worship so fantastically varied in its selling points that it could have been made possible only by a pastor whose "idea of culture" was as "encyclopaedic" as Howe says Parker's was (176).

What Howe describes as Parker's "many-sided power of appreciation" was reflected in the society's Sunday-morning meetings (176). Services spoke to congregants' eyes, ears, and minds, in a multisensory display of a religion that was not being offered in quite this same mixture—comprising equal parts lecture, prayer, music, and image—anywhere else in the city. To the Standing Committee, it was left to make arrangements for locating a permanent home for this one-of-a-kind worship. They chose the Melodeon, previously the home of the local Mechanics Institute, located on Washington Street, near West Street. For most of the 1840s, up to the time of the Twenty-Eighth Congregational Society's removal to larger quarters at Boston's Music Hall, in 1852, the Melodeon was the city's premier public space for concerts, lectures, and assorted entertainments. This remained the case after Parker's congregation signed a lease with the Handel & Haydn Society (at the time, the building's owners) in 1846, as the Melodeon continued to host a variety of different acts. Not all of these were "spiritual."[44] The Handel & Haydn Society itself presented Haydn's *The Creation* (1819) from the Melodeon's stage in 1846. A "Mr. Samuel Lover" gave the first of his "Irish evenings" in the fall of that same year, with the Steyermarkische Musical Company coming to town in 1848, the vocalist and pianist pairing of Madame Biscaccianti and Strakosch playing in 1849, and Donetti's Comic Troupe of Acting Monkeys arriving in 1852. Even the Twenty-Eighth Congregational Society got in on the act, as it retained the right to sublet the Melodeon's premises to other occupants. Thus, the society cohabited with a rotating cast of other rent-paying tenants. These included the members of the

Federal Street Baptist Society, a separate group of Anti-Sabbath conventioneers from March 1848, and, as an unexpected boon during the winter of 1850–51, the proprietor Josiah Perham and his crowd-pleasing presentation of artist William Burr's *Seven Mile Mirror,* a panorama of the northern lake country along the U.S.-Canadian border (figure 11).[45] Despite the Melodeon's being what one parishioner remembered as a "dingy hall"—the society concurred in this view, as they complained by letter to their landlords at the start of 1848—Parker's performances were unmatched by other area entertainments.[46] Howe, for example, remembers her minister keeping what she names "the spirit of the age" by means of "the living presence and the living utterance" that he projected from the stage (305). She further says that Parker "let out the metaphysical stops of his organ pretty freely" (311). The members of his society's Standing Committee voiced concerns that, as they wrote of their pastor in a report from April 1846, "some who hear his words from the pulpit, will be disposed to deny him the title of Christian, and attempt to affix on this Society the stigma of infidelity." But they were also "desirous that *all* should have an opportunity to come & hear what we believe to be the truth."[47]

Many did come. And, if they could withstand whatever pressure Parker's preaching applied to their personal orthodoxies, worshippers were treated to having their senses fed by a few modest extravagances. At a moment when there was, for example, what the *Boston Daily Advertiser* described as "a growing taste for Music in this community," even among those who, "a few years since, would have considered it beneath their dignity to patronise a concert," the society not only secured the services of a hired organist but also formed a small choir to accompany him in their renditions of traditional hymns.[48] There were fresh flowers adorning the pulpit every Sunday, too. In the words of one of the women who oversaw this ornamental ritual, it was in this way that members of the congregation who were "confined to the city, saw the columbine or the laurel or pond-lily for the first time."[49] Later in the society's life, there were additionally annual "Pic-Nic" excursions in the summer months to Waverley Grove, a short railway ride outside of Boston, providing what was said to be "a source of general satisfaction and pleasure to all who attended."[50] The former minister John T. Sargent, who had been removed from his pastorate at the city's Suffolk Street Chapel for exchanging pulpits with Parker well past the time of the latter's having fallen into disrepute with conservative Unitarians, liked to describe the "spell" that Parker cast over his "crowded audiences" as the effect of

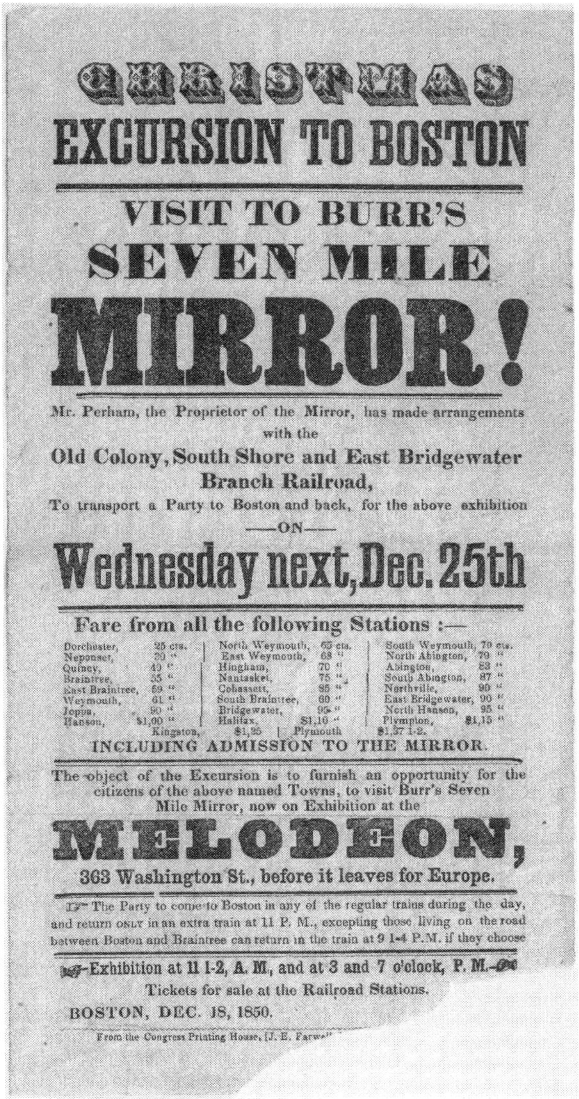

CHRISTMAS

EXCURSION TO BOSTON

VISIT TO BURR'S

SEVEN MILE

MIRROR!

Mr. Perham, the Proprietor of the Mirror, has made arrangements with the

Old Colony, South Shore and East Bridgewater Branch Railroad,

To transport a Party to Boston and back, for the above exhibition

—ON—

Wednesday next, Dec. 25th

Fare from all the following Stations :—

Dorchester,	25 cts.	North Weymouth,	65 cts.	South Weymouth,	70 cts.
Neponset,	30 "	East Weymouth,	68 "	North Abington,	79 "
Quincy,	40 "	Hingham,	70 "	Abington,	83 "
Braintree,	55 "	Nantasket,	75 "	South Abington,	87 "
East Braintree,	59 "	Cohassett,	85 "	Northville,	90 "
Weymouth,	61 "	South Braintree,	60 "	East Bridgewater,	90 "
Joppa,	90 "	Bridgewater,	95 "	North Hanson,	95 "
Hanson,	$1,00 "	Halifax,	$1,10 "	Plympton,	$1,15 "

Kingston, $1,25 | Plymouth $1,37 1-2.

INCLUDING ADMISSION TO THE MIRROR.

The object of the Excursion is to furnish an opportunity for the citizens of the above named Towns, to visit Burr's Seven Mile Mirror, now on Exhibition at the

MELODEON,

363 Washington St., before it leaves for Europe.

☞ The Party to come to Boston in any of the regular trains during the day, and return ONLY in an extra train at 11 P. M., excepting those living on the road between Boston and Braintree can return in the train at 9 1-4 P.M. if they choose

☞ Exhibition at 11 1-2, A. M., and at 3 and 7 o'clock, P. M. ☜

Tickets for sale at the Railroad Stations.

BOSTON, DEC. 18, 1850.

From the Congress Printing House, [J. E. Farwell

Figure 11. The Melodeon's presentation of the *Seven Mile Mirror* was popular enough that several regional railroads transported customers to and from Boston to see the panorama in person on Christmas Day 1850. From the printed broadside *Christmas Excursion to Boston* ([Boston]: Congress Printing House, 1850). Courtesy American Antiquarian Society.

an "Emersonian aesthetics."[51] But whether we think of the witchery of Parker's ministry as a marketable art form, or the scalable product of a cottage industry in urban belief, we arrive at the same conclusion: the originator of what more or less became the Parker *brand* had struck on a religious formula that worked in midcentury Boston. As the society's Standing Committee reported in April 1847, "Our meetings have been crowded from Sabbath to Sabbath, and the interest & attention which the exercises excite in the multitudes who attend show that the truths delivered by our beloved minister are exerting a widespread & deep influence upon the Community."[52]

For its part, the Standing Committee operated on a policy of relentless expansion. Board members were prevented from subdividing their Twenty-Eighth Congregation into franchises, one gathers, simply because there was no substituting for the one and only Theodore Parker, of whom they were the sole provider.[53] Even as the minister's popularity attracted more and more worshippers to his Sunday meetings, in the process stretching the seating at the Melodeon to maximum capacity, the committee continued to stress how imperative it was for the rank-and-file membership of the society to make what it said were the necessary "exertions to enlarge our number of subscribers."[54] This policy in turn impacted the reception of Parker's performances. It was apparently quite common, for instance, to find the swelling ranks of young male clerks—a recognizable urban type, in this period, of an aspirational middle class—securing seats for Sunday sermons at the society by arriving extra early, then wiling away the time by reading newspapers and pamphlets that might not be tucked courteously away when the minister began to preach. Nor, Julia Ward Howe's husband maintained, were the customary "impressions of reverence" and "decorum" reliably maintained. Audience members often arrived in the middle of the opening prayer, assuming there was one. Others came and went throughout the exercises, perhaps even making their way to the exit before a sermon's completion. And it was generally accepted that, as a matter of course, at least some of those present for Sunday worship with the society were mere thrill seekers rather than believers, or at best a discomfiting combination of the two.[55]

In response to these developments, the Standing Committee gave no sign of being unduly troubled by who was attending meetings, or how they comported themselves once they were there. If anything, board members expressed concern only over the fact that, as the committee reported in April 1852, "the expense of maintaining the public worship of the Society, has been borne by a comparative few (not over 150) of those who have enjoyed and still enjoy its benefits."[56] With a membership composed in no small part of young and urban office workers, tradesmen, and other local constituents of the middle and lower middling classes, the society was not about to see a sudden change in the habits or demographics of its primary donors. The more solidly prosperous members of the society, the middle- and upper-middle-class merchants and professionals on whose "moral condition" Parker preached in 1849, would continue to carry much of the financial burden of his ministry. It is evident that Parker's following in Boston would always include a substantial number of women, who may or may not have had a disposable income of their own to part with in support of his congregation. The city's laboring classes also made what contributions they could, in accordance with whatever their household finances allowed. But by and large, the people who turned up at the Melodeon or Music Hall for the full Parker experience had little from their own pockets that they could afford to subscribe to the society.[57] What few spare dollars and cents many of these men about town did possess they presumably spent, on demand, on a growing selection of urban entertainment options, more and more of which were becoming available as the century progressed. By contrast, the majority of the society's worshippers was far less sparing with its applause than it was with its money. Those who were in attendance made a demonstrative show of their support with an "intensity of feeling," in defiance of church conventions for Sunday services that, as one of Parker's longtime female congregants revealed, her minister had already violated by preaching on "the topics of the day."[58]

In a sermon from 1857, which he titled "Public Amusements, a Discourse," the Unitarian minister Edward Everett Hale (Harvard College class of 1839) suggested that none of this was necessarily heretical. As a member in good standing of the same Unitarian Association that had turned its back on Theodore Parker, and as the newly installed pastor, beginning in the spring of 1856, to Boston's South Congregational Church, Hale gave emphasis in the "Discourse" he later expanded and delivered at pulpits across the city to a religion that was responsive to the specific needs of the time and place in which it was practiced. "So long as we live in the country," he wrote, "the subject [of 'public amusements'] does not come up for discussion, for there God provides the best entertainment for everybody. Every boy can find it in the trout streams, and every girl among the buttercups." But in the city, Hale explained, the spiritual paradigm shifted. In his own words, "When we choose to bring people into crowded towns, to substitute pavement for the meadows, . . . we must substitute something for the relaxation and amusement which we have taken away." What Hale described was to some extent a way of catering to what he called the human need for "union." That is to say, he acknowledges that a "great part of the enjoyment" of a sermon, an orchestra, or a play (by way of example, Hale names *Much Ado about Nothing*, a Shakespearean favorite that enjoyed long runs in Boston) derives from the "contagious sympathy" it acquires when performed for "a large number of hearers." Nothing so much "amuses" us, Hale says, as what we undergo in common. At the same time, Hale recognizes that the "public" nature of such "amusements" as he endorses—and he is sensitive "not only to the restricting of bad public amusements," he writes, "but to the providing of good ones"—is of more than circumstantial importance to their enjoyment. Were these not available to everyone, equally, it would be "only the rich, the educated," Hale cautions, "who can supply, in their own homes, the necessity for entertainment."[59]

What Hale wanted was what Parker provided, the "education of the whole man,—body, mind and soul." But "instead of pretending," Hale insisted, "to teach people as they do," the guardians of the church would be better served in attending to the modern needs of modern people, for whom "the hours of rest are worth as much as the hours of labor." In the end, Hale decided that "the institutions of religion have no more power, more than the institutions of amusement, to work results finer than the motive power brought to bear" (1). Parker's society was built on a similar principle, with the added transcendental stipulation that the very best in "public" entertainment should originate with the great spiritual drama that was enacted *within* all persons of faith. In private, Parker grieved that even some of his supporters should have looked on his appearances at the Melodeon not as irreligious but as entirely unrelated to religion.[60] One of the minister's early defenders characterized this popular misconception as follows, writing that certain contemporaries felt Parker was little more than the host of a "Sunday Lyceum, where he harangued a promiscuous audience on all themes of thought, science, or politics."[61] Yet ultimately, Parker remained convinced that most people attended his sermons for some combination of religious, moral, or intellectual reasons. This appears to have been the case, despite the minister's reputation for being, as he said, "dis-reputable."[62]

In his Dudleian Lecture at the Harvard University Divinity School on November 11, 1976, the French philosopher Paul Ricœur warned of the "atheistic consequences" that could occur whenever "consciousness posits itself as the origin of meaning."[63] The occasion for Ricœur's making these remarks pertained neither to Parker nor to any other transcendentalist. Nor was the Frenchman interested, at least during his appearance on the leafy campus in Cambridge, in the historical conflicts involving irreligion that had been locally contested over the years prior to his arrival, conflicts that to some extent had determined what he called the "hermeneutic" ground from which he would be delivering his address. As Ricœur explained, he had come to Harvard "to recover a concept of revelation and a concept of reason that, without ever coinciding, can at least enter into a living dialectic and together engender something like an understanding of faith" (1). Emerson might be said to have attempted something similar in his own speaking engagement at the Divinity School, in 1838. Parker, too, had made the effort at achieving "something like an understanding of faith" into a regular undertaking with his Twenty-Eighth Congregational Society, in Boston, in the middle decades of the nineteenth century.

Where Ricœur parted ways with such transcendental predecessors as he never references in his lecture was in the posture he adopted toward what he names "this power of self-production" (30). There was a danger for Ricœur in a person's asserting his individual spirit too much. One result of the anomalous "authoritarian" position that could result from such an obstreperous display of selfhood—a show of bad faith, as far as Ricœur was concerned—the philosopher likens to a kind of bad grammar, whereby a believer made his own "consciousness" into a "subject," while subordinating his conception of "the divine" to a "predicate" of dependency (30, 1). Ricœur, it should be noted, maintains a studied distance from history as he conducts what he names his "meditation" on "revelation" (37). Yet he also recognizes (in an address that operates mostly at the level of "homology" and metaphor) the "presentation" of "historical testimony" as such as being pivotal to the "idea of a letting go," of the "letting go of self" that was the definitive condition for him of any religion (37, 32). There is, admittedly, a certain irony in our using the joyful surrender of Parker's followers in Boston to their captivating minister as a way to illustrate, historically, a city "letting go" of itself. But this is, in fact, the irony with which the Reverend Theodore Parker lived during the urban phase of his career. However much his "infidelity" related back to his theology, which was premised on Parker's belief in the boundlessness of *any* spiritual self, his ministry had in fact been raised (against Parker's wishes) on his congregation's tacit willingness to have whatever collective "consciousness" they possessed be absorbed by a minister who, for all his raw humility, was not immune from the tendency for self-aggrandizement of most paid performers. Ideally, Ricœur wanted religion to be what he described as an "expression of dependence without heteronomy"; that is to say, he understood religion to depend on our freedom from a subjection to forces outside of ourselves (37). It would have been hard for the transcendentalist Parker to imagine religion on any other terms, considering how he always, in the body of his sermons and writings, gave priority to the growth of the individual's spirit. At the same time, such history as he lived in his city ministry had helped to establish new standards of spiritual autonomy in New England that the phenomenologically minded postmodernist Ricœur never bothers to acknowledge. The spiritual selves of Parker's parishioners, in any case, came to "consciousness" within the context of a compact, consumerist urban society that had all but made the isolating "mean egotism" of Emerson's *Nature* seem a sylvan impossibility. There was simply to be no solitude (for the spirit, or any other aspect of selfhood) in the city, at least not on the traditional terms by which self-communion had earlier been understood. As the addled and unsteady religious life of Boston went, so went the transcendental meaning of belief that Parker would impart to such selves as filled the crowded seats of the Melodeon and Music Hall from week to week.

INFIDELITY IN THE CITY; OR, "FREE" RELIGION

Despite the upsurge in urban amusements in these years, not everyone had abandoned his religious will at the altar of entertainment. Occasionally, there was even someone who learned to assert his spiritual self by first submitting to such entertainment options as were on offer in a newly reconstituted free market of faiths, any one of which might have seemed that it could be swapped out for another without its owner noticing. For the American founder of "free" religion, Francis Ellingwood Abbot, the turning point from his being a purchaser to his becoming a provider of religious content began on Saturday, May 12, 1855, when he was just eighteen years old. "Frank," under which name the Unitarian-bred Abbot would later appear in the *Harvard College Class Book of 1859*, upon his graduation, was on this day (also his parents' twenty-fifth wedding anniversary) to be baptized alongside a sister and a brother at Boston's New South Church, located on the "Church Green" at the corner of Summer and Bedford Streets. "All the Cambridge folks came out," Abbot recorded in his daily planner, and "there were a good many other friends present beside." "It will," he continued, "begin a new era."[64]

Indeed it did. With his brother Edwin about to graduate from the college in June, a still callow Francis would be applying for admission to Harvard in July, with the usual two-day round of written and oral examinations to follow. Abbot passed that milestone as he had cleared the last formal obstacle standing between him and his faith, his recent baptism. Now his own man, he took an evident delight in dividing his attentions between such preoccupations as would characterize his entrance into adulthood. These included keeping a close watch on his mounting expenditures for cake, confectionery, cigars, and ice cream ("Me miserum! 12 cents ice cream," he complained in his diary), paying his annual assessment of one dollar to the Young Men's Christian Union, and availing himself of the area's store of entertainments. As for these last, Abbot was not too particular in deciding when or where or how he kept himself occupied, at least before he buckled down to his studies during his first fall term at the college. Among the pleasures he pursued—in somewhat random succession—over the months of spring, summer, and, yes, fall were the regular trips he made to the theater. He visited the opera, too, once to hear Mozart's *Don Giovanni,* then to catch Verdi's *Il trovatore.* He attended an antislavery lecture by the U.S. senator from Massachusetts, Charles Sumner. He was present for a pair of Sunday sermons by Samuel Abbot Smith (Harvard College class of 1849 and a graduate from the Divinity School in 1853). And he paid to see an unspecified "menagerie" as well.[65]

By the time of his senior year at Harvard, Abbot had begun to wean himself from the frenzied consumption of such merriment as these products afforded him. He now set about formulating the faith that, after he had risen to the position of pastor by the end of the next decade, would prove as much of an amusement for others as anything that Abner Kneeland or Theodore Parker had offered the religious market of Boston. At this point, Abbot settled on religion as his primary avocation, even as he set his sights on the ministry as the most likely field for his future endeavors. Both in and out of the classroom, Abbot's thinking had tended more and more toward the spiritual, by way of the philosophical, over the course of his undergraduate career.[66] Abbot's classmate Francis V. Balch announced in his Class Day oration from June 1859 that "the childish eagerness for amusement . . . shows itself more in the young man who is a Senior, than in the young boy who is a Freshman."[67] To read through the private "miscellanies" that Abbot recorded in *his* senior year is nonetheless to discover a spiritual seeker who was as earnest as any transcendentalist from a generation earlier. Perhaps Abbot had simply learned to "play" in a different way than Balch and the other members of his college class. We find, regardless, that at some moments Abbot's thoughts are most holy. "To divide one's heart between God and the world," he begins his diary for the school year of 1858–59, "is like Solomon's halving the harlot's infant—the moiety is utterly worthless." At others we can recognize quite plainly that he hewed to less orthodox views, as when he stepped beyond the predictable opinions of a straw man of "a skeptic" with his conviction that "the penny candle and burning Moscow are equal, when matched with the sun. [Spinoza says the same Epist. LVIII, Q10.]." In response to the "Mathematicians," moreover, whom Abbot alleges do "sometimes assert that Deity himself could not make twice two equal five," he concluded what none of his unoffending Harvard professors could have countenanced. "There is no alternative between a God omnipotent in the broadest sense of the word," Abbot writes, "and no God; between theism and atheism." In completing a college course of reading, then, which in addition to including Coleridge now featured such transcendental stalwarts as Kant and Cousin, the divinity student to be (Abbot lasted not one year at Harvard's Divinity School before switching to the Meadville Theological School, in Pennsylvania) was ready to announce what would be his creedless creed: "Every ultimate cause is spiritual; science is recognizing this truth more and more clearly day by day." Abbot, in short, was no longer satisfied by the "inferior conception of reason" that he felt held sway in Cambridge. He was ready for something more, or less, or both in the way of belief. The "math" didn't matter so much to Abbot, whose strange conjoining of the spiritual and empirical was something new under the sun in those days. As he maintained in his diary, in defiance "of all the subtle [*sic*] distinctions of theologians," "a finite object of worship is rejected by every mind."[68]

It would later take a court decree, from December 1868, to remove Abbot from his position as minister to the First Unitarian Society of Christians, in Dover, New Hampshire, where he had been installed only several years before. Now effectively excommunicated over what that state's Supreme Judicial Court said were his "disbeliefs, denials and doctrines subversive of the fundamental principles of Christianity as generally received and holden by the denomination of Christians known as Unitarians," Abbot was released to become the main spokesperson for a faith that, like transcendentalism before it, would incur the universal charge of "infidelity."[69] Whatever were his offenses against religious convention, Abbot had an undeniable appeal in certain progressive circles. The believers in spiritual mediums who read the *Banner of Light* newspaper, for example, said that he was "young" and "clear-headed" and "out-radicals the radicals."[70] Likewise in its report titled "Liberal Preaching," a writer from Abner Kneeland's *Boston Investigator,* still publishing after all these years, similarly praised Abbot for having "leaped the fence and got clear of sects." This was the paper's response to the "discourse" called "Religious Revivals" that Abbot had delivered back in Dover, after he observed the sudden rush of religious conversions that had recently occurred there. According to the *Investigator*'s account, Abbot had remarked that, "by repeated and well-dealt blows, any popular audience can be beaten up, like an egg, into a froth; but, when left to itself, the froth soon dies away. . . . The beating process imparts no weight, no religion; it imparts froth, and nothing more." Abbot, for his part, expected something much more substantive from his faith, something all-embracing and sustaining. "'It is a fearful thing,'" he said, quoting from scripture, "'to fall into the hands of the living God.'" But it would be more "fearful," Abbot contended, "to fall *out* of his hands. Hope and courage and aspiration are religion; despair is the worst Atheism."[71] Not for many more years did Abbot write his second full-length book, *The Way Out of Agnosticism; or, The Philosophy of Free Religion* (1890). But already he had signaled that his overriding purpose was to discover a route back *into* religion, not "out of" it.

Abbot made it his mission to circulate this message in person when- and wherever he could and through print in cases that called for less direct means of expression. Among the highlights of his early years out on the lecture circuit in New England was the talk he gave called "A Radical's Theology," which he delivered in the rooms of the Parker Fraternity, in Boston, on the evening of Sunday, February 3, 1867. Reprinted in the June edition of the liberal Unitarian monthly the *Radical,* a fledgling city paper that would have welcomed a contribution from a person of Abbot's enhanced stature, "A Radical's Theology" is the precise opposite of what it says it is.[72] "Like an edifice," Abbot says, "Theology is finished and stationary," whereas "Science," by contrast, "is organic and capable of indefinite growth" (585). Abbot isn't so much speaking of "Theology," then, as he's calling for "Theology" and "Science" to be "blended in what may be called . . . Theological Science or Scientific Theology" (585). His reasons for favoring this shift in our religious sensibilities is clear. "Science," he announces, "proclaims the principle of freedom, because freedom means observation and experiment, analysis and synthesis, criticism, philosophy, intuition, thought itself" (586). However anomalous a proposition was his combining "intuitive" transcendental idealism with a laboratory brand of scientific experimentalism, Abbot himself regarded his beliefs as, if not commonsensical, then utterly rational and defensible without ceasing to be spiritual, personal, and openly available to anyone and everyone who cared to partake of them.[73] The "radical's theology" was therefore anything but in Abbot's formulation. He in fact preferred to think of his religion as what he named "an anthropology of faith." For "my faith in man is so profound," Abbot writes, "that in all the vast compass of the known universe, I behold nothing so august and sublime as he" ("A Radical's Theology," 593). Where his "faith" would lead not even Abbot knew, and he accepted this uncertainty on principle as he did in practice. Abbot believed in nothing so much as he did in doubt, the intolerable alternative to which he regarded as the "fixed dogmas" of a church that had ostracized him (585). Hence his stated reasons for going his own religious road: "If the pathway of thought leads to scepticism, materialism, atheism, I will none the less walk in it; I am not of those who wish to be cheated 'for their own good.' Away with the faith that will not withstand the sharpest cross-fire of criticism and philosophy! If there is no God, faith is not skilled to create him. Nothing but truth is wholesome, and there is no guide to truth but thought" (586). This was the understanding of religion that Abbot brought before the Boston public in the aftermath of the U.S. Civil War. Some of the city's residents would fight him tooth and nail for trading "theology" for such effrontery as refused to renounce "skepticism" and "atheism" on sight. Others paid to hear him preach such words as they'd never heard preached before.

Soon enough Abbot became a key attraction in Boston's lecture halls. Although he was now based in Toledo, Ohio—following the rupture in his relationship with his former congregation, in New Hampshire, Abbot had since moved west to assume charge of the local Unitarian Society, which he in turn convinced to sever its connections with official Unitarianism—the apostle of what came to be known as "scientific theism" had managed to maintain close ties to New England's first city. This was primarily the result of Abbot's involvement with Boston's Free Religious Association. Abbot was one of the association's eight founders, many of whom had defected from organized Unitarianism in the aftermath of that denomination's second national conference, held in Syracuse, New York, in 1866. So-called free religionists like Kneeland had left the conference insisting on absolute freedom of thought and expression in matters of faith. From their vantage, their soon-to-be-erstwhile brethren had errantly aligned themselves with a codified set of beliefs, and so, on January 1 in the new year, they announced a meeting to discuss a rationale for establishing a new organization that would prove more accommodating to the diverse spiritual needs of free-minded believers at a time one of their number later named a "religious *Renaissance*."[74] That meeting took place on February 5 at the Boston home of Cyrus A. Bartol, a graduate of the Harvard Divinity School in 1835 and a sometime member of the Transcendental Club. About thirty people were in attendance. Many of these were dissident members of the Unitarian clergy, but there were also Universalists and Quakers, laywomen and -men, on hand as well. A small vanguard of their number having met the day prior, a Monday, at the city's Parker House hotel to draft a provisional constitution, the larger meeting was able to make short work (relatively speaking, as the free religionists were of as divided a mind as the transcendentalists had ever been) in their deliberations and called for a public convention to formally organize in Boston on May 30, 1867. Drafted by O. B. Frothingham, that call spoke of "the desire . . . to make a fellowship, not a party; to promote the scientific study of religious Truth, not to defend the legacy of Theological Tradition; to keep open the lines of spiritual freedom, not to close the lines of speculative beliefs."[75] But it was the people, more than the association's platform, that made the convention an area attraction. Among the invited speakers for May were a number of incipient celebrities who had established their reputations less, if at all, as learned clergy than as paid performers on the lecture circuit. Emerson was slated to speak, as was the seasoned social reformer Robert Dale Owen. The Quaker abolitionist Lucretia Mott appeared on the bill, as did the forward-thinking rabbi Isaac M. Wise. Abbot would take his turn at the lectern, too, contributing not for the last time to an event that was being widely advertised in both the city's religious and secular press. All reports indicate the chosen venue for the conference, Boston's newly rebuilt Horticultural Hall, was packed to overflowing.

At its subsequent annual meetings, also held in Boston, the association's Executive Committee, on which Abbot served as one of nine directors, returned often to the question of what the organization should actually *do*. The *Annual Report* that was produced and published after the first such meeting, held in the city's Tremont Temple on May 28, 1868, revealed that members remained unwavering in their commitment to "bringing the Association into more direct and active communication with the liberal religious sentiment of the country."[76] Beyond that commitment, things were unclear. There was one early proposal for a course of ten free religious lectures in Cambridge, to coincide by design with "the college term." Said lectures were to be delivered, again in the words of the *Annual Report,* "by persons representing progressive and rationalistic views in religion." Because only a small minority of the Executive Committee was present at this particular meeting, no official motion on the matter could pass. But the association's secretary, acting in what he called "his private rather than official capacity," did see this resolution through, the result being a short course of lectures—repeated afterward at lecture halls in Boston—given to what the *Report* describes as an "interested and attentive" audience composed of "the students of theology in Cambridge" (6–7). There were also suggestions for the publication of "essays and discourses for popular distribution." These would be tidily packaged pamphlet versions of the addresses speakers gave at the annual meetings, the intention of which talks, once more in the words of the *Report,* was to "consider religious questions from a purely rational, scientific, unsectarian, and undogmatic point of view, though in a thoroughly reverent spirit" (7). In addition, Abbot's *Index* would be up and running before too long, with its debut coming in January 1870. And meanwhile, there was the important work of organization building to undertake as well, as the association set about appointing a general agent, establishing a central office, soliciting members and contributions, and securing speakers for local venues across New England, the mid-Atlantic, and what we would refer to today as the American Midwest.

As far as the general populace of Boston was concerned, "free religion" was what was happening in Horticultural Hall, where, beginning in the 1868–69 season, the Free Religious Association began to sponsor a lecture series that would continue strong for the next twenty-five years. We might think that the average Bostonian had little cause to visit the hall, the home of the Massachusetts Horticultural Society. But with the rise of that society's operations and influence, it had been able to secure the site for a spacious new headquarters at 100–102 Tremont Street, between Bromfield Street and Montgomery Place. This became a popular gathering place for all of Boston (figure 12). The building's multiple stories, constructed from the white granite of Concord, New

Hampshire, facilitated a range of interests and activities right from the time of its opening, in 1865. Commercial stores occupied the building's ground floor. The society's library and administrative offices took up the second floor. And a large and elegantly appointed grand Exhibition Hall occupied the third floor. It was here, when meetings of the Unitarian Association (it was no coincidence that free religionists had elected to meet in the same place as loyal Unitarians) were not in session, that a selection of concerts, lectures, and other assorted entertainments were staged. The spirit of these would always range from the "serious" to the outlandish, as is suggested by an advertisement that appeared in 1897 for an "Oriental" tableau "entertainment," featuring a "Chinese Village and Theatre."[77] Such was the splendor of Horticultural Hall's ornate facade—the exterior of the structure was graced by statuary depicting Ceres, the ancient Roman goddess of agriculture, Flora, goddess of flowers, and Pomona, goddess of fruit trees—that it gave license to a writer from *Harper's Weekly* to say "the building is justly regarded as an ornament to the city."[78] It was the happenings *inside* this repurposed urban space that was causing such a commotion, however.[79]

Figure 12. *The New Horticultural Hall in Boston*, after a woodcut engraving by Samuel Smith Kilburn, 1865. From the Collection of the Boston Athenaeum, Prints and Photographs Department.

With its Sunday-afternoon lectures at Horticultural Hall, the Free Religious Association staked its claim to participating in the conversations on faith that had been ongoing in greater Boston since at least the start of the nineteenth century. The association's future president, William J. Potter, recalled the outlines of the free religionists' contribution to those conversations when he spoke, in 1892, of a religion that had decided, "according to the great doctrine of evolution . . . [that] the history of man is not Christo-centric, but *Cosmo-centric*."[80] Free religion was meant to be a *modern* religion and so provide its followers—no matter what their personal backgrounds or allotted stations in life—with new sources of religious truth derived from both the most up-to-date lessons of science and the ancient scriptures and enduring symbolic myths of a whole world's worth of religions, particularly in Asia.[81] By right of the influence he'd earned as an advocate of free religion, and because of the attention he'd won (not all of it flattering) for being an intrepid speaker, Abbot would ensure that free religion competed on an equal footing with the city's other leisure-time enticements, of which there were many. Abbot's spreading fame reached beyond the dues-paying members of the association. He was already regarded as someone, or something, worth seeing by the time he presented the fifth installment of the association's talks for the 1869 season. Of Abbot's lecture, from mid-February, titled "The Genius of Christianity and Free Religion," a writer from the *Boston Post* could say, "The reputation of the speaker drew together an unusually large audience, which for an hour and a half gave its undivided attention to his arguments." Our writer makes no mention of how listeners responded to Abbot's pronouncement that "the spirit of Christianity itself has become gradually more and more discordant with modern civilization and modern religion." Nor does he bother to register the effect of the speaker's decree that "Idealize and Transcendentalise the Christ as highly as you may, his power is gone the moment you make him aught less than a person."[82] What we can deduce, from a historical distance, is that Boston thought an appearance by Abbot was not to be missed.

City people had regular opportunities to attend his lectures, as he returned to town at least once each winter or spring (and sometimes more frequently) to challenge what he called any false "demonstration" of a "decisive authority in matters of belief."[83] This Abbot did in a string of presentations that, when taken together, constituted an advanced course in free religion. We might say the same of the twelve lectures that the Free Religious Association offered each calendar year (single tickets cost fifty cents, tickets for the entire course four dollars) between January and April, and as were highlighted by such luminaries as Thomas Wentworth Higginson, Wendell Phillips, Samuel Longfellow, the transcendentalist William Henry Channing, and Julia Ward Howe. Yet with Abbot, the association had its one true star. He spoke on Jesus and Socrates in 1870. Then came "Intuitionalism and the Scientific School of Free Religion," in 1871. The next year brought "God of Science," with the "Study of Religion," "Darwin's Theory of Conscience," and "Atomism in Religion" being offered at annual intervals thereafter. In its coverage of these events, the local press was game enough to engage on occasion with the content of Abbot's lectures, as when one paper went so far as to expand on the distinction the speaker had drawn between positivism (in which camp Abbot placed himself) and rationalism.[84] It was more often the case that beat writers simply quoted at length from Abbot's addresses, while providing a kind of metacommentary on their original delivery. The writer just mentioned, for example, was sure to let readers know that "Mr. Abbot does not look the Radical that he is; he has too peaceful and genial a face to be waging such furious warfare against time-honored institutions." Boston's *Investigator* agreed, in remarking that Abbot's "liberality" had made him "famous among the leading and progressive preachers of the time."[85] As for the reception side of the equation, "Many of the audience had not heard him [Abbot] before," we learn, so "there was a hush of expectancy as he came forward and began to speak."[86] A staff reporter for the *Republican* likewise wrote of Abbot's "statement of the attitude of science toward the religion of the future, which was . . . admirable for its clearness and vigor of expression," while another of Abbot's champions, at the *Banner of Light,* praised him for his "boldness of speech and belief." These qualities were said to have served the speaker well in addressing "quite a large audience." In fact, as the *Boston Post* observed of all of Abbot's "Sunday Services," there could not help but be "quite a large audience present to listen to such food for reflection as the lecturer furnished."[87]

Abbot's stock in trade was controversy, of course, and in this item he was seldom in short supply. As a warning, for instance, to the people of the neighboring city of Lowell, who had agreed to host a caravan of five speakers (the first of whom would be Abbot) from Horticultural Hall in March 1870, an unnamed writer for the local *Vox Populi* paper reported of the association's speakers prior to their arrival, "We do not presume they are very iniquitous, though probably some of them will be too liberal and others too visionary for the masses." At the same time, this same writer retreated far enough from his initial cautionary position to predict that, "in these days of liberal ideas, it is by no means surprising that an 'independent' course of lectures should meet with favor in Lowell." This was especially the case given what our writer called the speakers' "literary merit," which "will undoubtedly excel any course that has ever been given in this city."[88] Still, for a number of papers back in Boston, neither tolerance nor ambivalence was the proper response to what was transpiring late in the day on Sundays in *their* city. A writer for the *Universalist* reminded its readers that Abbot was "an avowed infidel." As for his "free religionist" associates, they, too, were said to favor "a total freedom from all religion."[89] A columnist from the Baptist *Watchman & Reflector* for his part found it "passing strange" that Boston should cede the stage to "an avowed rejecter of Christianity and calumniator of Christ." Another from the *Christian Register* found himself fighting on two fronts, as he sought to further distance Unitarians from the Free Religious Association after a mischievous Universalist accused the former denomination of having "sustained Atheists as preachers in their churches."[90] But even in conceding all of this, a writer for New York's *World*, after acknowledging that Abbot had succeeded in "cutting entirely loose from Christian creeds of every sort," professed an unqualified admiration for the "honest as well as earnest" Abbot. For this admirer, as for so many across the northeastern United States, Abbot's courageous "independence" made him what a purported "infidel" in that day could only be, "more conspicuous than others."[91] That in itself inspired a kind of faith, in *something*. And so, as the *Commonwealth* advised anyone with an interest in what the Free Religious Association represented "in the history of Boston culture," it was increasingly thought wise for those who'd "preserve its memories . . . not . . . to be absent from its weekly reunions of thoughtful and cultivated people."[92]

In his survey of the intellectual, social, and institutional "resources" that were available in nineteenth-century Boston "to sustain a public religious skepticism," the historian Christopher Grasso reminds us that "religious skepticism did not secularize America." This is not to deny, Grasso points out, "the more complicated effects that skepticism did have." It is simply to conceive of belief as a constantly shifting and contested ground.[93] By way of elaborating Grasso's claim, we might include among the "effects" he mentions not only a blurring of the distinction between the spiritual and secular in Boston, but also a reduction there of the difference between prayer time and playtime in this particular contemporary city. As we have seen, more and more New Englanders were becoming acculturated in these years to urban practices that dispensed with a traditional deference to the same old pieties that, until only recently, had once been the mainstay of the region. As a result, many city peoples gradually eased into inhabiting a more modern space than before, where the lingering impetus to shield whatever was deemed sacred had been relaxed enough to allow even nonradical "believers" in religions other than transcendentalism, "Parkerism," and free religion to resort to such outlets of religious expression as had once been considered forbidden.

Witness the postbellum look of religion in the *Boston Post* newspaper. In the page 2 column it reserved for "Entertainments," this long-running city daily could suggest, as of February 1869, that there was nothing to be lost by lumping together such of the area's coming attractions as the editors themselves apparently regarded as neither incompatible with nor antithetical to the new-look manner and matter of belief. In seriatim fashion, the *Post* reported that the "last work" of the German-born French composer Offenbach, *La Perichole*, was playing at the Boston Theatre. Stone & Murray's Circus was holding court at the Olympic. Over at Summer Hall, there was a lecture by Dr. O'Leary called "Health, Strength & Beauty." And in addition to the Harvard Musical Association's performance of its Eighth Symphony Concert, at the Boston Music Hall, readers were reminded that they could also look forward to the National Peace Jubilee and Musical Celebration, "to be held in Boston in June." After its launch in 1872, the rival *Boston Globe* would make some small effort to keep separate what the *Post* had implied was, if not identical, then closely enough associated to fall under the same heading. So, in side-by-side front-page columns, set immediately beneath the masthead, the *Globe* treated readers of its issues from December 1872 to a curated selection (moving from left to right) of the various urban pursuits from which they might choose. There are "Amusements" for some, "Concerts, &c." for others, and "Lectures, &c." for everyone else. It is difficult to say if anyone found the resulting syntax of the paper's page layout unseemly, considering that announcements for an "Odd Fellows' Fair" and "Novelties, Etc., for the Holidays" were bumping right up against an advertisement for an installment of the "Parker Fraternity Lectures" at Tremont Temple.[94] With the turn of the year, regardless, the paper ceased to make such fine distinctions. From this point forward, even an evening's benefit for the Young Men's Christian Association, at the Music Hall, would fall under the all-purpose category of "Amusements."[95]

These, then, were the *urban* conditions under which an old-school Unitarian, while taking an overview of religion in his city, in 1869, could observe for the *Christian Register,* "Now there has sprung up in Boston a whole generation of religious radicals." In this same writer's estimation, "Twenty years ago the city had one Theodore Parker. He stood alone." But of the then present day, our Jeremiah could say, "Nobody can read the newspapers without perceiving that during the last year, at least, religious radicalism has held high carnival in Boston." The list of offenses against fidelity was there for everyone to see. Today they read as one long lament over an assortment of vulgar "Novelties" to which our writer, unamused, must object. There is the Twenty-Eighth Congregational Society, alive and well under the pastoral care of the Reverend James V. Blake (Harvard College class of 1862 and a graduate from the Divinity School in 1866). A radical society of Universalists of two years' standing had also formed, led by the minister Rowland Connor, who was acting at that time as the vice president of the Free Religious Association. The liberal Unitarian congregation of the comparative religionist pastor W. R. Alger, "whose theology is probably as radical as Theodore Parker's, and whose tendencies lead him more and more away from established Unitarianism," was filling Boston's Music Hall on Sunday mornings, to the obvious approval of his parishioners. Sunday afternoon's "lectures" at Horticultural Hall continued unabated as well. Furthermore, not only had the *Radical* journal sprung up, in its devotion to spreading the word of a reformed religion, but the Radical *Club* was holding meetings (by invitation only) in the home of the Reverend John T. Sargent, at No. 13 Chestnut Street. And, as with its lectures, so, too, with the Free Religious Association's annual meetings, which bear comparison with the progressive celebrations of the Chardon Street Conventions, thirty years before.[96]

For the writer from the *Christian Register,* what he called "The Battle of Ideas in Boston" had been won. Of his radical adversaries he could write, "They control pulpits, conventions, parlors and periodicals."[97] Some five years later, another columnist from the *Christian Register* suggested the consequences of the radicals' victory, writing, "Thanks to modern toleration, one can almost be as heretical as he pleases now with almost entire impunity."[98] Since then, it has been the prerogative of those coming after the first, second, and third of New England's transcendental generations to sit back and watch this latest religious dispensation unfold.

AFTERWORD

The kinds of religious radicalism that appeared in New England in the nineteenth century carried costs for the people and communities that had lent them their time, energies, and attention. Francis Abbot, for one, was candid in saying that his religious views had exacted a heavy personal toll. As he wrote to a college classmate in 1865, even before his removal from the Unitarian Church, "You, I always thought, are as much a born missionary as I am a born Heathen, & what trifle of humanity I brought away from Harvard I owe to you, old fellow, God bless you."[1] At the same time, Abbot and other "free religionists" stood accused of the same charge of *negative* religion as had the transcendentalists in the 1830s, 1840s, and 1850s. They carried the burden, in other words, of having to provide "positive" proof that religious freedom, as they conceived it, amounted to more than the spiritual nullity with which they were often charged by their critics. Indeed, the *Christian Register* took note that *negativity* had become a point of dissension within the ranks of the Free Religious Association itself. A writer from the above publication related that the association's then secretary, William J. Potter, who entered Harvard's Divinity School in 1856 but never graduated, had mounted a "defense of the absence of affirmative expressions of the religious sentiment on the part of the Association." Meanwhile, Potter's colleague, his fellow cofounder Cyrus Bartol, insisted, "We cannot live on negations; and on no affirmations for its handful of advocates [to] agree, save the grand one of right to investigate." These in-house disagreements would have raised a smile from the writer from the *Register*, had Potter not also asserted that the association demonstrated at least as much "religious sentiment" as any other church organization. To this the nominal "Christian" in the debate could only respond with skepticism. "Has there ever been a prayer offered at a Free *Religious* convention?" he asked. In fact, there had, as the many ordained ministers among the association's membership would have ensured. "Have the members of such a body ever joined in the singing of a theistic hymn?" the writer from the *Register* continued. Again an accurate answer would have been yes, as the association, in its later iterations from the 1880s and 1890s, turned its annual meetings into "festivals," where attendees sang hymns that one associationist said had been "adapted to our broad, liberal views."[2] For anyone inside the association, the freedom in which they believed, like the freedom they had chosen to practice, could only ever be imagined as belonging *with* religion. That religion was not a "nothing."

Whatever else was Abbot's legacy, and however much he might have tempered transcendental intuition with a hardheaded faith in scientific observation, he insisted from the founding of the Free Religious Association that the work of worship was first and last an affirmation: of life, liberty, and the far-reaching power of belief. To this extent, Abbot very much falls within the "heretical" lineage of transcendentalism. He was replacing the faith that he was rejecting, in equal (but not opposite) measure. Abbot made his intentions plain within the pages of the *Index*. In his "Prospectus" for the newspaper, which he composed in Toledo on November 1, 1869, he stated outright, "The Index will aim at a two-fold object, positive and negative." As to the former, his paper aimed "to increase pure and genuine Religion in the world,—to develop a nobler spirit and higher purpose both in society and the individual." As for the latter, his *Index* sought "to increase Freedom in the world,—to destroy every species of spiritual slavery, to expose every form of superstition, to encourage independence of thought and action in all matters that concern belief, character or conduct."[3]

Were this not "affirmative" enough a statement of faith, Abbot in fact opened the inaugural issue of the *Index* with a list called "Fifty Affirmations." These he subdivided into discrete categories. Under "Religion," for example, he defined his terms ("Religion is the effort of man to perfect himself"), identified priorities ("The root of religion is universal human nature"), and established parameters ("Historical religions are all one, in virtue of this one common root"). Under "Christianity," meanwhile, Abbot let it be known that he was and wasn't a subscriber to the "liberal" kind, which he describes as both "the highest development of the free spirit of protest against authority which is possible within the Christian church" and, at the same time, "the lowest possible development of faith in the Christ,—a return to the Christian Confession in its crudest and least developed form." And under the heading "Free Religion" (Abbot reserves his final category for the "Relation of Christianity to Free Religion"), he made such affirmations as Parker ("The great law of Free Religion is the still, small voice of the private soul") and Emerson ("The great peace of Free Religion is spiritual oneness with the infinite One") had made in their respective testaments to Absolute Religion and the "Over-Soul."[4] From an orthodox view, there was plenty to take exception with in Abbot's list. But Abbot was not writing for an audience of the orthodox, not primarily, at least. To truly qualify as "affirmative," his writing would in any case need to be less of a response to free religion's critics than a positive statement of what he *did* believe. Otherwise, he would be subject to the same accusations as had beset such of his predecessors as Theodore Parker, whom the Unitarian minister turned Episcopalian priest Samuel Osgood (Harvard College class of 1832) had said was just another of transcendentalism's "eloquent destructives."[5] Thus, unlike the title of Abbot's piece from three years earlier, "A Radical's Theology," that of "Fifty Affirmations" did not belie the effective argument of its contents. The author of this list didn't just believe in *one* thing; he believed in *many* things, the totality of which he had spelled out in full.

There is something rather sad, then, in the discordant note on which Abbot's career would end. By 1880 he was worn down from the leadership roles that he had assumed with the *Index* and the Free Religious Association. And so, Abbot's heart followed where his mind had led him, back to the formal study of philosophy. He earned his Ph.D. from Harvard in 1881, but, because of his long affiliation with religious radicalism, he was unable to secure an academic teaching position in the United States. Instead, he supported himself and family by running a classical school for young men, the Home School for Boys, in Cambridge, Massachusetts. Abbot was to have his share of successes in the meantime. His first book, *Scientific Theism*, a critique of German idealistic philosophy, appeared in 1885. It was received especially well in Europe, even undergoing a German translation. In 1887, moreover, Abbot was appointed as a temporary replacement in Harvard's Philosophy Department for Professor Josiah Royce, who was on sick leave for the upcoming academic year. Abbot in some respects made the most of his opportunity, teaching an advanced offering on "scientific theism" for Philosophy 13, a core course at the college. His instructor's notes for his class meeting on February 15 reveal that Abbot had gained a platform for "free religion" at the very seat of liberal Protestantism in New England. That, at least, is how he interpreted whatever mandate his terminal position gave him. "No dogma proposed here," he informed his students. "No appeal except to free intelligence, applied to the facts of Nature according to scientific method. Freedom, yet positiveness, of all science, as a body of established truths. My one aim to show that Science establishes Theism." That same day in February—this was, after all, an "advanced" course—Abbot would go on to say a word about the "wide and rapid spread of *Agnosticism*." So far as he was concerned, "Such a system, if mere negation can be a system at all, can have no long future."[6] We can only guess as to whether such a reassurance put students' fears to rest, assuming they did not already trust *affirmatively* in the "future."

Difficult days lay ahead for Abbot. His Harvard "experiment," notably, would not yield the happiest of results. The man he'd replaced, Josiah Royce, was well aware of Abbot's work even before the latter's appointment as his short-term stand-in. Writing in the journal *Science* in 1886, Royce had taken Abbot to task in his review of *Scientific Theism,* the "positive doctrine" of which the full-time Harvard faculty member said relied on the questionable "presuppositions" that "the world as a whole must be one rationally comprehensible system of relations" and that "the universe *per se* is an infinite self-consciousness." From where Royce stood, Abbot had not (and could not) demonstrate "*how* an individual consciousness" such as he'd described "can know a real world" from which the self was inextricable. And thus Royce implied that Abbot had based his religion—if that's what it was—on a shaky foundation, which neither Abbot nor any other "objective idealist" could defend.[7] Abbot responded to Royce in the preface to the third edition of his book. Yet the tensions between the two philosophers increased after Royce reviewed Abbot's *The Way Out of Agnosticism* in the October 1890 issue of the *International Journal of Ethics*.[8] In the *Public Appeal* that Abbot issued in 1891, he asked Harvard for redress from Royce, arguing that the latter had misled the readers of his review into thinking that Abbot's philosophy was "essentially idealistic" in its method and meaning, when Abbot, of course, regarded himself as an "intuitive" empiricist through and through. Harvard having declined to take this step against a member of its own faculty, Abbot followed up with another pamphlet, the rhetorically titled *Is Not Harvard Responsible for the Conduct of Her Professors, as Well as of Her Students? A Public Remonstrance Addressed to the Board of Overseers of Harvard University* (1892). Here, the aggrieved Abbot contends, in his own words, that "Harvard is responsible to mankind for the general moral conduct, not only of her students, but still more of her instructors" (7). We can probably say that the author who wrote those words did so with the full force of his convictions.

AFTERWORD

As for the rest of his beliefs, Abbot was too swept up in the controversy at hand to give much thought, on this occasion, to posterity. But he would always keep the faith. He continued to affirm his belief in the negative future that transcendentalism had opened before him.

Abbot was not the last New Englander from the nineteenth century to find that the religion passed down to him from his ancestors had proved inadequate in satisfying his personal spiritual needs. Nor did he come close to qualifying as the first, as the preceding pages have made clear. Abbot was instead a representative example of a New England tradition in the period, by which the religious conventions of the past were revised or rejected not so much from a desire to escape the deep-seated claims that faith made upon his own person, but rather as an initial step—perhaps even a radical one—in restoring to a historic Protestant reformation of several centuries' standing a strong dose of the *reformist* element with which it began. Like all of the believers, "free" or otherwise, who appear in this study, Abbot was always looking backward as much as he was looking forward. By the same token, he was working within the context of a regional religious culture that transcendentalism, by the start of the Civil War, had already markedly changed, and in ways that would lead Abbot and others who were outside (and sometimes inside) the fold of the "like-minded" to offer up fresh resistance to a new set of spiritual norms that they'd inherited. To the extent, then, that transcendentalism was as much a restoration as it was a reformation, the spiritual life that the "New Views" placed before the New England public represented the fulfillment of liberal religion's all but impossible dream. In building back up a practice of belief that it had been so eager to pull down, transcendentalism turned the negative work of criticism into a positive alternative of change.

Transcendental Heresies has been organized according to what we can regard as the four representative instances of transcendental religion in "action." Each of these is associated with a place as much as it is with a person or a people. The most salient of these places are Cambridge, Concord, the "country," and the city. At the same, this book has shown that, no matter where or when it was happening, transcendentalism both was and was not responsible for the withering effect it was often said to have on religious belief in the nineteenth century. Whatever faith had been in New England before the time of transcendentalism's regional emergence, it was already evolving in response to both internal and external pressures for change. Transcendentalism unquestionably added to those pressures. But in doing so, it also quickened the religious impulses of anyone who was able to regard the criticism of religion as a beginning, and not an end, of belief. For a select few, the spiritual promise that a critical transcendental religion made possible was great enough for them to want to preach, and practice, among their contemporaries the "new" religion that had transformed their own lives. For all of the differences (not the least of them being religious) between Emerson and Thoreau, Fuller and Parker, and Abbot and everyone among his forebears who likely would have struggled to fully assimilate his postromantic empiricism, they were bound together by their readiness to speak a religious word—and to live a religious life—on behalf of the miracle of spiritual consciousness. Not all of their listeners believed as they did. Nor would transcendentalism's most vocal proponents have wanted them to, in keeping with their trust in the individual as the necessary locus of all belief. Such a religion didn't require fifty affirmations. It needed only one.

NOTES

ARCHIVAL COLLECTIONS

ANDOVER-HARVARD THEOLOGICAL LIBRARY, HARVARD DIVINITY SCHOOL (MH-AH)
    Francis Ellingwood Abbot Papers, 1815–1940
    Theodore Parker Papers
    Twenty-Eighth Congregational Society (Boston), Records, 1845–89
    Unitarian Universalist Association, Minister files, 1825–2010

BOSTON ATHENAEUM
    Rare Newspapers
    Prints and Photographs
    Theater Collection

BOSTON PUBLIC LIBRARY
    John Park, Diary, 1791–1852, five volumes

CONCORD FREE PUBLIC LIBRARY
    Prichard, Hoar, and Related Family Papers, 1799–1948
    Records of the First Church in Concord, 1739–1857
    Records of the Middlesex County Criminal Cases Kept by Justice of the Peace Abiel Heywood at Concord, 1798–1823
    Report of the Selectmen of the Town of Concord, Relative to the Expenses of the Town up to March 24, 1837

HARVARD UNIVERSITY ARCHIVES
    Francis Ellingwood Abbot, College Themes and Forensics, 1856–57
    Francis Ellingwood Abbot, Notes of Lectures on Scientific Theism: Given in the Advanced Course, Philosophy 13, Harvard College, 1887–88
    Papers of Francis Ellingwood Abbot, 1841–1904
    Harvard College Class Books for 1825–50
    Library Charge Records, Harvard College
    John Langdon Sibley, Diary

HOUGHTON LIBRARY, HARVARD UNIVERSITY
    Boston Religious Union of Associationists, Records, 1847–51
    William Ellery Channing Papers, 1819–52

James Freeman Clarke Correspondence (LS)
Ralph Waldo Emerson Journals and Notebooks, 1820–80
Margaret Fuller Family Papers, 1662–1970
George Ripley, Commonplace book
Ellen H. Sturgis Papers

HUNTINGTON LIBRARY, SAN MARINO, CALIFORNIA
Thoreau-Sewall Papers, 1790–1917

MASSACHUSETTS HISTORICAL SOCIETY (MHS)
Boston Debating Society, Minutes, 1832–36
William Ellery Channing Papers, 1791–1892, five microfilm reels
D. F. Child Collection
Christopher Pearce Cranch Papers
Lamb Family Papers
Theodore Parker Papers
George Ripley Papers, 1834–92
Rotch Family Papers
Louisa Lee Waterhouse, Journal, 1839–41

SCHLESINGER LIBRARY, RADCLIFFE INSTITUTE FOR ADVANCED STUDY, HARVARD UNIVERSITY (SL)
Almy Family Papers
Ames Family Historical Collection, 1762–2006
Browne Family Papers
Cabot Family Papers
Ednah Dow Cheney Papers
Dana Family Papers
Ellis Gray Loring Papers
Frances Merritt Quick Papers
Poor Family Papers
Sarah Alden Bradford Ripley Papers
Robinson-Shattuck Papers

THOREAU INSTITUTE AT WALDEN WOODS, LINCOLN, MASSACHUSETTS
Raymond Adams Collection in the Thoreau Society Collections
Henry S. Salt Collection

INTRODUCTION

1. James C. Turner, *Without God, Without Creed: The Origins of Unbelief in America* (Baltimore: Johns Hopkins University Press, 1986), xiii.
2. See Perry Miller, *The Transcendentalists: An Anthology* (Cambridge, Mass.: Harvard University Press, 1950), 89; and Lawrence Buell, *Literary Transcendentalism: Style and Vision in the American Renaissance* (Ithaca, N.Y.: Cornell University Press, 1973), 4–5.

3. *Journals and Miscellaneous Notebooks of Ralph Waldo Emerson*, vol. 9, *1843–1847*, ed. Ralph H. Orth and Alfred R. Ferguson (Cambridge, Mass.: Belknap Press of Harvard University Press, 1971), 381.
4. Turner, *Without God, Without Creed*, xiv.
5. On culture as a *practice*, see Michel de Certeau, *The Practice of Everyday Life*, trans. Steven F. Rendall (1980; reprint, Berkeley: University of California Press, 2011), xv–xvi. See also Nancy Tatom Ammerman, *Sacred Stories, Spiritual Tribes: Finding Religion in Everyday Life* (New York: Oxford University Press, 2013), 56–90. David D. Hall provides a historical survey of the practice of religion in his edited volume *Lived Religion in America: Toward a History of Practice* (Princeton, N.J.: Princeton University Press, 1997).
6. Daniel Walker Howe, *The Unitarian Conscience: Harvard Moral Philosophy, 1805–1861* (Cambridge, Mass.: Harvard University Press, 1970), 1.
7. Elisabeth Hurth, *Between Faith and Unbelief: American Transcendentalists and the Challenge of Atheism* (Boston: Brill, 2007), 2.
8. Turner, *Without God, Without Creed*, xv, 43, 80, 82; Charles Taylor, *A Secular Age* (Cambridge, Mass.: Belknap Press of Harvard University Press, 2007), 25–27; John Lardas Modern, *Secularism in Antebellum America* (Chicago: University of Chicago Press, 2011), 2; and Peter Coviello and Jared Hickman, "Introduction: After the Postsecular," *American Literature* 86, no. 4 (2014): 645–54.
9. Mario Bowman and Ülo Valk, "Introduction: Vernacular Religion, Generic Expressions and the Dynamics of Belief," in *Vernacular Religion in Everyday Life: Expressions of Belief*, ed. Mario Bowman and Ülo Valk (New York: Routledge, 2014), 5.
10. William James, *The Varieties of Religious Experience: A Study in Human Nature* (1902; reprint, New York: Longmans, Green, 1917).
11. The total population of New England in 1890 was 4.7 million; some 1.1 million of these people lived in rural communities, about a quarter of the total population. The U.S. Census in the nineteenth century considered any settlement of greater than 2,500 people to be "urban." From Alexander E. Cance, "The Decline of the Rural Population in New England," *Publications of the American Statistical Association* 13, no. 97 (1912): 96.
12. Barbara L. Packer, *The Transcendentalists* (Athens: University of Georgia Press, 2007), 129.

CHAPTER 1: EMERSON AND THE EVOLUTION OF BELIEF IN NEW ENGLAND

1. Ralph Waldo Emerson, "Spiritual Laws," in *The Collected Works of Ralph Waldo Emerson* (hereafter cited parenthetically in the text as *CW*), vol. 2, *Essays: First Series,* ed. Joseph Slater, Alfred R. Ferguson, and Jean Ferguson Carr (Cambridge, Mass.: Belknap Press of Harvard University Press, 1979), 77.
2. Ralph Waldo Emerson, "The Transcendentalist" (1841), in *The Collected Works of Ralph Waldo Emerson,* vol. 1, *Nature, Addresses, and Lectures,* ed. Robert E. Spiller (Cambridge, Mass.: Belknap Press of Harvard University Press, 1971), 56–57.
3. Nathan O. Hatch, *The Democratization of American Christianity* (New Haven, Conn.: Yale University Press, 1989), 172.
4. Noah Worcester, *A Review of Atheism for Unlearned Christians* (Boston: J. Munroe, printed for the American Unitarian Association, 1836). In 1813 Worcester accepted an invitation to be the founding editor of Boston's *Christian Disciple,* a periodical that was influential in Unitarian and transcendentalist circles. Under the pen name "H. O. N.," Ralph Waldo Emerson placed his first published work in this journal in 1822, "Thoughts on the Religion of the Middle Ages."
5. Andrews Norton, *A Discourse on the Latest Form of Infidelity* (Cambridge, Mass.: John Owen, 1839).
6. Norton never mentions *transcendentalism* as such, but he does associate the "transcendental generalities" of New England's "new school" with the philosophical idealism that was then emanating from Germany (38).
7. Robert D. Richardson, *Emerson: The Mind on Fire* (Berkeley: University of California Press, 1995), 288. As Richardson writes, "Never content just to attack what he disapproved, Emerson puts the case for positive religious feeling." For a discussion of Emerson as a "connected critic," see Richard F. Teichgraeber III, *Sublime Thoughts/Penny Wisdom: Situating Emerson and Thoreau in the American Market* (Baltimore: Johns Hopkins University Press, 1996), xi–xii, 31.
8. As the Unitarian minister William Batchelder Greene (a graduate of the Harvard Divinity School in 1845) explained, "So the word Transcendentalism relates not to a system of doctrines but to a point of view." Greene, *Transcendentalism* (West Brookfield, Mass.: Oliver S. Cooke, 1849), 14.

9. In writing from West Roxbury, Massachusetts, on January 3, 1839, the Unitarian minister Parker made these remarks in a letter to his fellow pastor George E. Ellis. Noting that a number of area clergymen were asking "whether he [Emerson] was a Christian?" Parker records a variety of offsetting responses that are typical of transcendentalism's reception in this period: "Greenswood said he was not and defended his position rather poorly, you may suppose. Pierpoint maintained he was an Atheist—a downright Atheist. But nobody doubted he was a virtuous and most devout man—one who would enter Heaven when they were shut out." Theodore Parker Papers, Massachusetts Historical Society (hereafter cited as MHS).

10. Clarke articulated his distinction between "negative transcendentalism" and "positive transcendentalism" in "Discourse of Matters Pertaining to Religion," an article that he published under his own auspices after its rejection by the flagship transcendentalist journal the *Dial*. In his essay, Clarke depreciated Parker's teaching as "the new gospel of shallow naturalism," although in later years he would revise his estimation of Parker's work enough to undertake a collection of Parker's writings. John White Chadwick, *Theodore Parker: Preacher and Reformer* (Boston: Houghton Mifflin, 1900), 127.

11. David M. Robinson, *Emerson and the Conduct of Life: Pragmatism and Ethical Purpose in the Later Work* (1993; reprint, New York: Cambridge University Press, 2009), 27.

12. Branka Arsić, *On Leaving: A Reading in Emerson* (Cambridge, Mass.: Harvard University Press, 2010), 2, 9.

13. *Journals and Miscellaneous Notebooks of Ralph Waldo Emerson* (hereafter cited parenthetically in the text as *JMN*), vol. 3, *1826–1832*, ed. William H. Gilman and Alfred R. Ferguson (Cambridge, Mass.: Belknap Press of Harvard University Press, 1963), 77. Writing from St. Augustine, Florida, Emerson also entertained on this same trip the more orthodox religious positions of his youth. On March 11, 1827, he wrote, "To believe too much is dangerous, because it is the near neighbour of unbelief. Pantheism leads to Atheism." *Journals and Miscellaneous Notebooks of Ralph Waldo Emerson*, vol. 1, *1819–1822*, ed. William H. Gilman, Alfred R. Ferguson, George P. Clark, and Merrell R. Davis (Cambridge, Mass.: Belknap Press of Harvard University Press, 1960), xxvi.

14. Convers Francis, at the time a Unitarian minister in Watertown, wrote in his journal that "the straitest [*sic*] sect of Boston conservatism" had come "to abhor and abominate R. W. Emerson as a sort of mad dog" following his address. Joel Myerson, ed., *Emerson and Thoreau: The Contemporary Reviews* (New York: Cambridge University Press, 1992), 28. Even Emerson's uncle Samuel Ripley tried to persuade him in July 1838 not to publish his address, because he did not "want to see you classified with Kneeland [the American atheist Abner Kneeland], [Thomas] Paine &c, bespattered and belied." Samuel Ripley to Ralph Waldo Emerson, August 1838, in *The Letters of Ralph Waldo Emerson,* ed. Ralph L. Rusk (New York: Columbia University Press, 1939), 2:148n169.
15. Bruce A. Ronda, *The Fate of Transcendentalism: Secularity, Materiality, and Human Flourishing* (Athens: University of Georgia Press, 2017), 3. The transcendentalists resembled the Unitarians in this "critical" respect. As Lawrence Buell writes of the latter, "Seldom have the recognized leaders of a denomination been so critical of it." Buell, *Literary Transcendentalism: Style and Vision in the American Renaissance* (Ithaca, N.Y.: Cornell University Press, 1973), 48.
16. Ralph Waldo Emerson, "The Divinity School Address" (July 15, 1838), in *CW,* 1:71–94.
17. Philip F. Gura, *American Transcendentalism: A History* (New York: Hill and Wang, 2007), 102–5.
18. Word of Emerson's address spread more quickly than did the lecture in its limited published format. The handful of students who attended the lecture took immediate steps to have it published *privately,* as not all of them were prepared to endorse its contents. Shortly thereafter, Emerson revised the manuscript in compliance with the advice of friends, upon which the same group of students as before had one hundred revised copies published.
19. By contrast, the editors of the first volume of Emerson's *Collected Works* claim that "The Divinity School Address" is "essentially centrifugal in impulse" (1:73).
20. Only six of these students were in attendance for Emerson's address.
21. David M. Robinson, "'A Religious Demonstration': The Theological Emergence of New England Transcendentalism," in *Transient and Permanent: The Transcendentalist Movement and Its Contexts,* ed. Charles Capper and

Conrad Edick Wright (Boston: Massachusetts Historical Society, 2000), 52–57 (quote on 57).

22. Henry Ware Jr., *The Personality of the Deity* (1838), in *The Works of Henry Ware, Jr.* (Boston: James Munroe, 1847), 3:38. In a letter Ware mailed to Emerson on October 3, 1838, he wrote of his regret that the two friends and former associates should be involved in "a sort of public opposition." John Ware, M.D., *Memoir of the Life of Henry Ware, Jr.* (Boston: James Munroe, 1846), 397.

23. Andrews Norton, "The New School in Literature and Religion," *Boston Daily Advertiser*, August 27, 1838, in *Transcendentalism: A Reader*, ed. Joel Myerson (New York: Oxford University Press, 2000), 246–50.

24. *Journals and Miscellaneous Notebooks of Ralph Waldo Emerson*, vol. 7, *1838–1842*, ed. A. W. Plumstead and Harrison Hayford (Cambridge, Mass.: Belknap Press of Harvard University Press, 1969), 110–11.

25. The response to Emerson's "Divinity School Address" was not entirely negative, as the reactions recorded in the following make clear: Cyrus Bartol, *Radical Problems* (Boston: Roberts Brothers, 1872), 68; Theodore Parker, in a letter from August 7, 1838, to George Ellis, in O. B. Frothingham, *Theodore Parker: A Biography* (Boston: J. R. Osgood, 1874), 106; and Orestes Brownson, "Mr. Emerson's Address," *Boston Quarterly Review* 1 (1838): 500–514. On the general reaction to Emerson's address, see Gura, *American Transcendentalism: A History*, 102–10.

26. Sharon Cameron, "The Way of Life by Abandonment: Emerson's Impersonal," *Critical Inquiry* 25, no. 1 (1998): 1–31.

27. Josiah Quincy, *The History of Harvard University* (Cambridge, Mass.: J. Owen, 1840), 13.

28. James C. Turner, *Without God, Without Creed: The Origins of Unbelief in America* (Baltimore: Johns Hopkins University Press, 1986), xii–xiii.

29. Octavius B. Frothingham, "Attitudes of Unbelief," in *The Rising and the Setting Faith and Other Discourses* (New York: G. P. Putnam's Sons, 1878), 185–87.

30. O. B. Frothingham, *Transcendentalism in New England: A History* (New York: G. P. Putnam's Sons, 1876), 302, 136–37.

31. In *Village Atheists: How America's Unbelievers Made Their Way in a Godly Nation* (Princeton, N.J.: Princeton University Press, 2016), Leigh Eric Schmidt writes that it was not until the final quarter of the nineteenth

century that unbelief became a legitimate religious position in the United States (xv). Today, Robert C. Fuller claims that only one in seven Americans is "indifferent" to religion. He further estimates the number of "nonreligious" Americans at between 8 percent and 15 percent of the total U.S. population, while suggesting that some 21 percent is "unchurched." Fuller, *Spiritual but Not Religious: Understanding Unchurched America* (New York: Oxford University Press, 2001), 2–4.

32. Alexis de Tocqueville, *Democracy in America,* trans. Henry Reeve and ed. Phillips Bradley, 2 vols. (New York: Vintage, 1945), 1:314–16, 324.

33. George H. Williams, *The "Augustan Age": Religion in the University, the Foundations of a Learned Ministry and the Development of the Divinity School,* vol. 2 of *Divinings: Religion at Harvard from Its Origins in New England Ecclesiastical History to the 175th Anniversary* (Gottingen, Germany: Vandenhoeck & Ruprecht, 2014), 37–39.

34. *Report of a Committee of the Overseers of Harvard College, January 6, 1825* (Cambridge, Mass.: Hilliard and Metcalf, 1825).

35. Cited in Perry Miller, *Nature's Nation* (Cambridge, Mass.: Belknap Press of Harvard University Press, 1967), 125.

36. For a short history of natural religion at Harvard, refer to Williams, *Divinings*, 1:285–330.

37. *Journals and Miscellaneous Notebooks of Ralph Waldo Emerson,* vol. 9, *1843–1847,* ed. Ralph H. Orth and Alfred R. Ferguson (Cambridge, Mass.: Belknap Press of Harvard University Press, 1971), 381.

38. Emerson wrote these lines in an essay, "The Sovereignty of Ethics," *North American Review* (May 1, 1878): 404–21. See *The Complete Works of Ralph Waldo Emerson: Lectures and Biographical Sketches,* centenary ed. (Boston: Houghton Mifflin, 1903–4), 10:183–214. The lines in question come from page 204 of the centenary edition.

39. This was the Unitarian minister John Pierce's (Harvard College class of 1793) response to a query made, by letter, from William Henry Channing (Harvard College class of 1829, Harvard Divinity School class of 1833) about the religious climate at Harvard in the aftermath of the French Revolution. Pierce's letter of September 6, 1843, appears in the William Ellery Channing Papers, MHS.

40. Stephen P. Shoemaker, "The Emerging Distinction between Theology and Religion at Nineteenth-Century Harvard University," *Harvard Theological Review* 101, nos. 3–4 (2008): 419–20.

41. *Report of a Committee* (1825), 6–9; *Fourth Annual Report of the President of Harvard University to the Overseers, on the State of the Institution, for the Academical Year 1828–9* (Cambridge, Mass.: E. W. Metcalf, 1830), Appendix A, i–ii. The admission requirement of the "Four Gospels" was "Discontinued" in 1842, according to the *Report of a Committee of the Overseers of Harvard University, Concerning the Requirements for Admission to the University* (Salem, Mass.: printed at the Gazette office, 1845), 11.
42. Theodore Parker to Columbus Greene, April 2, 1834, Parker Papers, MHS.
43. From the reprint of Parker's address, *Transcendentalism: A Lecture* (Boston: Free Religious Association, 1876), 26; and *A Discourse of Matters Pertaining to Religion* (Boston: Charles C. Little and James Brown, 1842), 437, 469. In a chapter from the latter volume, "The Moral and Religious Character of Jesus of Nazareth," Parker names his first section heading "The Negative Side, or the Limitations of Jesus" (290).
44. "Pythologion" [1819–21] MSS; Cambridge, April 1819–May 1821, Ralph Waldo Emerson journals and notebooks, 1820–80, MS Am 1280h (3), Ralph Waldo Emerson Memorial Association deposit, Houghton Library, Harvard University.
45. Andrew Peabody, James Freeman Clarke, and Henry Lee speak, respectively, to the history of Holden Chapel, Harvard Hall, and University Hall in *The Harvard Book: A Series of Historical, Biographical, and Descriptive Sketches* (Boston: Houghton, Osgood, 1878), 58–60, 75, 87. The quotations from Lee appear on pages 87–88, 105. The volume in question was collected and published by the Harvard class of 1874.
46. Even though University Hall was not completed until 1815, the chapel itself opened in 1814.
47. *Proceedings of the Overseers of Harvard University, the Report Accepted, and the Resolutions Adopted by Them on the 25th of August, 1834, Relative to the Late Disturbances in that Seminary* (Boston: James Loring, 1834), 19, 5.
48. *Seventh Annual Report of the President of Harvard University to the Overseers, on the State of the Institution, for the Academical Year 1831–2* (Cambridge, Mass.: E. W. Metcalf, 1833), Appendix A, xix.
49. *Sixteenth Annual Report of the President of Harvard University to the Overseers, on the State of the Institution, for the Academical Year 1840–41* (Cambridge, Mass.: Thomas G. Wells, 1842), appendix; *Seventeenth Annual Report . . . for the Academical Year 1841–42* (Cambridge, Mass.: Metcalf, Keith, and Nichols, 1843), appendix, iv; *Twenty-Second Annual Report . . .*

for the Academical Year 1846–47 (Cambridge, Mass.: Metcalf, 1848), 36, 38; *Twenty-First Annual Report . . . for the Academical Year 1845–46* (Cambridge, Mass.: Metcalf, 1847), 28–30.

50. *Report on the Rules and Statutes of the Office of "Preacher to the University and Plummer Professor of Christian Morals," at Harvard College, with the Proceedings of the Overseers Thereon, April 12, 1855* (Boston: T. R. Marvin, 1855), 4–6, 9–10, 13–14.

51. During the seventeenth century, more than 50 percent of the recipients of Harvard's A.B. degree became parish ministers, with many of them receiving an additional A.M. degree in recognition of their continuing studies in divinity under the tutelage of one or more seasoned pastors. For the period 1800–1830, only 15 percent of Harvard's A.B. candidates pursued specialized study in theology and pastoral care. For the period 1830–50, the number falls to 10 percent. Not one single student from the Harvard College class of 1855 would declare himself a candidate for the ministry. Lawrence Buell calculates these percentages in *Literary Transcendentalism*, 49.

52. Hasbrouck Davis, *The Subterfuge of Infidelity: A Sermon Delivered at Waltham, on Sunday, Sept. 4, 1853* (Boston: Benjamin H. Greene, 1853), 3–6.

53. Charles Godfrey Leland, *Memoirs* (New York: D. Appleton, 1893), 77–79.

54. Nathaniel Hawthorne, *The House of the Seven Gables* (1851), in *The Centenary Edition of the Works of Nathaniel Hawthorne*, ed. William Charvat (Columbus: Ohio State University Press, 1965), 181.

55. Samuel Gridley Howe, "Atheism in New-England," pts. 1–2, *New-England Magazine* (December 1834): 501; (January 1835): 54–55.

56. Thomas M. Clark, *Modern Infidelity, a Price Lecture: Delivered in Trinity Church, Boston, March 15, 1848* (Boston: Samuel H. Parker, 1848), 8, 10.

57. Nathaniel Hall, *The Unbelief of Christendom: A Sermon Preached at the Ordination of Mr. Frank P. Appleton, as Pastor of the First Unitarian Church in Danvers, January 14th, 1846* (Danvers, Mass.: G. B. Carlton–Courier Press, 1846), 17.

58. As Theodore Parker explains in a letter from September 24, 1855, to the Unitarian minister George R. Noyes (Harvard College class of 1818, Harvard Divinity School class of 1839), the Boston *Atlas* newspaper ran a series of pieces in 1834 that accused the *Christian Examiner* of countenancing various forms of infidelity. Theodore Parker Papers, MHS.

59. Amos Smith (Harvard Divinity School, 1842), "What in your opinion are some of the most important causes of infidelity in modern times," 1, 6. HUC 8841.318.2. Francis Charles Williams (Harvard Divinity School, 1844), "What are the principal causes of the infidelity of modern times, especially the infidelity of literary men," 1, 11–12. HUC 8844.318. Augustus Woodbury (Harvard Divinity School, 1848), "Causes of Modern Infidelity," 1, 5. HUC 8848.318. Harvard University Archives, Archives Stacks.

60. Orestes A. Brownson, *The Convert: or, Leaves from My Experience* (1857), in *The Works of Orestes A. Brownson*, ed. Henry F. Brownson (Detroit: Thorndike Nourse, 1884), 5:75–76.

CHAPTER 2: HENRY DAVID THOREAU, VILLAGE ATHEIST

1. In 2005 Robert Gross wrote of the religious scholarship on Thoreau, "Students of Henry David Thoreau have finally gotten religion." Gross, "Faith in the Boardinghouse: New Views of Thoreau Family Religion," *Thoreau Society Bulletin* 250 (Winter 2005): 1. See also Alan D. Hodder, *Thoreau's Ecstatic Witness* (New Haven, Conn.: Yale University Press, 2001), 1–5; and "The Religious Horizon," in *Henry David Thoreau in Context*, ed. James S. Finley (New York: Cambridge University Press, 2017), 78–88.
2. Hodder, "The Religious Horizon," 80.
3. Thoreau's contemporary Mrs. Daniel Chester French recorded this anecdote in her volume *Memories of a Sculptor's Wife* (1928). See Raymond Adams, "Thoreau and His Neighbors," *Thoreau Society Bulletin* 44 (Summer 1953): 3.
4. Robert A. Gross, "'That Terrible Thoreau': Concord and Its Hermit," in *A Historical Guide to Henry David Thoreau*, ed. William E. Cain (New York: Oxford University Press, 2000), 184.
5. Adams, "Thoreau and His Neighbors," 1.
6. In 1849 the Thoreau family settled in what came to be known as their "Yellow House," in the thick of a Concord neighborhood that Leslie Perrin Wilson describes as "vibrant and close-knit." Wilson, "Concord," in *Henry David Thoreau in Context*, 8.
7. Letter to the editor from "O," *Yeoman's Gazette,* September 16, 1826, 1.
8. Gross, "Faith in the Boardinghouse," 3.
9. John Shepard Keyes, *A Brief History of Concord.* Keyes's volume was originally published as part of D. Hamilton Hurd's *History of Middlesex County,*

Massachusetts, with Biographical Sketches of Many of Its Pioneers and Prominent Men (Philadelphia: J. W. Lewis, 1890), 2:587.

10. Gross, "Faith in the Boardinghouse," 3.
11. "Moral and Religious," *Middlesex Observer,* June 21, 1822, reprinted from the *Keene (N.H.) Sentinel.*
12. All of the following appear in the *Yeoman's Gazette:* "The Atheist and the Artificial Globe," September 23, 1826; advertisement for Unitarian tracts, October 21, 1826; "Dedication," December 2, 1826; "Young Children at Church," December 9, 1826; "Miseries at Church," December 9, 1826; "Religion a Solace to the Afflicted," December 23, 1826; and "Anecdote of Rev. Dr. Lathrop," December 23 and 30, 1826. A more complete announcement of the dedication of Concord's Trinitarian Church appeared on December 9, 1826, in a summary. Furthermore, "The Atheist and the Artificial Globe" would reappear in the paper on January 10, 1829. Also note that "Young Children at Church" is reprinted from the *Christian Register;* "Miseries at Church" is taken from the *Old Colony Memorial;* and "Religion a Solace to the Afflicted" originally ran in the *Dover (N.H.) Gazette.*
13. From the *Yeoman's Gazette,* see Edward Everett, "Hymn," January 31, 1829; and George Gordon, Lord Byron, "The Vampyre," January 31, 1829. In the *Concord Freeman,* refer to "Ministers in Old Times," July 29, 1837; and "A Hint to the Opponents of Materialism and Infidelity," October 7, 1837. From the *Republican,* finally, see "Elijah's Interview with God," January 15, 1841; "From the Dial. Religion.," January 1, 1841; and "Young Men's Association," January 15, 1841. Monica Elbert provides an informative historical account of the *Concord Freeman* in "Nathaniel Hawthorne, *The Concord Freeman,* and the Irish 'Other,'" *Éire-Ireland* 29, no. 3 (1994): 60–73 (quote on 60). For more on Theodore Parker's sermon "A Lesson for the Day; or, The Christianity of Christ, of the Church, and of Society," consult Dean Grodzins, *American Heretic: Theodore Parker and Transcendentalism* (Chapel Hill: University of North Carolina Press, 2002), 210. Note that this chapter's broader construction of everyday culture as a "practice"—a practice inclusive of religion—comes from the French theorist Michel de Certeau, *The Practice of Everyday Life,* trans. Steven F. Rendall (1980; reprint, Berkeley: University of California Press, 2011).
14. Gross, "'That Terrible Thoreau,'" 195.

15. Alexis McCrossen, "Sabbatarianism: The Intersection of Church and State in the Orchestration of Everyday Life in Nineteenth-Century America," in *Religious and Secular Reform in America: Ideas, Beliefs, and Social Change*, ed. David K. Adams and Cornelius A. Van Minnen (New York: New York University Press, 1999), 137.
16. As the *Yeoman's Gazette* reported on March 6, 1830, the Concord Lyceum hosted lectures by such religiously inclined speakers as a "Mr. Swett, of Cambridge Theological School," whose talk, the paper says, "was listened to with great attention, by a crowded audience." Among the lectures offered to a subscribing public were these: "Is the Immortality of Man taught by the Light of Nature?" and "Is it probable that man, unaided by Revelation, would ever have attained to the knowledge of the true God, or a future state?" See the *Gazette*'s "Concord Lyceum" notice for January 19, 1833, and December 5, 1835.
17. Robert C. Fuller, *Spiritual but Not Religious* (New York: Oxford University Press, 2001), 8. Fuller's citation from James comes from *The Varieties of Religious Experience* (1902; reprint, New York: Longmans, Green, 1917), 382.
18. Fuller, *Spiritual but Not Religious*, 17.
19. Lemuel Shattuck, *A History of the Town of Concord* (Boston: Russell, Odiorne, 1835), 191.
20. "For the Yeoman's Gazette," *Yeoman's Gazette*, February 8, 1834; William B. Gallagher, "Harvest Hymn," *Concord Freeman*, November 20, 1840; "June Term of Common Pleas," *Concord Freeman*, July 13, 1838.
21. In *Literary Transcendentalism*, Lawrence Buell suggests that Thoreau and his brother are effectively breaking the Sabbath on Sunday as they sail their boat in *A Week* (216).
22. William E. Nelson, "Emerging Notions of Modern Criminal Law in the Revolutionary Era: An Historical Perspective," in *American Law and the Constitutional Order*, ed. Lawrence Mier Friedman and Harry N. Scheiber (Cambridge, Mass.: Harvard University Press, 1988), 166–67.
23. The 2016 Massachusetts General Laws: Part IV, Crimes, Punishments and Proceedings in Criminal Cases; Title I, Crimes and Punishments; Chapter 272, Crimes against Chastity, Morality, Decency, and Good Order. Universal citation: MA Gen L ch 272 § 36 (2016).
24. From the *Yeoman's Gazette*, refer to the following: "Indictment for Blasphemy," January 25, 1834; "From the Boston Transcript," February 1, 1834,

and "Abner Kneeland," July 7, 1838. On the legal history of blasphemy in eighteenth- and nineteenth-century Massachusetts, see James S. Kabala, *Church-State Relations in the Early American Republic, 1787–1846* (New York: Routledge, 2015), 107, 125.

25. Gross, "'That Terrible Thoreau,'" 184, 186, 190–94.
26. *Yeoman's Gazette,* "Oh! Steal Not Thou My Faith Away," July 14, 1838. The Episcopal minister and Christian songwriter James Gilborne Lyons published his most popular title, "Oh! Steal Not Thou My Faith Away," in 1831, sometime after his emigration to the United States from Ireland. Lyons went on to publish his collection *Christian Songs* in Philadelphia in 1848.
27. Henry David Thoreau, "Walking" (1862), in *Excursions,* from *Writings,* ed. Joseph J. Moldenhauer (Princeton, N.J.: Princeton University Press, 2007), 202.
28. David M. Robinson, *Natural Life: Thoreau's Worldly Transcendentalism* (Ithaca, N.Y.: Cornell University Press, 2004), 11.
29. Laura Dassow Walls, *Henry David Thoreau: A Life* (Chicago: University of Chicago Press, 2017), xix, 49.
30. Joshua Kotin, *Utopias of One* (Princeton, N.J.: Princeton University Press, 2018), 4, 19.
31. Maria Thoreau to Prudence Ward, February 28, 1849, Thoreau-Sewall Papers, 1790–1917, HM 64932; and March 15, 1849, Thoreau-Sewall Papers, 1790–1917, HM 64933, Huntington Library, San Marino, Calif.
32. Parker solicited Lowell's review as the editor of the *Massachusetts Quarterly Review.* He was himself pleased with *A Week,* a surprising response given the unfavorable impression he'd formed of the book's author. This portion of Lowell's review appears in *Emerson and Thoreau: The Contemporary Reviews,* ed. Joel Myerson (New York: Cambridge University Press, 1992), 357. Joel Myerson attributes the anonymous review of *A Week* that appeared in the *New-York Tribune* to the paper's editor Horace Greeley, who otherwise championed Thoreau's cause as a writer. The cited passages here are from *The Contemporary Reviews,* 341–42.
33. Dassow Walls, *Henry David Thoreau,* 272.
34. Robert Milder, *Reimagining Thoreau* (New York: Cambridge University Press, 1995), 33.
35. Robert D. Richardson Jr. describes Thoreau's Harvard in *Henry Thoreau: A Life of the Mind* (Berkeley: University of California Press, 1986), 8–11.

Further statistics on Thoreau's graduating class appear in the *Twelfth Annual Report of the President of Harvard University to the Overseers, on the State of the Institution, for the Academical Year 1836–37* (Cambridge, Mass.: Folson, Wells, and Thurston, 1838), appendix, xvii. See also Thoreau's Harvard essay from 1837 "Barbarism and Civilization," in *Writings: Early Essays and Miscellanies,* ed. Joseph J. Moldenhauer and Edwin Moser (Princeton, N.J.: Princeton University Press, 1976), 108, 110.

36. H. Daniel Peck, *Thoreau's Morning Work: Memory and Perception in "A Week on the Concord and Merrimack Rivers," the Journal, and "Walden"* (New Haven, Conn.: Yale University Press, 1990), 8.

37. Jonathan Bishop, "The Experience of the Sacred in Thoreau's *Week,*" *ELH* 33, no. 1 (1966): 71, 77.

38. As he would also do in the "Monday" section of *A Week,* Thoreau made these remarks by way of noticing the increased commercial traffic that the Concord River experienced on Mondays, at the start of the workweek. See Thoreau's journal entry for July 20, 1859, from *Journal,* vol. 12, March 2, 1859–November 30, 1859, in *The Writings of Henry David Thoreau,* ed. Bradford Torrey (Boston: Houghton Mifflin, 1906), 247.

39. Robert M. Thorson, *The Boatman: Henry David Thoreau's River Years* (Cambridge, Mass.: Harvard University Press, 2017), xv.

40. John C. Broderick, "The Movement of Thoreau's Prose," *American Literature* 33, no. 2 (1961): 136.

41. John Weiss, "Thoreau," *Christian Examiner* 79 (July 1865): 99.

42. The greatest spike in Thoreau's absences from chapel and Sabbath services occurred during his sophomore year. From a high of nineteen excused and six unexcused absences during the third term of his freshman year, Thoreau recorded thirty-five excused and three unexcused absences during the second term of his sophomore year. These numbers dropped during Thoreau's junior year, which was interrupted by his prolonged leave from illness, before returning to freshman-year levels (save for his third and final term, when they jumped upward again) during his senior year. Kenneth Walker Cameron has compiled these attendance records in *Thoreau's Harvard Years: Materials Introductory to New Explorations, Record of Fact and Background* (Hartford, Conn.: Transcendental Books, 1966), 13.

43. Thoreau composed these essays in the courses he took with Edward Tyrrel Channing, who at the time was Harvard's Boylston Professor of Rhetoric and Oratory. See Cameron, *Thoreau's Harvard Years,* 2:8–13. In saying there

was "a sprightlier side" to Thoreau at Harvard than many of his memorialists cared to remember, Raymond Adams also notes that the young college graduate was often cautious to the point of conformity. From Raymond Adams, "Thoreau at Harvard: Some Unpublished Records," *New England Quarterly* 13, no. 1 (1940): 27, 29.

44. Josiah Quincy to Ralph Waldo Emerson, Cambridge, Mass., June 25, 1837, as cited in Cameron, *Thoreau's Harvard Years*, 19. In reporting that 95 of the 103 college graduates that Concord counted between the years 1642 and 1876 came from Harvard, the Concord-born physician Edward Jarvis (Harvard College class of 1826) would write that "the people of Concord have justly had the reputation of superior culture and manners for several generations and especially for the last fifty years." Jarvis, *Traditions and Reminiscences of Concord, Massachusetts, 1779–1878* (1880; reprint, Amherst: University of Massachusetts Press, 1993), 100, 107, 237.

45. Thoreau had already begun the study of German language and literature at Harvard in the first term of his junior year, before his acquaintance with Brownson began. Thoreau enrolled in four full semesters of German instruction while at Harvard.

46. Robinson, *Natural Life*, 12–13.

47. Bronson Alcott, "The Forester," *Atlantic Monthly*, April 1862, 443–44.

48. Hodder, *Thoreau's Ecstatic Witness*, 4–5.

49. *The Contemporary Reviews*, 342.

50. Richardson, *Henry Thoreau*, 248; Robinson, *Natural Life*, 7–8; Hodder, *Thoreau's Ecstatic Witness*, 7, 11.

51. Jarvis recalled Thoreau from their Concord days in his *Traditions and Reminiscences of Concord, Massachusetts* (1880). Robert Gross cites these recollections in "'That Terrible Thoreau,'" 212.

52. For a full rehearsal of this anecdote, refer to Gross, "'That Terrible Thoreau,'" 182.

53. Emerson made this statement in his famous eulogy for his friend, "Thoreau," which originally appeared in the August 1862 issue of the *Atlantic Monthly*. The full line reads, "He was a protestant *à l'outrance* and few lives contain so many renunciations." From *Collected Works*, vol. 10, *Uncollected Prose Writings*, ed. Ronald A. Bosco and Joel Myerson (Cambridge, Mass.: Harvard University Press, 2013), 414.

54. "The Legislature," *Yeoman's Gazette*, February 7, 1829.

55. Matthew Hale, "The Sum of Religion," *Yeoman's Gazette,* February 14, 1829.
56. Report of the Selectmen of the Town of Concord, Relative to the Expenses of the Town up to March 24, 1837 (Concord Free Public Library).
57. In an essay from 1903 in the *Atlantic Monthly* magazine, the popular nature writer John Burroughs said of the writer of *A Week,* "Thoreau was not a born naturalist, but a born supernaturalist." This cited line appears in "Thoreau as 'a Born Supernaturalist,'" *Current Opinion* 67, no. 1 (1919): 44. See also Gorham B. Munson, "A Dionysian in Concord," *Outlook,* August 29, 1928, 690, 692.
58. *The Correspondence of Henry D. Thoreau,* vol. 1, *1834–1848,* ed. Robert N. Hudspeth (Princeton, N.J.: Princeton University Press, 2013), 69, 89.
59. Concord's First Parish remained the town's publicly supported church until 1855, when the municipal corporation announced that it would cease to conduct "parochial business."
60. *Journal,* vol. 9, in *The Writings of Henry David Thoreau,* ed. Bradford Torrey (Boston: Houghton Mifflin, 1906), 331–32. The name of Sanborn's landlord at the time was "Holbrook."
61. Raymond Adams, "Thoreau's Growth at Walden," *Christian Register,* July 1945, 268.
62. As Robert Gross writes in "'That Terrible Thoreau,'" this is the name that some of Thoreau's neighbors reserved for him behind his back (182).
63. F. B. Sanborn, "The Religion of Thoreau" (1906), from an unidentified newspaper clipping held at the Thoreau Institute in Lincoln, Mass.
64. *The Journal of Henry David Thoreau,* ed. Bradford Torrey and Francis Allen, 14 vols. (Boston: Houghton Mifflin, 1906). The cited passage is from 11:113.
65. Commenting on Thoreau and his "philosophy of life," Ella Gilbert Ives wrote at the turn of the twentieth century, "It became his business to preach and practise [sic] these truths." Ives, "The Gospel of the Open: Studies of Some of Its Preachers," *Boston Evening Transcript,* April 24, 1901.
66. Frank Luther Mott, *A History of American Magazines,* vol. 3, *1865–1885* (Cambridge, Mass.: Harvard University Press, 1938), 78. Among the contributors to the *Radical* were three disciples of Theodore Parker. These included Thoreau's Harvard classmate John Weiss, the Unitarian minister and transcendentalist author David Atwood Wasson, and the Unitarian clergyman Samuel Johnson (Harvard College class of 1842 and a graduate

from the Divinity School in 1846). Also included in the *Radical*'s stable of authors were the late-generation transcendentalists Moncure Conway and O. B. Frothingham.

67. "Religion," *Radical,* September 1865, 1.
68. From the Records of the First Church in Concord, 1739 to 1857 (Concord Free Public Library), for the following dates: July 20 and November 30, 1823; October 30, 1825; February 22 and March 30, 1828; and February 20, 1842.
69. On Sabbath breaking, see the Records of the First Church in Concord, 1739 to 1857, for September 1, October 9, and December 4, 1825. The church records make mention of the work of the town's Bible Societies on January 25, 1829. The topic of temperance arises on July 1, 1832, while the approved upgrade to four "silver plated" collection plates to be used for communion service appears on February 20, 1842.
70. *Remarks on the Existing State of the Laws of Massachusetts, Respecting Violations of the Sabbath* (Boston: printed by Nathaniel Willis, 1816), 3.
71. As with Sabbath breaking, there are no recorded instances to be found of women in Concord using the Lord's name in vain. From the Records of the Middlesex County criminal cases kept by Justice of the Peace Abiel Heywood at Concord, 1798–1823 (Concord Free Public Library), for the following dates: January 15, 1814; June 27, 1815; October 1, 1817; March 31, 1819; and, in two separate cases, January 1, 1823.
72. Refer to the following dates from the Records of the Middlesex County criminal cases: May 6 and July 9 and 16, 1815 (including four separate charges, two of them involving brothers); and the previously noted dates of September 1 and October 9, 1825.
73. "Religion," 1.
74. Leonard N. Neufeldt, *The Economist: Henry Thoreau and Enterprise* (New York: Oxford University Press, 1989), 53–54.
75. Stanley Cavell, *The Senses of Walden* (1972; reprint, Chicago: University of Chicago Press, 1992), 6–11.
76. "An Ideal for Freethinkers," *Truth Seeker,* June 24, 1893, 387. In this unnamed writer's view, "The Christian multitude complains, finds fault, accuses; Thoreau kept silence, uncriticisingly selected, and taught by example" (388).
77. Ives, "Gospel of the Open."

78. Dassow Walls, *Henry David Thoreau*, 191–92.
79. Catherine Albanese, *Corresponding Motion: Transcendental Religion and the New America* (Philadelphia: Temple University Press, 1977), 52.
80. Perrin Wilson, "Concord," 4.
81. The earlier-referenced unidentified newspaper clipping on Thoreau from 1906 contains the subheadlines "Obviously Heterodox Thoughts on God" and "Tolerant and Intolerant Ideas on the Church."
82. Leigh Eric Schmidt, *Village Atheists: How America's Unbelievers Made Their Way in a Godly Nation* (Princeton, N.J.: Princeton University Press, 2016), 14–15, 30–31.
83. Nathaniel Bolton, *A Poem: On Infidelity* (Greenwich, Mass.: John Howe, printer, 1808).
84. Remarking on the Englishman Paine's famous statement of Enlightenment skepticism, *The Age of Reason* (1794), Henry A. Beers said that "well-thumbed copies" of this work "passed from hand to hand in many a rural tavern or store, where the village atheist wrestled in debate with the deacon or the school-master." Beers, *An Outline Sketch of American Literature* (New York: Chautauqua Press, 1887), 65.
85. Emerson, *Collected Works of Ralph Waldo Emerson*, vol. 10, *Uncollected Prose Writings*, ed. Ronald A. Bosco and Joel Myerson (Cambridge, Mass.: Belknap Press of Harvard University Press, 2013), 427.
86. Weiss, "Thoreau," 108.
87. Edward A. Horton, "Love of Nature," in *Noble Lives and Noble Deeds: A Series of Lessons for Sunday Schools, by Various Writers, Illustrating Christian Character*, no. 36 (Boston: Unitarian Sunday-School Society, 1893), 2–3.
88. The term "whitewashed" appears in the earliest extant correspondence from Thoreau, dating to his sophomore year at Harvard, in 1834. In this letter, Thoreau and his Cambridge roommate addressed the campus steward to request that their room be "painted and whitewashed." Note that Thoreau's roommate in Hollis 32, James Richardson, described himself to Harvard's class secretary as a "preacher of theology and religion or righteousness." From *Correspondence of Henry D. Thoreau*, 1. The senior essay from Thoreau referenced here is from May 26, 1837; it was written in response to the assigned topic, "Whether Moral Excellence tend directly to increase Intellectual Power." See *Writings: Early Essays and Miscellanies*, ed. Moldenhauer and Moser, 106–8.

89. Gross, "Faith in the Boardinghouse," 1.
90. Robert D. Richardson Jr., "Thoreau and Concord," in *The Cambridge Companion to Henry David Thoreau*, ed. Joel Myerson (New York: Cambridge University Press, 1995), 14.
91. Dating back a generation, the Thoreau family's home library contained a book that might have informed Henry David Thoreau's practical conception of religion. In 1811 his paternal aunt, Jane Thoreau, inscribed her name in a copy of Hannah More's *Practical Piety; or, The Influence of the Religion of the Heart on the Conduct of Life, by Hannah More . . . in Two Volumes*, vol. 2 (Boston: Munroe and Francis, 1811). The volume retained its place in the household occupied by the adult author of *Walden*.
92. Milder, *Reimagining Thoreau*, 60.
93. Dassow Walls, *Henry David Thoreau*, 274.
94. Henry David Thoreau, *The Journal of Henry D. Thoreau* (Princeton edition *Journal*), 8 vols. to date (Princeton, N.J.: Princeton University Press, 1981–), 3:306. This particular entry appears for July 16, 1851.
95. Dassow Walls, *Henry David Thoreau*, 302–3, 400.

CHAPTER 3: TRANSCENDENTAL WOMEN "LOSING" THEIR RELIGION

1. Caroline Healy Dall, *Transcendentalism in New England: A Lecture* (Boston: sold by Roberts Brothers, 1897), 24.
2. Susan Phinney Conrad says the characteristically "nonaggressive" aspects of romanticism appealed to women as much as they did to men. Conrad, *Perish the Thought: Intellectual Women in Romantic America, 1830–60* (New York: Oxford University Press, 1976), 10–11.
3. Charles Capper, "'A Little Beyond': The Problem of the Transcendentalist Movement in American History," in *Transient and Permanent: The Transcendentalist Movement and Its Contexts*, ed. Charles Capper and Conrad Edick Wright (Boston: Massachusetts Historical Society, 2000), 22–23.
4. Among the more noteworthy recent examples of Fuller's "masculinization" is from Ann Douglas, *The Feminization of American Culture* (1977; reprint, New York: Farrar, Straus and Giroux, 1998), 261–62.
5. Phyllis Cole and Jana Argersinger, introduction to *Toward a Female Genealogy of Transcendentalism*, ed. Jana L. Argersinger and Phyllis Cole (Athens: University of Georgia Press, 2014), 21.

6. Fuller met Mary Moody Emerson at Newburyport, Massachusetts, in 1841. The exchange left both women disappointed. Fuller's comments on Emerson, which she made to her Concord friend Elizabeth Hoar, appeared after her death in 1850, in *Memoirs of Margaret Fuller Ossoli*, ed. James Freeman Clarke, Ralph Waldo Emerson, and W. H. Channing, 2 vols. (Boston: Phillips, Sampson, 1852), 1:315 (hereafter cited as *MMF*). In *Genealogy* Fuller's dismissal of M. M. Emerson's intellectual pretensions appears in Noelle A. Baker, "'Let Me Do Nothing Smale': Mary Moody Emerson and Women's 'Talking' Manuscripts," 51.
7. Eric Gardner makes the related observation that, among transcendentalists, it was sometimes assumed that "those interested in concrete reform could not also engage with Transcendentalism's idealism" (294). Gardner, "'Each Atomic Part': Edmonia Goodelle Highgate's African American Transcendentalism," in *Genealogy*, ed. Argersinger and Cole, 277–99. Tiffany K. Wayne makes a comparable claim in her study of transcendentalism and feminism, *Woman Thinking: Feminism and Transcendentalism in Nineteenth-Century America* (Lanham, Md.: Lexington Books, 2005).
8. Phyllis Cole, "Stanton, Fuller, and the Grammar of Romanticism," *New England Quarterly* 73, no. 4 (2000): 538.
9. Susan Jacoby writes of the connection between early American feminism (and abolitionism) and anticlericalism, which certain contemporaries interpreted as evidence of an inseparable relation between women's rights and irreligion. From Jacoby's *Freethinkers: A History of American Secularism* (New York: Holt, 2004), 69.
10. Fuller's Boston Conversations were unscripted by design. As Fuller wrote to one correspondent, "The best part of life is too spiritual to bear recording." Thomas Wentworth Higginson, *Margaret Fuller Ossoli* (Boston: Houghton Mifflin, 1884), 118.
11. Ralph Waldo Emerson felt that even women of Fuller's comparative independence were too implicated in the lives of others to capitalize on their personal spiritual resources. Hence, they would have been unable to accept the spiritual challenge he'd issued in his early writings and lectures. See Phyllis Cole, "Woman Questions: Emerson, Fuller, and New England Reform," in *Transient and Permanent*, 413.
12. Kathleen Ann Lawrence, "Soul Sisters and the Sister Arts: Margaret Fuller, Caroline Sturgis, and Their Private World of Love and Art," *ESQ: A Journal of the American Renaissance* 57, nos. 1–2 (2011): 79.

13. Sara Lyons associates this correlation between "Art" and unbelief with two prominent Victorians, the poet Algernon Swinburne and the aesthetic theorist Walter Pater. Lyons, *Algernon Swinburne and Walter Pater: Victorian Aestheticism, Doubt and Secularisation* (New York: Routledge, 2015), 6.
14. Eliza Susan Morton Quincy, *Memoir of the Life of Eliza S. M. Quincy* (Boston: printed by J. Wilson and Son, 1861), 100.
15. Charles Capper, "Margaret Fuller as Cultural Reformer: The Conversations in Boston," *American Quarterly* 39, no. 4 (1987): 512.
16. Sarah Clarke to James Freeman Clarke, November 17, 1839, "Letters of a Sister," MS Am 1569, Houghton Library, Harvard University. The quoted passage appears in Capper, "Margaret Fuller as Cultural Reformer," 512.
17. Nancy Craig Simmons, "Margaret Fuller's Boston Conversations: The 1839–40 Series," *Studies in the American Renaissance* (1994): 204 (hereafter cited as "Conversations"). While Peabody is largely credited as the source of these transcriptions, the records themselves are in the hand of Elizabeth Hoar.
18. Wesley T. Mott and David M. Robinson, "Transcendentalism," in *Encyclopedia of Transcendentalism*, ed. Wesley T. Mott (Westport, Conn.: Greenwood Press, 1996), 224–29.
19. Both "faith" and "reverence" received consideration during the first season's sixth Conversation. See "Conversations," 208–9.
20. During the Conversations' first series, beginning in November 1839, many of the women who assembled with Fuller earlier in the day would reappear in the evening at Emerson's winter lecture series, "The Present Age."
21. Capper, "Margaret Fuller as Cultural Reformer," 517.
22. Sarah Hodges to Esther Mack, December 16, 1842[?], MS Am 1086, Margaret Fuller Manuscripts and Works, box A, vol. 10. Houghton Library, Harvard University.
23. According to her friend and fellow transcendentalist William Henry Channing, Fuller "felt too profoundly the vastness of the universe and of destiny ever to presume that with her span rule she could measure the Infinite" (*MMF,* 2:81).
24. Higginson, *Margaret Fuller Ossoli,* 174–75.
25. In her Providence journal from the late 1830s, Fuller said that Emerson's "sermons" were "like landmarks of my spiritual history" (*MMF,* 1:194).
26. Lydia Maria Child, "Letter XI," December 9, 1841, in *Letters from New York* (Boston: James Munroe, 1843), 67.
27. Lydia Maria Child, "Letter XIII," April 24, 1844, in *Letters from New York, Second Series* (Boston: J. H. Francis, 1845), 125.

28. Sarah Ann Wider, "'How It All Lies before Me To-day': Transcendentalist Women's Journeys into Attention," in *Genealogy*, ed. Argersinger and Cole, 164.
29. Sandra M. Gustafson, "Choosing a Medium: Margaret Fuller and the Forms of Sentiment," *American Quarterly* 47, no. 1 (1995): 35–36.
30. Claudia Stokes, *The Altar at Home: Sentimental Literature and Nineteenth-Century American Religion* (Philadelphia: University of Pennsylvania Press, 2014), 1–3.
31. Tracy Fessenden, *Culture and Redemption: Religion, the Secular, and American Literature* (Princeton, N.J.: Princeton University Press, 2007), 3. In *A Secular Age* (Cambridge, Mass.: Belknap Press of Harvard University Press, 2007), Charles Taylor names this proliferation of the "ever-widening variety of moral/spiritual options" the "supernova effect" (299). This "effect" is most conspicuous for Taylor in the period after the Second World War.
32. José Casanova, "A Secular Age: Dawn or Twilight?," in *Varieties of Secularism in a Secular Age*, ed. Michael Warner, Jonathan VanAntwerpen, and Craig Calhoun (Cambridge, Mass.: Harvard University Press, 2010), 273.
33. Grant Shreve, "Fragile Belief: Lydia Maria Child's *Hobomok* and the Scene of American Secularity," *American Literature* 86, no. 4 (2014): 657–58.
34. Conrad Edick Wright, *Beginnings of Unitarianism in America* (Hamden, Conn.: Archon Books, 1976), 241. In his remarks to the college chapter of Phi Beta Kappa, Kirkland, who served as Harvard's president from 1810 to 1828, warned against what he described as "the poison of the skeptical and disorganizing philosophy, which is now perverting and corrupting man." John T. Kirkland, *An Oration, Delivered, at the Request of the Society of ΦBK* (Boston: John Russell, 1798), 21. More's remarks appear in her book *Practical Piety; or, The Influence of the Religion of the Heart on the Conduct of Life, by Hannah More . . . in Two Volumes* (Boston: Munroe and Francis, 1811), 1:71, 2:150.
35. Ernestine L. Rose, "A Defense of Atheism," *Boston Investigator*, May 8, 1861. Rose originally delivered this address in Boston's Mercantile Hall on April 10, 1861.
36. Eliza Clapp, *Studies in Religion* (New York: C. Shepard, 1845), 9–10, 218. At the request of Emerson, Clapp, a resident of Dorchester, Massachusetts, contributed three hymns and two poems to the *Dial* in 1841.
37. Phyllis Cole, "Elizabeth Peabody in the Nineteenth Century: Autobiographical Perspectives," in *Genealogy*, ed. Argersinger and Cole, 135.

Peabody's remarks appear in her diary from 1822, as cited in Mary Van Wyck Church, "Biography of Elizabeth Palmer Peabody, 1869–1921," 18.
38. Megan Marshall, "Elizabeth Palmer Peabody: The First Transcendentalist?," *Massachusetts Historical Review* 8 (2006): 1–15.
39. *Letters of Elizabeth Palmer Peabody: American Renaissance Woman,* ed. Bruce A. Ronda (Middletown, Conn.: Wesleyan University Press, 1984), 247.
40. Elizabeth Palmer Peabody, *Reminiscences of William Ellery Channing, D.D.* (Boston: Roberts Brothers, 1880), 57.
41. Cole, "Elizabeth Peabody in the Nineteenth Century," 140–41; Monika M. Elbert, "Elizabeth Palmer Peabody's Problematic Feminism and the Feminization of Transcendentalism," in *Reinventing the Peabody Sisters,* ed. Monika M. Elbert, Julie E. Hall, and Katharine Rodier (Iowa City: University of Iowa Press, 2006), 200, 208.
42. From Peabody's diary for 1822, referenced in Church, "Biography of Elizabeth Palmer Peabody," 32–33.
43. Elbert, "Peabody's Problematic Feminism," 200.
44. Peabody to Eliza Guild, in Church, "Biography of Elizabeth Palmer Peabody," 340–41.
45. Elizabeth Palmer Peabody, "Spirit of the Hebrew Scriptures, No. III, Public Worship: Social Crime, and Its Retribution," *Christian Examiner* 17, no. 1 (1834): 85; and "Spirit of the Hebrew Scriptures," *Christian Examiner* 16, no. 2 (1834): 177.
46. Both articles appeared in modified form in Peabody's later book *Last Evening with Allston, and Other Papers* (Boston: D. Lothrop, 1887). The author derived the first of these, "The Atheism of Yesterday," from her article "The Being of God," which originally appeared in the *Christian Examiner* for September 1858. Peabody's companion piece on atheism, "Egotheism, the Atheism of To-day," first ran in the *Religious Magazine* during the same month and year as "Yesterday."
47. Ralph Waldo Emerson, "The Transcendentalist" (1841), in the *Collected Works of Ralph Waldo Emerson* (hereafter cited as *CW*), vol. 1, *Nature, Addresses, and Lectures,* ed. Robert E. Spiller (Cambridge, Mass.: Belknap Press of Harvard University Press, 1971), 10.
48. Elizabeth Cady Stanton, Susan B. Anthony, and Matilda Joslyn Gage, ed., *History of Woman Suffrage,* 3 vols. (Rochester, N.Y.: Charles Mann, 1887), 1:802.

49. Cole, "Stanton, Fuller, and the Grammar of Romanticism," 549, 546.
50. Margaret Fuller, "The Great Lawsuit. Man *versus* Men. Woman *versus* Women," *Dial* 4 (July 1843): 1–47.
51. On the phrase "Christian transcendentalist," see Ronald V. Wells, *Three Christian Transcendentalists: James Marsh, Caleb Sprague Henry, Frederic Henry Hedge* (1943; reprint, New York: Octagon Books, 1972). Hedge's "atheist" statement appears in Joel Myerson, "Frederic Henry Hedge and the Failure of Transcendentalism," *Harvard Library Bulletin* 23, no. 4 (1975): 403.
52. In her opening editorial statement for the *Dial*, Fuller made clear that the transcendental journal she headed would "embrace much more than criticism." Fuller, "The Editors to the Reader," *Dial* (July 1840): 3–4.
53. Susan Belasco Smith, introduction to *Summer on the Lakes, in 1843*, by Margaret Fuller (Urbana: University of Illinois Press, 1991), ix.
54. Thomas Wentworth Higginson recalls watching the author at work in the college library, "where I can well remember to have seen Miss Fuller sitting, day after day, under the covert gaze of the undergraduates who had never before looked upon a woman reading within those sacred precincts." Higginson, *Margaret Fuller Ossoli*, 194.
55. On Fuller's attitudes toward the literary representation of the American Indian, see Laura L. Mielke, *Moving Encounters: Sympathy and the Indian Question in Antebellum Literature* (Amherst: University of Massachusetts Press, 2008), 99–103.
56. Ronald J. Zboray and Mary Saracino Zboray, "Transcendentalism in Print: Production, Dissemination, and Common Reception," in *Transient and Permanent*, 321–22.
57. Almy Family Papers, diary of Hannah Lowell (Jackson) Cabot, September 4, 1839, typed transcript, carbon copy, 1839–42, Schlesinger Library (hereafter cited as SL), Radcliffe Institute, Harvard University.
58. Rotch Family Papers, diary of Isabel Morgan, June 22–23, 1845, Massachusetts Historical Society (hereafter cited as MHS).
59. Sarah Alden Bradford Ripley Papers, Ripley to George F. Simmons, March 7, 1844, SL. Ripley's correspondent, who at the time was studying in Germany, had served previously as an assistant minister in Ripley's Waltham.
60. "'Treasure in My Own Mind': The Diary of Martha Lawrence Prescott, 1834–1836," ed. Leslie Perrin Wilson, *Concord Saunterer* 11 (2003): 128.

Prescott entered these observations into her diary at 5:30 p.m. on April 5, 1836.
61. *Concord Saunterer* 11 (2003): 113.
62. In the King James Bible, the line to which Prescott alludes reads, "But one thing is needful: and Mary hath chosen that good part, which shall not be taken away from her."
63. Dana Family Papers, diary of Sarah Watson Dana, August 25, September 8, September 15, and October 27, 1833, SL. Refer as well to the letter from Fanny [Webb?] to Sarah Watson (who by this time was residing in Hartford, Connecticut) from February 12, 1838, in which the writer misnames the chapter from Carlyle's book "Natural Supernaturalized." Dean Grodzins's description of *Sartor Resartus* appears in his *American Heretic: Theodore Parker and Transcendentalism* (Chapel Hill: University of North Carolina Press, 2002), 65.
64. Ames Family Historical Collection, 1762–2006, MC 773, diary of Catherine Robbins, October 22, 1836, SL.
65. Catherine's sister, Ann Jean, corresponded with Emerson in these years.
66. Louisa Lee Waterhouse, journal, ca. April 19, 1840, MHS. At a later date, the Massachusetts mill girl turned writer and educator Lucy Larcom would similarly write by letter to a friend that "Emerson is 'coming out' in the Atlantic, isn't he? Poor 'Brahma!'" The "Atlantic" to which Larcom refers is the *Atlantic Monthly*, which began publishing in Boston in 1857. By "Brahma," Larcom would indicate Emerson's poem from 1856 by that same name. From the papers of Harriet Jane Hanson Robinson and Harriette Lucy Robinson Shattuck, Lucy Larcom to Harriet Hanson Robinson, December 18, 1857, SL. On an earlier occasion, Larcom admitted to what she called her "Puritan *penchants*," which led her to regard Emerson as "very much like the old heathen philosophers." She continued, "How such a head grew up among Yankee cabbages, I don't understand." Papers of Harriet Jane Hanson Robinson and Harriette Lucy Robinson Shattuck, Lucy Larcom to William Steven Robinson, January 13, 1853, SL.
67. Additional papers of the Albert Gallatin Browne Family, Sarah Smith (Cox) Browne, account book, and Sarah Smith (Cox) Browne to Albert Gallatine Browne, June 29, 1855, SL. Browne's reference is likely to Daniel Defoe's *The Political History of the Devil* (1726), an irreverent examination by the author of the origins of evil. Browne additionally wrote that American

author Harriet Beecher Stowe "has a little too much of theology," which "makes me shudder."

68. Papers of Harriet Jane Hanson Robinson and Harriette Lucy Robinson Shattuck, Lucy Larcom to Harriet Hanson Robinson, November 21, 1856, and December 18, 1857, SL. Larcom stated her views on "philosophers" with Emerson in mind, of whom she wrote, "What I like best in Emerson is that he always gets you a thinking" (December 18, 1857).

69. Papers of Harriet Jane Hanson Robinson and Harriette Lucy Robinson Shattuck, William S. Robinson and Harriet Hanson Robinson, diary, [n.d.] 1855 and July 30, 1856, SL. For her part, Robinson regarded Emerson as "most a divine man, besides being so great a genius" (June 5, 1856).

70. Cabot Family Papers, 1786–2013, A-99, papers of Elisabeth (Dwight) Cabot, diary for September 25, 1859, SL.

71. Ibid., Cabot to Ellen (Dwight) Twisleton, December 16, 1860, SL. A member of Ephraim Peabody's congregation at King's Chapel (that is, Stone Chapel) in Boston, Elisabeth Dwight would marry there in 1857. In her correspondence, she voices her opinions on the transcendentalist acquaintances of her husband, the lawyer and editor (and graduate from Harvard's Law School, in 1845) James Eliot Cabot. In time, James Cabot became Emerson's biographer and literary executor.

72. Ibid., commonplace book, 1851–74, SL.

73. Ellis Gray Loring Papers, A-160, commonplace book of Louisa (Gilman) Loring, ca. 1830–32, SL. Loring does not mention the source of her quotation from Novalis, although this same passage appeared in the *New Monthly Magazine* for July 1830. Loring's husband, the Boston-born lawyer and abolitionist Ellis Gray Loring, entered Harvard College in 1819 but did not graduate after being dismissed in 1823 for his participation in an undergraduate disturbance.

74. The biblical line reads, "For we wrestle not against flesh and blood, but against principalities, against powers, against the rulers of the darkness of this world, against spiritual wickedness in high places."

75. Frances Merritt Quick Papers, diary for September 19, 1858, SL.

76. Ibid., diary for September 20, 1858, SL. Quick's biblical reference is to 1 Cor. 3:13—"Every man's work shall be manifest; for the day of the Lord shall declare it, because it shall be revealed in fire; and the fire shall try every man's work, of what sort it is." For the strict denominationalist

Quick, mere "contact with Unitarians" warranted a mention in her diary, since she felt that Unitarianism "has so many phases, and reveals itself so variously at different times and to different persons, that it gives you no chance for a vital attack upon its falsities" (October 3, 1858).

77. Poor Family Papers, 1791–1921, A-132, Feroline (Pierce) Fox to Mary Pierce Poor, August 12, 1842, SL.
78. Ibid., Mary (Pierce) Poor to Henry Varnum Poor, April 3, 1841, SL.
79. Ibid., April 17, 1841, SL.
80. Mary Moody Emerson (MME) to William Emerson, May 20, 1826, in *The Selected Letters of Mary Moody Emerson*, ed. Nancy Craig Simmons (Athens: University of Georgia Press, 1993), 210. Mary wrote this letter to William, Waldo's older brother, from Vale (which Mary called "Elm Vale"), a 150-acre farm close to the White Mountains near Waterford, Maine.
81. MME to Charles Chauncy Emerson, May 1827, and to William Emerson, June 13, 1840. All references are to *Letters,* 227–28, 418, 280–81.
82. Sarah Alden Bradford Ripley Papers, Ripley to George F. Simmons, October 7, 1844, SL.
83. Ibid., February 29, 1844, SL. The quoted line in Sarah's letter is from George Herbert's poem "Virtue" (1633).
84. Ibid., April 8, 1844, SL. The Ripleys, Sarah and her husband, Samuel, retired to Concord in 1846.
85. Ibid., June 26, 1844, SL.
86. Ibid., January 9, 1845, SL. Sarah uses the phrase "spectral illusion" in her letter from February 29, 1845.
87. Dorri Beam, *Style, Gender, and Fantasy in Nineteenth-Century American Women's Writing* (New York: Cambridge University Press, 2010), 37, 46.
88. Wider, "'How It All Lies before Me To-day,'" 167–68.
89. Cranch's decision to leave the ministry was informed by his increasing dedication to landscape painting. As he wrote to Emerson on September 12, 1841, "I become more and more inclined to sink the minister in the man, and abandon my present calling *in toto* as a profession." Leonora Cranch Scott, *The Life and Letters of Christopher Pearse Cranch* (Boston: Houghton Mifflin, 1917), 60. Part of Cranch's difficulties as a minister stemmed from the trouble he had in overcoming *self* in attending to the spiritual needs of his parishioners. He was seeking, moreover, for a greater intensity in his

religious life than what he felt the Unitarian Church provided. As he wrote to his father on July 11, 1840, he needed something "more satisfying to the soul" (50). Nancy Stula maintains that, although Cranch "was by no means as radical in his views as Emerson," he did "encounter censure as a result of his affiliation with Transcendentalism" (23). His fellow transcendentalist John Sullivan Dwight (Harvard College class of 1832, Harvard Divinity School 1836) would warn Cranch by letter on April 20, 1840, "Let me advise you . . . to repent of your heresies, to renounce R. W. E. and all his evil work and return to good old fashioned Unitarianism" (Cranch Papers, MHS). Cranch himself said that Emerson's writings were "considered very heretical by most persons, and by many as downright atheism, mysticism, or perhaps nonsense" (Scott, *Life and Letters,* 47). Undeterred in his artistic work, Cranch, as a landscape painter of some renown, practiced a transcendental aestheticism that paired painting with prayer. See Nancy Stula, "Transcendentalism: The Path from Preaching to Painting," in *At Home and Abroad: The Transcendental Landscapes of Christopher Pearse Cranch (1813–1892)* (New London, Conn.: Lyman Allyn Art Museum, 2007), 15–56.

90. Sarah Freeman Clarke to James Freeman Clarke, February 11, 1838, MS Am 1569, James Freeman Clarke Correspondence (hereafter cited as LS), V, letters to and from Sarah Freeman Clarke, Houghton Library, Harvard University.

91. Although she became a confirmed Christian some nine years before her marriage, Lidian Jackson Emerson was sympathetic to transcendentalism as a necessary correction to Unitarianism, which she is recorded as having described as "cold and hard, with scarcely a firmament above." On L. J. Emerson's religious views, see Delores Bird Carpenter, "The Life of Lidian Jackson Emerson by Ellen Tucker Emerson" (Ph.D. diss., University of Massachusetts, 1978), 81. For the remarks from Emerson's "Transcendental Bible," see Delores Bird Carpenter, "Lidian Emerson's 'Transcendental Bible,'" *Studies in the American Renaissance* (1980): 91–92.

92. Rather than read transcendental aestheticism as an *enlargement* of the spiritual self, Barbara Novak writes of a transcendental tradition of American landscape painting that aimed for "a more complete elimination of the ego." Novak, *Nature and Culture: American Landscape Painting, 1825–1875* (New York: Oxford University Press, 1980), 272.

93. Elizabeth Palmer Peabody, "Introduction: The Word 'Aesthetic,'" in *Aesthetic Papers,* ed. Elizabeth Peabody (New York: G. P. Putnam, 1849), 1.
94. Elizabeth Palmer Peabody, "The Dorian Measure, with a Modern Application," ibid., 104. Although he was briefly a transcendentalist, Ward opted to become a banker rather than pursue a literary vocation, and he later became a cofounder of New York's Metropolitan Museum of Art. In the *Aesthetic Papers,* see his essay "Criticism," 5–24.
95. Margaret Fuller, from her journal for September 17, 1842, from Joel Myerson, ed., "Margaret Fuller's 1842 Journal: At Concord with the Emersons," *Harvard Library Bulletin* 21, no. 3 (1973): 326.
96. Robert D. Habich, ed., "Margaret Fuller's Journal for October, 1842," *Harvard Library Bulletin* 33, no. 3 (1985): 281–82.
97. Sarah Clarke to James Freeman Clarke, October 27, 1839, LS.
98. Parker made this statement in a letter written from Boston on February 1, 1855. His correspondent was Miss Helen P. Mills of Chatham, Massachusetts. Theodore Parker Papers, MHS.
99. The transcendentalists' first noteworthy encounter with Allston's work came in the spring of 1839, when the painter, a member of Boston's conservative Shepard Congregational Church, mounted an exhibition of forty-five of his canvases in the city gallery of portraitist Chester Harding. Of these paintings, eight were representations of women. See Albert J. von Frank, "The Visual Arts," in *The Oxford Handbook of Transcendentalism,* ed. Joel Myerson, Sandra Harbert Petrulionis, and Laura Dassow Walls (New York: Oxford University Press, 2010), 442–44.
100. Peabody, *Last Evening with Allston,* 46–47; Sarah Clarke, "Our First Great Painter, and His Works," *Atlantic Monthly* 15 (1865): 131.
101. Margaret Fuller, "A Record of Impressions Produced by the Exhibition of Mr. Allston's Pictures in the Summer of 1839," *Dial* (July 1840): 76.
102. Lydia L. A. Very, "What Is It to Be Religious?," in *Poems* (Boston: W. F. Draper, 1856), 167–68.
103. Jones Very maintained that a divine visitation had left him with a deeper appreciation of the twenty-fourth chapter of the Gospel according to Matthew, while claiming that Christ's Second Coming was "in him." See Carlos Baker, *Emerson among the Eccentrics: A Group Portrait* (New York: Viking, 1996), 122.

104. Jones Very served as a tutor in Greek at his alma mater before entering the Harvard Divinity School in the fall of 1836. Although he never completed his studies for the ministry, he would, in later years, hold temporary pastorates in Maine, Massachusetts, and Rhode Island as he pursued what proved an erratic literary career. On Very's mother, see Barbara L. Packer, *The Transcendentalists* (Athens: University of Georgia Press, 2007), 70.

CHAPTER 4: TRANSCENDENTALISM, URBANISM, AND UNBELIEF

1. Abner Kneeland, *A Review of the Trial, Conviction, and Final Imprisonment in the Common Jail of the County of Suffolk of Abner Kneeland: for the Alleged Crime of Blasphemy, Written by Himself* (Boston: George A. Chapman, 1838), 46.
2. These were the words of Lemuel Shaw, chief justice of the Massachusetts Supreme Court and future father-in-law of U.S. author Herman Melville. From *Commonwealth v. Kneeland*, 37, *Massachusetts Reports*, 206 ff. (1838).
3. In what he called his "Philosophical Creed," composed at Hebron, New Hampshire, on May 28, 1833, Kneeland wrote of his "beliefs" as follows: "I believe that the whole universe is NATURE, and that the word NATURE embraces the whole universe, and that God and Nature, so far as we can attach any rational idea to either, are perfectly synonymous terms. Hence I am not an Atheist, but a Pantheist; that is, instead of believing there is no God, I believe that in the abstract all is God." Kneeland, *Review*, 21. Kneeland gave an early survey of the pejorative names assigned him in *A Review of the Evidences of Christianity; in a Series of Lectures, Delivered in Broadway Hall, New York, August, 1829* (Boston: Office of the Investigator, 1831). These names also applied to "all others who do not bow down to the golden image of orthodoxy" (30–31).
4. In his *Review of the Prosecution against Abner Kneeland, for Blasphemy, by a Cosmopolite* (Boston, 1835), David Henshaw acknowledged that simply reviewing the case in question risked "shocking the prejudices of the truly pious" (3). For a review of Kneeland's multiple trials, see Leonard W. Levy, "*Commonwealth v. Kneeland*," in *Religion and American Law: An Encyclopedia*, ed. Paul Finkelman (New York: Routledge, 2013), 100–102. For Kneeland's own position on the basis of "belief," refer to Abner Kneeland,

Speech of Abner Kneeland, Delivered before the Full Bench of Judges of the Supreme Court, in His Own Defence, for the Alleged Crime of Blasphemy (Boston: J. Q. Adams, 1836), v.
5. *Evidences of Christianity*, 7.
6. Solicitation for subscriptions to the *Boston Investigator* newspaper, from the edition for November 24, 1834.
7. Martin Green, *The Problem of Boston: Some Readings in Cultural History* (New York: W. W. Norton, 1966), 41. Ronald Story likewise describes Boston in the nineteenth century as being composed by what he calls the overlapping "branches" of a cultural and entrepreneurial elite. Story, *The Forging of an Aristocracy: Harvard & the Boston Upper Class, 1800–1870* (Middletown, Conn.: Wesleyan University Press, 1980), 71.
8. E. L. Godkin, as cited in Green, *Problem of Boston*, 41.
9. Paul DiMaggio, "Cultural Entrepreneurship in Nineteenth-Century Boston: The Creation of an Organizational Base for High Culture in America," *Media, Culture & Society* 4, no. 1 (1982): 34.
10. James W. Cook, *The Arts of Deception: Playing with Fraud in the Age of Barnum* (Cambridge, Mass.: Harvard University Press, 2001).
11. With special reference to the latter half of the nineteenth century, Jackson Lears writes of a "vernacular ethic of fortune," which in his view promoted "a healthy skepticism regarding the human capacity for mastering fate, recalled the wisdom of Ecclesiastes, and offered relief from the closed system of work and reward." Lears, *Something for Nothing: Luck in America* (New York: Viking Penguin, 2003), 156–57.
12. For a discussion of Kneeland's ties to Emerson, see Robert E. Burkholder, "Emerson, Kneeland, and the Divinity School Address," *American Literature* 58, no. 1 (1986): 1–14.
13. Robert Gross, "Transcendentalism and Urbanism: Concord, Boston, and the Wider World," *Journal of American Studies* 18, no. 3 (1984): 363.
14. John Kasson, *Amusing the Million: Coney Island at the Turn of the Century* (New York: Hill & Wang, 1978). In *Electric Dreamland: Amusement Parks, Movies, and American Modernity* (New York: Columbia University Press, 2012), Lauren Rabinovitz similarly contends that, "at the turn of the last century, America got serious about amusement" (1).
15. Colin Jager, *Unquiet Things: Secularism in the Romantic Age* (Philadelphia: University of Pennsylvania Press, 2014), 3.

16. The response to Catholicism by much of Boston's Protestant establishment was hardly accommodating. With the end of the Napoleonic Wars in 1815, the rising incidence of Irish Catholic immigration was greeted by many in the city as evidence of a papal conspiracy to establish the dominance of the Roman Catholic Church in the New World. See Jenny Franchot, *Roads to Rome: The Antebellum Protestant Encounter with Catholicism* (Berkeley: University of California Press, 1994), 5–6, 62; and Thomas H. O'Connor, *Boston Catholics: A History of the Church and Its People* (Boston: Northeastern University Press, 1998), 55, 57. On the softened nineteenth-century New England strain of revivalism known as the "New Measures," refer to James D. Bratt, "Religious Anti-revivalism in Antebellum America," *Journal of the Early Republic* 24, no. 1 (2004): 68–70. On "Associationism" as a Boston-oriented religious expression, see Carl J. Guarneri, "The Associationists: Forging a Christian Socialism in Antebellum America," *Church History* 52, no. 1 (1983): 36–49.

17. Mary Kupiec Cayton, "The Making of an American Prophet: Emerson, His Audiences, and the Rise of the Culture Industry in Nineteenth-Century America," *American Historical Review* 92, no. 3 (1987): 600, 604; Bonnie Carr O'Neill, *Literary Celebrity and Public Life in the Nineteenth-Century United States* (Athens: University of Georgia Press, 2017), 3, 87–88.

18. In his *Conversations with Children on the Gospels* (Boston: J. Munroe, 1837), Alcott made the substance of his experimental pedagogy a matter of public record. Among the topics he treated in this publication were such sensitive matters as birth and circumcision. Alcott's sometime assistant Elizabeth Peabody composed a less controversial account of the Temple School in her *Record of a School: Exemplifying the General Principles of Spiritual Culture* (Boston: Russell, Shattuck, 1836).

19. Having drafted their petition (authored principally by Ellis Gray Loring) early in 1838, Channing and his signers directed their remarks to the governor of Massachusetts. Among their stated reasons for supporting Kneeland was the belief that, "by punishing infidel opinions, we shake one of the strongest foundations of faith, namely, the evidence which arises to religion from the fact, that it stands firm and gathers strength amidst the severest and most unfettered investigations of its claims." William Ellery Channing Papers, 1819–52, MS Am 1428, Houghton Library, Harvard University. The Unitarian Universalist Association would issue a subsequent petition

on Kneeland's behalf on February 23, 1975. See the Unitarian Universalist Association, Minister Files, 1825–2010, bMS 1446/107, Abner Kneeland, Andover-Harvard Theological Library, Harvard Divinity School, Harvard University (hereafter cited as MH-AH).
20. Andrew Peabody, *Harvard Reminiscences* (Boston: Ticknor, 1888), 198–99.
21. Ibid., 9–10.
22. Kenneth Walker Cameron, *Thoreau's Harvard Years: Materials Introductory to New Explorations, Record of Fact and Background* (Hartford, Conn.: Transcendental Books, 1966), 2:125.
23. The announcement for Brownson's talk appeared in the *Christian Register*, November 27, 1836. The announcement for Emerson appeared in the "Commercial Record" of the *Boston Daily Advertiser*, January 19, 1837.
24. Ralph Waldo Emerson, *Journals and Miscellaneous Notebooks of Ralph Waldo Emerson*, vol. 5, *1835–1838*, ed. Merton M. Sealts Jr. (Cambridge, Mass.: Belknap Press of Harvard University Press, 1965), 545.
25. Catherine Albanese, *Corresponding Motion: Transcendental Religion and the New America* (Philadelphia: Temple University Press, 1977), 33.
26. The second Chardon Street Convention was held on March 30, 1841, while the third, by now removed to Boston's Masonic Temple, occurred on March 29, 1842.
27. James Porter, *Modern Infidelity, Alias Come-out-ism, as Taught by Ultra Non-resistants, Transcendentalists, Garrisonians, and Other Revolutionists: In Three Lectures* (Boston: Waite, Peirce, [1845]), 4.
28. Ralph Waldo Emerson, "The Chardon Street Convention," in *The Complete Works of Ralph Waldo Emerson: Lectures and Biographical Sketches*, centenary ed. (Boston: Houghton Mifflin, 1903–4), 10:375.
29. Lawrence Levine names the nineteenth-century shift in the United States toward a vaunted conception of art the "sacralization of culture." Levine, *Highbrow, Lowbrow: The Emergence of Cultural Hierarchy in America* (Cambridge, Mass.: Harvard University Press, 1988).
30. Michael Broyles, "Music and Class Structure in Antebellum Boston," *Journal of the American Musicological Society* 44, no. 3 (1991): 452.
31. John Sullivan Dwight, "Address, Delivered before the Harvard Musical Association, August 25, 1841," *Musical Magazine* 3 (1841): 263–64. As a resident of Brook Farm, the utopian reform commune in West Roxbury, during the mid-1840s, Dwight contributed "sacred music" on piano at meetings

of the Boston Religious Union. As we learn from the minutes of a union meeting held on Sunday evening, March 7, 1847, one attendee was reported to have passed "through various forms of scepticism to find at last complete satisfaction in the hopes of the Associative doctrines." Sterling Delano, "A Calendar of Meetings of the 'Boston Religious Union of Associationists,' 1847–1850," *Studies in the American Renaissance* (1985): 201–2.

32. Although he trained as a composer, singer, and soloist in Europe, Russell toured frequently in the United States, and he served as the organist at the First Presbyterian Church of Rochester, New York, from 1833 to 1841. See Russell, *Words of the Oratorio of "The Skeptic"* ([Boston]: Kidder & Wright, printers, [between 1838 and 1842]).

33. John Brazer, *Sermons* (Boston: Crosby and Nichols, 1849), 93–95.

34. As cited in Dean Grodzins, *American Heretic: Theodore Parker and Transcendentalism* (Chapel Hill: University of North Carolina Press, 2002), 264.

35. Ibid., 267.

36. One local observer went out of his way to differentiate between the "free gospel" he found at Parker's Boston congregation in 1858 and what he calls "the excesses of the revival movement" that he discovered elsewhere in the city (276, 274). See "Excesses of the Revival—Theodore Parker's Case," from the *Boston Daily Bee*, March 17, 1858, in *The Collected Works of Theodore Parker* (London: Trübner, 1875), 3:274–78.

37. Elizabeth Peabody to John Sullivan Dwight, June 10, 1841, in *Letters of Elizabeth Palmer Peabody: American Renaissance Woman*, ed. Bruce A. Ronda (Middletown, Conn.: Wesleyan University Press, 1984), 253.

38. By December 19, 1868, the *Register* was reporting on "Theatre Meetings" in a special page 2 column. By the very next week, this column became a recurring feature of the paper, under the revised heading "Theatre Preaching." Here the *Register* reported on such assembly room sermons and lectures as were held in the nation's largest cities, notably Boston and New York.

39. "Spiritual Deadness" or "Spiritual Indifference." Theodore Parker Papers, 1836–62, series II, vol. 2, sermons 24–67, 1837, bMS 101/5 (1), MH-AH. Parker originally delivered this sermon in West Roxbury on September 3, 1837.

40. Ibid., series I, journal, vol. 3, May 19, 1851–October 4, 1856, bMS 101/3 (1), MH-AH. In times of his own illness, Parker diagnosed himself as "dull," a description from which he recoiled.

41. Ibid., vol. 1, July 13, 1838–December 31, 1840, bMS 101/1 (2), MH-AH. Parker delivered this sermon in June 1840.
42. Parker's letter is dated October 29, 1847. From the Twenty-Eighth Congregational Society (Boston) Records (hereafter cited as 28R), 1845–89, bMS 7/1 (10), box 1, folder 1, MH-AH.
43. Julia Ward Howe, *Reminiscences, 1819–1899* (Boston: Houghton Mifflin, 1899), 149–50.
44. Even before his appointment as pastor to the Twenty-Eighth Congregational Society, Parker had been a regular lecturer at the Melodeon. At 7:00 p.m. on January 2, 1845, for example, Parker, at the request of the Warren Street Chapel Association, took to the Melodeon's stage to deliver an address titled "Roman Slavery," with tickets costing twenty-five cents. See "Commercial Record," *Boston Daily Advertiser,* January 2, 1845.
45. See Loren R. Lerner and Mary F. Williamson, *Art and Architecture in Canada: A Bibliography and Guide to the Literature to 1981* (Toronto: University of Toronto Press, 1991), 28; and Joseph Earl Arrington, "William Burr's Moving Panorama of the Great Lakes, the Niagara, St. Lawrence, and Saguenay Rivers," *Ontario History* 51 (Summer 1959): 141–62. Burr's panorama proved a good piece of business for the society. According to a report from the Standing Committee on April 6, 1851, "The various expenses of the year have been discharged promptly, & some sources of income then not looked for, from the use of the Hall for the exhibition of the Panoramas of W. Burr, has left a surplus in hand somewhat larger than at the close of last year." 28R, box 1, folder 4.
46. Ednah Dow Littlehale Cheney, *Reminiscences of Ednah Dow Cheney (Born Littlehale)* (Boston: Lee & Shepard, 1902), 109. In a letter to the Handel & Haydn Society from January 31, 1848, John Ayres, at that time clerk to the Twenty-Eighth Congregational Society, informed the owners of the premises of "the bad condition of the Melodeon on Sundays." As Ayres writes, "Last Sunday we had no fires, the doors without fastenings, matts [sic] full of wet mud & wholly unfit for any good purpose—Kettle drums are left in front of the organ and the seats in a very dirty condition." 28R, box 1, folder 3.
47. Report of the Standing Committee, April 6, 1846, 28R, box 1, folder 4.
48. "Music," *Boston Daily Advertiser,* January 16, 1845. After its move to Boston's Music Hall, in 1852, the Twenty-Eighth Congregational Society ceased to

contract with an individual organist. By the terms of a new contract made with the Boston Music Hall Association, completed on November 15 of this same year, the society arranged with its new landlords for the supply of a permanent organist as well as a choir of "seven or eight good singers." 28R, box 1, folder 3.

49. Cheney, *Reminiscences*, 106–7.
50. Report of the Standing Committee, April 4, 1858, 28R, box 1, folder 4.
51. Sargent made these remarks in a letter he wrote to Parker on July 13, 1858. At the time, Sargent was working as the head of the Boston Providence Association, a local charitable organization in the city. 28R, box 1, folder 2. As he announced earlier, in a pamphlet defense of his friend, Sargent stood by Parker, despite his having "become, as it were, the embodiment of Ultra Unitarianism." John T. Sargent, *The True Position of Rev. Theodore Parker: Being a Review of Rev. R. C. Waterston's Letter in the Fourth Quarterly Report of the Benevolent Fraternity of Churches* (Boston: Andrews, Prentiss & Studley, 1845), 21–22.
52. Report of the Standing Committee, April 4, 1847, 28R, box 1, folder 4.
53. Because Parker had been excluded from pulpit exchanges with his Unitarian peers, the committee resolved on March 5, 1849, "that no objection would be entertained by this Society, if discourses by laymen should occasionally be substituted for the usual services at the Melodeon." In the event that such an arrangement could not be reached, the committee further resolved that "the Society would cheerfully consent to such occasional discontinuance of Mr. Parker's Sunday labors as the state of his health may from time to time seem to him to require." 28R, box 1, folder 1.
54. Report of the Standing Committee, April 6, 1846. The committee persisted in its membership drive, despite having declared, in the spring of 1847, that "the problem whether or not a really independent pulpit would be sustained in Boston, seems thus to have been satisfactorily solved." Report of the Standing Committee, April 4, 1847. Nor did attendance numbers at Sunday meetings dwindle thereafter. As the Standing Committee reported on April 4, 1852, "Notwithstanding efforts in many quarters to create distrust, & enlist prejudice, the attendance has certainly not declined, but has rather steadily increased." 28R, box 1, folder 4. Attendance at Sunday meetings continued to rise in the years between 1853 and 1855, after the society relocated to Boston's Music Hall.

55. Howe, *Reminiscences*, 244; Cheney, *Reminiscences*, 109–10; Grodzins, *American Heretic*, 478.
56. The committee issued this statement in its report from April 4, 1852. 28R, box 1, folder 4.
57. This profile of Parker's Boston audience is based on the society's original list of subscribers from 1845. Heading this list is a fair representation of the city's mercantile elite, the "merchants," "land agents," and dealers in "wholesale goods" who contributed as much as $100 or $200 per year to the support of the society. Among the next tier of support are the enterprising professionals and businessmen who managed, in their respective callings as doctors, lawyers, and tailors and dealers in hardware, "dry goods," and books, to contribute anywhere from $15 to $80 per annum to the society. Next in the number of subscribers are manual laborers, the carpenters and pavers for whom a contribution of $5 or $10 could have represented an entire week's wages. Alongside them were the fledgling members of the lower middle classes, the clerks, printers, engravers, and teachers whose formal educations were extensive enough to impart to them at least the appearance, if not the promise, of upward mobility. See the entirety of the society's original subscription list in 28R, box 1, folder 4, bms 7/1 (3). Note that women are well represented in a separate, undated notebook listing members of the society.
58. Cheney, *Reminiscences*, 110.
59. Edward Everett Hale, "Public Amusements, a Discourse," *Christian Register*, December 19, 1868.
60. In his diary, Parker called this charge "the most painful of my ministry." See Parker's Journal O (December 1851), 155–57. For a discussion of the spiritual, as opposed to topical, emphasis of Parker's preaching, see Dean Grodzins and Joel Myerson, "The Preaching Record of Theodore Parker," *Studies in the American Renaissance* (1994): 58–60.
61. Ednah Dow Littlefield Cheney makes these remarks in John Weiss, *Life and Correspondence of Theodore Parker* (Boston: D. Appleton, 1864), 1:414–21.
62. As cited in Dean Grodzins, "Theodore Parker and the 28th Congregational Society: The Reform Church and the Spirituality of Reformers in Boston, 1845–1859," in *Transient and Permanent: The Transcendentalist Movement and Its Contexts*, ed. Charles Capper and Conrad Edick Wright (Boston: Massachusetts Historical Society, 2000), 76.

63. Paul Ricœur, "Toward a Hermeneutic of the Idea of Revelation," *Harvard Theological Review* 70, nos. 1–2 (1977): 30. Ricœur originally delivered this lecture to the "Symposium sur l'idée de la révélation" at the Faculté Universitaire St. Louis in Brussels, on February 17, 1976.
64. Papers of Francis Ellingwood Abbot, 1841–1904, HUG 1101, box 12, College Material, Harvard University Archives. See also the *Harvard College Class Book of 1859*, HUD 257.714 F, Harvard University Archives, Archives Stacks.
65. See Abbot's planner for the period running from February through December 1855. Papers of Francis Ellingwood Abbot, HUG 1101, box 12, College Material, Harvard University Archives.
66. The arc of Abbot's religious thinking can already be seen in his sophomore year. In response to a series of prompts from his Composition course for 1856–57, Abbot moves from defending what he calls "the fundamental doctrines of our common religion" to a mild chastising of "the moral and religious character of Coleridge," before maintaining, in a subsequent exercise, "that Mahometanism was a necessary pioneer of Christianity, one onward step in human progress." Francis Ellingwood Abbot, College Themes and Forensics, 1856–57, HUC 8856.386, Harvard University Archives, Archives Stacks.
67. Francis V. Balch and William R. Huntington, *Oration and Poem, Delivered by Francis V. Balch and Wm. R. Huntington, Class Day, 1859* (Boston: Alfred Mudge & Son, 1860), 12.
68. "Miscellanies" from Abbot's Private Notebook, 1858–59, Senior Year, Papers of Francis Ellingwood Abbot, HUG 1101, box 12, College Material, Harvard University Archives.
69. "The Dover Unitarian Society Case," *Christian Register*, April 3, 1869.
70. "Rev. Francis E. Abbot's Position," *Banner of Light*, April 17, 1869.
71. "Liberal Preaching," *Boston Investigator*, May 5, 1869.
72. Francis Ellingwood Abbot, "A Radical's Theology," *Radical*, June 1867, 585–86. Horace Traubel, the confidant of poet Walt Whitman, wrote in his eulogy of this paper's editor, Sidney Morse, "What *The Dial* was to Transcendentalism *The Radical* was to Free Religion." Traubel, "Sidney Morse: The Best of Him," *Conservator*, March 1903.
73. In Abbot's eyes, what separated free religion from transcendentalism was the latter's reliance on intuition as the sole basis for belief. He elaborated

this position in a lecture at Horticultural Hall in 1877, "Free Religion versus Transcendentalism." Abbot published his talk under the same name in the April 19 issue of the *Index*, 186–87. In his gloss on Abbot's Horticultural Hall talk, titled "Intuitionalism versus Science," from February 1871, a reporter for the *Boston Daily Advertiser* relates the speaker's saying that "the intuitional school bases faith on direct revelation of Divine Being by means of a special faculty of the soul called the 'higher reason.'" The exclusionary nature of this "faculty" was problematic for Abbot, who, in the words of the *Daily Advertiser*'s correspondent, worried that people in possession of only "the ordinary faculties of the mind" would be left "ignorant" of spiritual "truths" in consequence. This same writer redacted Abbot's verdict on the transcendentalists, as follows: "The simple fact is, that they have imported into free religion some relic of the dogmatism of orthodoxy." "The Civil War in Free Religion," *Boston Post*, February 6, 1871.

74. William J. Potter, *The Free Religious Association, Its Twenty-Five Years and Their Meaning: An Address for the Twenty-Fifth Anniversary of the Association, at Tremont Temple, Boston, May 27th, 1892* (Boston: Free Religious Association of America, 1892), 7.

75. Frothingham's statement reappeared much later in the pages of the *Index*. See the edition for April 12, 1877, 175.

76. *Annual Report of the Executive Committee of the Free Religious Association* (Boston: W. F. Brown, 1868), preface 2.

77. Advertisement from the *Boston Globe*, December 29, 1897.

78. "Horticultural Hall, Boston," *Harper's Weekly*, April 13, 1867, 226.

79. Built in 1845, the original headquarters for the Massachusetts Horticultural Society was located on Boston's School Street, at what had previously been the site of the city's old Latin School. The society would relocate again in 1901, after moving to Back Bay.

80. Potter, *Free Religious Association*, 26.

81. David M. Robinson, "'The New Epoch of Belief': The *Radical* and Religious Transformation in Nineteenth-Century New England," *New England Quarterly* 79, no. 4 (2006): 559, 561; Stow Persons, *Free Religion: An American Faith* (New Haven, Conn.: Yale University Press, 1947), 42–54.

82. "The Horticultural Hall Meetings," *Boston Post*, February 15, 1869. The entirety of Abbot's talk reappeared in the premiere issue of the *Index*, from January 1, 1870, 2–4.

83. Abbot, as cited in "Horticultural Hall," *Boston Post,* February 6, 1871.
84. "Boston Lectures," *Commonwealth,* June 4, 1870, 1. Abbot himself had written on the finer points of applied scientific reason in his article "Positivism in Theology," *Christian Examiner* (March 1866): 234–67.
85. "The Sunday Question," *Boston Investigator,* September 8, 1869.
86. "Boston Lectures," 1.
87. "Horticultural Hall Lectures," *Republican,* February 6, 1871; "Jesus and Socrates," *Banner of Light,* March 12, 1870; "Sunday Services," *Boston Post,* February 28, 1870. The reporter from the *Post* wrote that Abbot's most recent lecture "was attentively listened to and his remarks evidently were well received" (1).
88. "The Independent Course of Lectures," *Vox Populi,* March 2, 1870. According to a report in Boston's *Commonwealth,* the "Orthodox" superintendent of the Sunday school in Lowell warned the parishioners at his church against the speakers from Horticultural Hall, telling them, "There is to be a series of lectures in Huntington Hall by the devil and his emissaries." "Brief Notes," *Commonwealth,* March 5, 1870.
89. "Socrates Compared with Jesus," *Universalist,* March 12, 1870.
90. "Rev. Mr. Clarke and Mr. Abbot," *Watchman & Reflector,* March 24, 1870; "Brevities," *Christian Register,* September 30, 1871.
91. "Intuitionalism vs. Science," *World,* February 6, 1871.
92. "Brief Notes," 2.
93. Christopher Grasso, *Skepticism and American Faith: From the Revolution to the Civil War* (New York: Oxford University Press, 2018), 356.
94. *Boston Daily Globe,* December 2, 1872.
95. *Boston Daily Globe,* February 19, 1873.
96. "The Battle of Ideas in Boston," *Christian Register,* June 26, 1869.
97. Ibid.
98. "Modern Martyrdom Again," *Christian Register,* November 14, 1874.

AFTERWORD

1. Abbot to Charles Adams Allen (Harvard College class of 1858), April 27, 1865, Papers of Francis Ellingwood Abbot, 1841–1904, HUG 1101, box 43, Correspondence, Harvard University Archives.
2. *Souvenir Festival Hymns* (Boston: Free Religious Association, 1899), 5. As the introduction to this volume explained, "Free Religion, while not

casting away old songs which still express the universal thought, has felt the need of its own expression" (5).
3. Francis Ellingwood Abbot, "Prospectus," *Index,* January 1, 1870, 5.
4. Abbot's friend, the Unitarian minister, abolitionist, and Civil War soldier Thomas Wentworth Higginson (Harvard College class of 1841), said that Abbot's "affirmations" "seemed to me the most important statement of religious truth since Luther." Higginson made this remark in a letter to Abbot, dated March 16, 1870. Abbot Papers, box 43, Correspondence. See also Francis E. Abbot, "Fifty Affirmations," *Index,* January 1, 1870, 1. Abbot's list of "affirmations" is indeed numbered. The selective survey that appears here includes portions of numbers 1–3, 29, and 39–40. See also Emerson's essay "The Over-Soul" (1841), in *The Collected Works of Ralph Waldo Emerson,* vol. 2, *Essays: First Series,* ed. Joseph Slater, Alfred R. Ferguson, and Jean Ferguson Carr (Cambridge, Mass.: Belknap Press of Harvard University Press, 1979), 159–78.
5. Osgood passed this judgment on Parker in his published review of *A Discourse of Matters Pertaining to Religion.* The reviewer went on to observe, "It requires very little talent to say smart things against the cherished opinions of the Church." See also "Parker's Discourse," *Monthly Miscellany* 7 (August 1842): 151.
6. Abbot Papers, Notes of Lectures on Scientific Theism: Given in the Advanced Course, Philosophy 13, Harvard College, 1887–88, HUC 8887.270.13, Harvard University Archives, Archives Stacks.
7. Josiah Royce, "Abbot's Scientific Theism," *Science* (April 9, 1886): 335–37.
8. Josiah Royce, "Dr. Abbot's 'Way Out of Agnosticism,'" *International Journal of Ethics* 1, no. 1 (1890): 98–113.

INDEX

Page references in *italics* refer to figures and photos.

Abbot, Edwin, 175
Abbot, Francis Ellingwood: "Atomism in Religion," 183; "Darwin's Theory of Conscience," 183; "Fifty Affirmations," 183, 188–89; on free religion vs. transcendentalism, 231–32n73; Free Religious Association of, 13, 154–55, 178–84, 186–89; "The Genius of Christianity and Free Religion," 182; "God of Science," 183; at Harvard, 175–76, 189–90, 231n66; Home School for Boys, 189; *Index* of, 154, 180, 188–89; "Intuitionalism and the Scientific School of Free Religion," 183; *Is Not Harvard Responsible for the Conduct of Her Professors, as Well as of Her Students?*, 190; legacy of, 187–92; "A Radical's Theology," 177–78, 189; "Religious Revivals," 177; removal from First Unitarian Society of Christians, 176–77; *Scientific Theism*, 189, 190; *The Way Out of Agnosticism*, 177, 190
Adair, James, 122
Adams, Hannah, 54–55
Adams, Raymond, 51, 207–8n43
Aesthetic Papers (journal), 138
aesthetic transcendentalism: *Aesthetic Papers* and, 137–38; *Beatrice*, 141–42, *142*; *Le Brigand*, 139–41, *140*; spiritualism vs., 138–39; *Summer on the Lakes*, Clarke's illustrations, 143–46, *144*, *145*; "transparent eye-ball" of Emerson's *Nature*, 135–37, *136*; visual arts popularity, 102–3, 134–35
Age of Reason, The (Paine), 211n84
Albanese, Catherine, 158
Alcott, Amos Bronson, 103, 141, 154, 156, 225n18
Alcott, Louisa May, 110
Alger, W. R., 186
Allston, Washington, 141–43, *142*, 216n46, 222n99
American Heretic (Grodzins), 153
"American Scholar" (Emerson), 3, 16
American Unitarian Association, 17, 57, 81, 196n4
Analogy of Religion, Natural and Revealed (Butler), 32
Andover Theological Seminary, 6
Annual Reports (Harvard Committee of the Overseers), 29, 36–40, *38*
Appeal to Common Sense and the Constitution, An (Kneeland), 148
Argersinger, Jana L., 97–98
Arsić, Branka, 21
atheism: Emerson on, 44; etymology of, 17; spread of secularism in antebellum United States, 7; Thoreau as Concord's "village atheist," 9–10, 49–53, 66, 88
"Atheism in New-England" (S. G. Howe), 44
"Atheism of Yesterday, The" (Peabody), 115
At Home and Abroad (Stula), 221n89

Atlantic Monthly: inception of, 218n66; on Thoreau, 209n57
Atlas (Boston), on infidelity, 202n58
"Atomism in Religion" (Abbot), 183

Baker, Carlos, 222n103
Balch, Francis V., 175–76
Banner of Light (Boston), on Abbot, 177, 183
Barnum, P. T., 150–51, 161
Bartol, Cyrus A., 13, 179, 187
"Battle of Ideas in Boston, The" (*Christian Register*), 147
Beam, Dorri, 134
Beatrice (Allston), 141–42, *142*
Beers, Henry A., 211n84
Beginnings of Unitarianism in America (Wright), 215n34
Blake, James V., 186
Boston: Concord's proximity to, 64; size of (1838), 158; transcendentalism as entertainment in, 150–53, 157, 159–61, 183–86; as transcendentalist center, 4. See also transcendentalism, urbanism, and unbelief; *individual Boston newspapers*
Boston Daily Advertiser: Norton and, 26; on Parker, 168, 232n73
Boston Evening Transcript, on Thoreau, 209n65
Boston Globe, on postbellum religion, 185
Boston Investigator, Rose in, 112
Boston Post: on Abbot, 182; on postbellum religion, 185
"Brahma" (Emerson), 218n66
Brazer, John, 161–63
Brigand, Le (Lessing), 139–41, *140*
Browne, Albert Gallatine, 218–19n67
Browne, Sarah Smith (Cox), 129, 218–19n67
Brownson, Orestes, 46, 113, 156, 158
Broyles, Michael, 160
Buell, Lawrence, 198n15, 205n21
Burr, William, 168
Burroughs, John, 209n57
Bushnell, Horace, 128

Butler, Joseph, 32
Byron, George Gordon, 58

Cabot, Elisabeth (Dwight), 130
Cabot, James Eliot, 219n71
Cameron, Kenneth Walker, 158, 207n42, 208n44
Cameron, Sharon, 26–27
Capper, Charles, 96, 97, 103
Carlyle, Thomas, 128
Carpenter, Delores Bird, 221n91
Casanova, José, 111
Channing, Ann, *142*
Channing, Edward T., 118, 207–8n43
Channing, William Ellery, 113, 114, 124, 125, 156, 225n19
Channing, William Henry, 183, 200n39, 213n6, 214n23
Chardon Street Conventions, 159–60, 226n26
Child, Lydia Maria, 109–10, 111, 116, 134
Christian Disciple, Emerson's first published work in, 196n4
Christian Examiner (Unitarian Church): as flagship journal, 45; infidelity accusations, 202n58; Norton as editor of, 114
Christian Register (Unitarian Church): on Abbot, 183, 184, 186; on negative religion, 187; Potter and, 187–88; on "Theatre Meetings," 227n38; on "Theatre Preaching," 165–66
Christian Songs (Lyons), 206n26
Church of the Disciples, 164–65
"Circles" (Emerson), 20
Clapp, Eliza, 112
Clark, Thomas, 44
Clarke, James Freeman: aesthetic transcendentalists and, 137, 146; Church of the Disciples, 164–65; Conversations and, 104, 106; Fuller's travel with, 119; *Memoirs of Margaret Fuller Ossoli,* 213n6; on Parker, 20, 197n10; on "Positive Transcendentalism," 21
Clarke, Sarah Freeman: aesthetic transcendentalism and, 135, 137, 139, 141–

46, *144, 145*; on Conversations, 104; legacy of, 102; *Summer on the Lakes* and, 119, 143–46, *144, 145*
Cole, Phyllis, 97–98, 100, 113, 213n11
Coleridge, Samuel Taylor, 113, 176
Collected Works of Ralph Waldo Emerson, The (Slater, Ferguson, & Carr), 47
Commonwealth (Boston) on Abbot, 183, 184, 233n88
"Compensation" (Emerson), 21
Concord: annual report of expenses (1837), 75–76; Concord Day (1906), 80; lapse of traditional religious observance in, 9, 59–64, 74–75, 83–84; map of, *65*; "O" in *Yeoman's Gazette* on religious schism in, 53–57; population (1850), 64; proximity to Boston, 64; secular societies and institutions of, 60–61, 85, 205n16; *Third Meeting House in Concord*, 80; Thoreau as "village atheist" of, 9–10, 49–53, 66, 88; Thoreau's sympathies toward religious folkways of, 67–68; Trinitarian church established in, 54–60; *Walden* and depiction of, 79–91; *A Week* and depiction of, 68–69, 73–79, 207n38. See also *Walden*; *Week on the Concord and Merrimack Rivers, A*; *Yeoman's Gazette*; *individual names of churches*
Congregational Church of Commonwealth of Massachusetts, 5
Connor, Rowland, 186
Conrad, Susan Phinney, 212n2
Conversations (Fuller), 10, 94, 101–10, 125, 213n10, 214n17, 214n19
Conversations with Children on the Gospels (Alcott), 225n18
Conway, Moncure, 210n66
Cranch, Christopher Pearse, *39*, 135–37, *136*, 138, 220–21n89
Culture and Redemption (Fessenden), 215n31

Dall, Caroline Healy, 95–96, 99
Dana, Richard Henry, Jr., 127
Dana, Sarah Watson, 218n63

Darwin, Charles, 13
"Darwin's Theory of Conscience" (Abbot), 183
Davis, Hasbrouck, 42–43
"Defense of Atheism, A" (Rose), 112, 215n35
De Veritate Religionis Christianae (Grotius), 32
Dial: aesthetic transcendentalists and, 143; Emerson on Chardon Street Convention in, 159–60; Fuller's writing in, 117, 217n52; Poor on, 131
Dimaggio, Paul, 150
Discourse of Matters Pertaining to Religion, A (Parker), 33, 131, 163
Discourse on the Latest Form of Infidelity, A (Norton), 2, 18–20, 26–28, *39*, 196n6
Discourse on the Transient and Permanent in Christianity, A (Parker), 163, 164
"Divine Providence" (Swedenborg), 130
"Divinity School Address, The" (Emerson), 18, 20–27, 36, 44, 45, 64, 97, 114, 134, 151, 198n14, 198nn18–19, 199n22, 199n25
"Dorian Measure, with a Modern Application, The" (Peabody), 222n94
Douglas, Ann, 212n4
Dudleian Lectures on Natural Religion (Harvard), 30
Dunbar, Louisa, 74
Dwight, Elisabeth, 219n71
Dwight, John Sullivan, 156, 160, 226–27n31

"Each Atomic Part" (Gardner), 213n7
"Egotheism, the Atheism of To-day" (Peabody), 115
Ellis, George E., 197n9
Emerson, Charles Chauncy (brother), 132
Emerson, Ellen Tucker (daughter), 221n91
Emerson, Lidian Jackson (wife), 137, 221n91
Emerson, Mary Moody (aunt), 98, 132, 213n6, 220n80

Emerson, Ralph Waldo: on atheism, 44; Cabot, J. E, as biographer of, 219n71; on Chardon Street Convention, 159–60; Concord as home of, 49; Cranch and, 220–21n89; on "faith," 15–20; as Free Religious Association member, 13; Harvard's changing interpretation of religion and, 27, 28; as Harvard student, 33; Josiah Quincy's letter to, 208n44; Kneeland supported by, 12; legacy of, 189, 192; on "negativity," 21–24; on "New Views," 3; Richardson, R. D., on, 41; Thoreau and, 3, 9, 72, 74, 88, 91, 208n53; as Unitarian minister, 15, 21, 25. *See also* Emerson, Ralph Waldo, titles of works

Emerson, Ralph Waldo, titles of works: "American Scholar," 3, 16; "Brahma," 218n66; in *Christian Disciple*, 196n4; "Circles," 20; "Compensation," 21; "The Divinity School Address" (1838) of, 18, 20–27, 36, 44, 45, 64, 97, 114, 134, 151, 198n14, 198nn18–19, 199n22, 199n25; Harvard speech (1846), 2, 31; Josiah Quincy's letter to, 208n44; "Lectures on the Times," 19, 46–48; *Memoirs of Margaret Fuller Ossoli*, 213n6; *Nature*, 46, 72, 87, 90, 109, 116, 127, 135, 174; in *North American Review*, 200n38; "The Over-Soul," 26; "The Present Age," 214n20; "Religion" (lecture series), 158; "The Sovereignty of Ethics," 200n38; "Spiritual Laws," 15; Thoreau as protégé of, 9, 72, 91; Thoreau characterized by, 74; Thoreau's eulogy by, 88, 208n53; "The Times," 47; "The Transcendentalist," 19, 22, 47–48

Emerson, Ralph Waldo, women transcendentalists and: aesthetic transcendentalists and, 138, 141; "Brahma," 218n66; Emerson on women's role in transcendentalism, 213n11; Emerson's legacy and, 93, 94, 97; feminine infidelity and, 114–16; Fuller on influence of Emerson, 214n25; Larcom on, 218n66, 219n68; *Nature* and effect on, 109; "transparent eye-ball" of Emerson's *Nature*, 135–37, *136*; women's reception of transcendentalism, 127, 128, 130

Emerson, William (brother), 132
Emerson among the Eccentrics (Baker), 222n103
Emerson and Thoreau: The Contemporary Reviews (Myerson), 206n32
Emerson: The Mind on Fire (R. D. Richardson), 196n7
Everett, Edward, 31, 40–41, 58
Exposition of the Old and New Testaments (Henry), 131

Federal Street Baptist Society, 168
Felton, Cornelius C., 118, 139
feminine infidelity, 109–23; Child's legacy of, 109–10; Fuller's legacy of, 116–23; importance of printed works by women, 110–11; Peabody's legacy of, 113–16; secularism in United States vs. Europe, 111–12; unbelief as belief position, 112. *See also* Peabody, Elizabeth Palmer
Feminization of American Culture, The (Douglas), 212n4
Fessenden, Tracy, 215n31
"Fifty Affirmations" (Abbot), 188–89
First Parish Church (Concord): Concord's religious schism and, 53–64; psalms and hymns of, 82; Records of, 210n69; Sabbath breaking and, 74, 83; Thoreau's and family's affiliation with, 50, 56–57, 60, 61, 78–79, 85, 90; town support ended for, 209n59; *A Week* and depiction of, 76
First Unitarian Society of Christians (New Hampshire), 176–77
Forging of an Aristocracy, The (Story), 224n7
Fox, Feroline (Pierce), 131, 132
Francis, Convers, 198n14

INDEX

Free Religious Association, 13, 154–55, 178–84, 186–89
Friend (journal), Peabody and, 113
Friends of Theodore Parker, 164, 165
Friends of Universal Reform, 159–60
"From the Dial. Religion." (Parker), 58–59, 204n13
Frothingham, Octavius B., 28–29, 179, 210n66
Fuller, Margaret: aesthetic transcendentalists and, 102, 139–45; Conversations, 10, 94, 100–110, 125, 213n10, 214n19; *Dial,* 217n52; "The Great Lawsuit," 101, 117–19, 120, 122; on infidelity, 110, 113, 116–18, 119–22; on influence of Emerson, 214n25; legacy of, 93, 94, 96, 98–99, 154, 192; *Margaret Fuller Ossoli,* 213n10, 217n54; "Margaret Fuller's Boston Conversations," 214n17; "masculine" attributes assigned to, 97, 212n4; *Memoirs of Margaret Fuller Ossoli,* 213n6; Peabody's legacy and, 113; religious beliefs of, 106–7; *Summer on the Lakes,* 119–23, 143–46, *144, 145*; women's reception of transcendentalism, 125, 134
Fuller, Robert C., 199–200n31

Gardner, Eric, 213n7
Garrison, William Lloyd, 159
General Court of the Commonwealth of Massachusetts, 63
"Genius of Christianity and Free Religion, The" (Abbot), 182
Godkin, E. L., 150
"God of Science" (Abbot), 183
Gospel of Matthew, 222n103
"Gospel of the Open, The" (Ives), 209n65
Grasso, Christopher, 184
"Great Lawsuit, The" (Fuller), 101, 117–19, 120, 122
Greeley, Horace, 107, 206n32
Green, Martin, 150

Greene, William Batchelder, 196n8
Grimké sisters, 110
Grodzins, Dean, 128, 153, 165
Gross, Robert, 51, 151, 209n62
Grotius, Hugo, 32
Guild, Eliza, 114
Gura, Philip, 23
Gustafson, Sandra, 110

Habich, Robert, 139
Hale, Edward Everett, 171–72
Hall, Nathaniel, 44–45
Handel & Haydn Society, 167
Hardenberg, Georg Philipp Friedrich Freiherr von ("Novalis"), 130, 219n73
Harding, Chester, 222n99
Harper's Weekly, on Horticultural Hall, 181
Harvard College (University): Abbot and, 175–76, 189–90, 231n66; *Annual Reports,* 29, 31, 35–41, *38*; Appleton Chapel, 40–41; Brazer and, 162; Committee of the Overseers, 30–31, 35; "The Divinity School Address" (1838), 18, 20–27, 36, 44, 45, 64, 97, 114, 134, 151, 198n14, 198nn18–19, 199n22, 199n25; Emerson's speech to Divinity School (1846), 2, 31; Harvard Musical Association, 160; Kirkland as president of, 112, 157, 215n34; "On Devotional Exercises and the Observance of the Lord's Day" (code of laws), 35; parish ministers among alumni, 202n51; Professor of the Philosophy of the Heart, 41–42; Quincy, J., as president of, 103; revised code of laws (Corporation and Overseers), 35; Ricœur's lecture (1976), 172–73; students' interest in urbanism/Boston events, 155–58; Thoreau as student of, 51, 67, 71–72, 89, 206–7n35, 207–8nn42–43, 208n45, 211n88; as transcendentalist incubator, 4; transition of religious culture at, 3–6, 8–9, 27–42, *38, 39,* 201n41; University Hall,

Harvard College (continued)
33–36, *34*, 40, 201n46; women's exclusion from, 110
Hatch, Nathan, 16
Hawthorne, Nathaniel, 44
"Hebrew Scriptures" series (Peabody), 114–16
Hedge, Frederic Henry, 117
Henry, Matthew, 131
Henry Thoreau: A Life of the Mind (R. D. Richardson), 206–7n35
Henshaw, David, 223n4
Herbert, George, 220n83
Higginson, Thomas Wentworth, 107, 183, 213n10, 217n54, 234n4
Highbrow, Lowbrow (Levine), 226n29
Himes, Joshua V., 131
Histoire de l'art moderne en Allemagne (Raczyski), 139
History of the American Indians (Adair), 122
Hodges, Sarah, 105–6
Holyoke, Edward, 30
Home School for Boys, 189
Hooper, Ellen Sturgis, 108, 130
Horticultural Hall (Boston), 154–55, 179–83, *181*, 186, 232n79
House of the Seven Gables, The (Hawthorne), 44
Howe, Daniel Walker, 4
Howe, Julia Ward, 167, 168, 170, 183
Howe, Samuel Gridley, 44
Hurth, Elisabeth, 4–5
Hutchinson, Anne, 96, 99
"Hymn" (Everett), 58

Index (weekly paper), Abbot and, 154, 180, 188–89
Indian Encampment (S. F. Clarke), 143, *144*
infidelity: *Atlas* on, 202n58; blasphemy charges against Kneeland, 12, 63, 147–51, 223–24n4; defined, 2–3; as "increasing," 42–48; Norton on, 2, 18–20, 26–28, *39*, 56, 196n6; Smith, A., on, 203n59. *See also* Emerson, Ralph Waldo; Kneeland, Abner; Thoreau, Henry David; transcendentalism, urbanism, and unbelief; women and transcendentalism
International Journal of Ethics, 190
"Intuitionalism and the Scientific School of Free Religion" (Abbot), 183
Investigator (Boston): on Abbot, 183; Kneeland and, 148–49, 156, 177, 183
Is Not Harvard Responsible for the Conduct of Her Professors, as Well as of Her Students? (Abbot), 190
Ives, Ella Gilbert, 209n65

Jackson, Hannah Lowell, 124, 125
Jacoby, Susan, 213n9
Jager, Colin, 152
James, William, 8
Jarvis, Edward, 208n44
Johnson, Samuel, 209–10n66

Kasson, John, 152
Kilburn, Samuel Smith, *181*
Kirkland, John T., 112, 157, 215n34
Kneeland, Abner: blasphemy charges/trials of, 12, 63, 147–51, 223–24n4; Emerson's support of, 12; incarceration of, 155–59; *Investigator* of, 148–49, 156, 177, 183; "Philosophical Creed," 223n3; Ripley, S., on, 198n14; Unitarianism second national conference (1866) and, 179

Larcom, Lucy, 129, 218n66, 219n68
Lardner, Nathaniel, 113
Last Evening with Allston, and Other Papers (Peabody), 216n46
Lawrence, Kathleen, 102, 141
Lears, Jackson, 224n11
"Lectures on the Times" (Emerson), 19, 46–48
Lee, Henry, 34
legal issues of religious worship: Blackstone, William, on, 62; General Court of the Commonwealth of Massachusetts on blasphemy, 63; Hale

on, 75; of Sabbath breaking, 9, 62, 74, 82–84, 205n21, 210n69, 210n71. *See also* Kneeland, Abner
Leland, Charles Godfrey, 44
Lessing, Karl Friedrich, 139–41, *140*
Letters from New York (Child), 109
Levine, Lawrence, 226n29
Liberator, Garrison and, 159
Life and Letters of Christopher Pearse Cranch, The (Scott), 220–21n89
"Life of Lidian Jackson Emerson, The" (E. T. Emerson), 221n91
Literary Transcendentalism (Buell), 205n21
Locke, John, 32, 126
Longfellow, Samuel, 183
Loring, Ellis Gray, 219n73
Loring, Louisa (Gilman), 130, 219n73
Lowell, James Russell, 66, 206n32
Lyceum (Concord), 60–61, 85, 205n16
Lyons, James Gilborne, 206n26

Mack, Esther, 106
Mackinaw Beach (S. F. Clarke), 144, *145*
Malcolm, Howard, 129
Margaret Fuller Ossoli (Higginson), 213n10, 217n54
"Margaret Fuller's Boston Conversations" (Simmons), 214n17
Massachusetts Horticultural Society. *See* Horticultural Hall
Massachusetts Quarterly Review, Parker as editor of, 206n32
Massachusetts Senate, 75
Melodeon (Boston), 12–13, 167–74, *169*, 228n46
Memoirs of Margaret Fuller Ossoli (Clarke, Emerson, & Channing), 213n6
Miller, Perry, 3, 96–99, 160
"Minerva & Vulcan" (Conversations, Fuller), 104, 108
Modern, John Lardas, 7
"Morbid Appetite for Excitement" (Brazer), 162–63
More, Hannah, 112, 212n91
Morgan, Isabel, 124–25

Mott, Lucretia, 13, 179
Mott, Wesley, 105
Murat, Achille, 21–22
Music Hall (Boston), 167–74
Musical Magazine, Dwight in, 226–27n31
Myerson, Joel, 206n32, 222n99

Nation, on Boston, 150
Native Americans, Fuller on, 121–22, 144
Nature (Emerson), 46, 72, 87, 90, 109, 116, 127, 135, 174
negative religion: Abbot and contemporaries accused of, 187; Clarke, J. F., on "negative" and "positive transcendentalism," 20, 197n10; Emerson on "negativity," 21–24; Thoreau on religion and contradiction, 52–53; women transcendentalists and, 115–16; Worcester on, 17–18, 20
New England, population of (1890), 195n11
New-England Magazine, "Atheism in New-England," 44
New England Quarterly, "Thoreau at Harvard," 208n43
New England religious belief, evolution of. *See* religious belief in New England, evolution of
New Horticultural Hall in Boston, The (Kilburn), *181*
"New Measures," 225n16
New Monthly Magazine, Novalis quote in, 219n73
"New Views" and changing culture. *See* transcendentalism, urbanism, and unbelief; women and transcendentalism
New York Independent, Davis's article, 43
New-York Tribune, on Thoreau, 206n32
North American Review, Emerson's article in, 200n38
North Church (Salem), 162
Norton, Andrews: Allston and, 141; *A Discourse on the Latest Form of Infidelity,* 2, 18–20, 26–28, *39,* 196n6; women transcendentalists and, 114, 116
Novak, Barbara, 221n92

Novalis (Hardenberg), 130, 219n73
Noyes, George R., 202n58

"Oh! Steal Not Thou My Faith Away" (Lyons), 64, 206n26
Osgood, Reverend Dr., 128
Osgood, Samuel, 189
"Over-Soul, The" (Emerson), 26
Owen, Robert Dale, 179
Oxford Handbook of Transcendentalism, The (Myerson, Petrulionis, & Walls), 222n99

Packer, Barbara, 12, 223n104
Paine, Thomas, 211n84
Paley, William, 32
Palfrey, John G., 25
Parker, Theodore: Brazer and, 161–63; characterization of preaching by, 165–67; Clarke, J. F., on, 20; *A Discourse of Matters Pertaining to Religion*, 33, 131, 163; *A Discourse on the Transient and Permanent in Christianity*, 163, 164; on Emerson, 20, 25, 197n9; "free gospel" of, 227n36; Friends of Theodore Parker, 164, 165; "From the Dial. Religion.," 58–59, 204n13; "A Lesson for the Day," 59; letter to Noyes, 202n58; as *Massachusetts Quarterly Review* editor, 206n32; at Melodeon and Music Hall venues, 12–13, 167–74, 228n46; *Radical* contributors and, 209–10n66; religion in Concord and, 58–59, 60, 66; "Religion" (lecture series), 165; "Spiritual Deadness," 165–66; "Transcendentalism," 33; *Transcendentalism: A Lecture*, 201n43; Twenty-Eighth Congregational Society of, 153–54, 164–65, 229nn53–54, 230n57; women transcendentalists and, 116, 125, 131, 141, 222n98
Peabody, Andrew Preston, 33, 157
Peabody, Elizabeth Palmer: aesthetic transcendentalists and, 102, 137–38, 141; "The Atheism of Yesterday," 115; "The Dorian Measure, with a Modern Application," 222n94; "Egotheism, the Atheism of To-day," 115; as first transcendentalist, 113; Fuller's Conversations hosted by, 100–101, 104–6, 109; "Hebrew Scriptures" series, 114–16; *Last Evening with Allston, and Other Papers*, 216n46; legacy of, 93, 94; Parker and, 165; "Public Worship," 115; published works of, 101
Peabody, William B. O., 127
Perham, Josiah, 168
Perish the Thought (Conrad), 212n2
Personality of the Deity, The (Ware Jr.), 25–26
Petrulionis, Sandra Harbert, 222n99
Phillips, Wendell, 183
"Philosophical Creed" (Kneeland), 223n3
Philosophical Dictionary (Voltaire), 148
Pierce, John, 200n39
Poems (L. L. A. Very), 146
Poor, Mary Pierce, 131–32
Porter, James, 159
Portinari, Beatrice, 142
Potter, William J., 182, 187
Practical Piety (More), 212n91
Prescott, Martha Lawrence, 125–27, 218n62
"Present Age, The" (lecture series, Emerson), 214n20
Protestant faith. *See* religious belief in New England, evolution of; Trinitarians; Unitarianism; *individual denominations*
"Public Amusements, a Discourse" (Hale), 171–72
Public Appeal (Abbot), 190
"Public Worship" (Peabody), 115

Quick, Frances Merritt, 131, 132, 219–20n76
Quincy, Eliza Susan Morton, 103–4
Quincy, Josiah, 27, 103, 208n44

Raczyski, Atanazy, 139
Radical: contributors to, 81, 209–10n66; inception of, 186; "A Radical's

Theology," 177–78, 189; Thoreau's theories and, 84
"Radical's Theology, A" (Abbot), 177–78, 189
"Religion" (lecture series, Emerson), 158
"Religion" (lecture series, Parker), 165
religious belief in New England, evolution of, 15–48; Emerson on "faith" and, 15–20; Emerson's "Divinity School Address" (1838) and, 18, 20–27, 36, 44, 45, 64, 198n14, 198nn18–19, 199n22, 199n25; Harvard's changing religious position and, 3–6, 8–9, 27–42, *38, 39*; infidelity, 2–3, 12, 18–20, 26–28, *39*, 42–48, 56, 63, 147–51, 196n6, 202n58; modern-day statistics, 199–200n31; negative religion, 17–18, 20–24, 52–53, 115–16, 187, 197n10; New England population statistics (1890), 195n11. *See also* Emerson, Ralph Waldo; feminine infidelity; Harvard College; infidelity; legal issues of religious worship; Sabbath worship; unbelief; Unitarianism
Religious Freedoms Act (1811), 5
"Religious Revivals" (Abbot), 177
Reminiscences (W. E. Channing), 114
Republican (Boston), on Abbot, 183
Review of Atheism for Unlearned Christians, A (Worcester), 17–18
Review of the Trial, Conviction, and Final Imprisonment in the Common Jail of the County of Suffolk of Abner Kneeland, A (Kneeland), 149, 155–57
revivalism, "New Measures," 225n16
Richardson, James, 211n88
Richardson, Robert D., 19, 23, 41, 196n7, 206–7n35
Ricœur, Paul, 172–74
Ripley, Ezra, 125, 126
Ripley, George, 156
Ripley, Samuel, 198n14
Ripley, Sarah Alden Bradford, 125, 132–34, 217n59
Robber and His Child, The (Lessing), *140*
Robbins, Catherine, 128, 218n65
Robinson, David, 20–21, 105

Robinson, Harriet Jane Hanson, 129, 218n66, 219nn68–69
Robinson, William S., 219n69
Rolling Prairie of Illinois (S. F. Clarke), 144–45, *145*
Ronda, Bruce, 22
Rose, Ernestine, 112, 215n35
Royce, Josiah, 189, 190
Russell, Henry, 161, 227n32

Sabbath worship: Parker on, 59; Sabbatarian movement, 60; Sabbath breaking, 9, 62, 74, 82–84, 205n21, 210n69, 210n71; Thoreau on, 49
Sargent, John T., 168, 170, 186, 229n51
Sartor Resartus (Carlyle), 128
Schmidt, Leigh Eric, 199–200n31
Science (journal), on Abbot, 190
Scientific Theism (Abbot), 189, 190
Scott, Leonora Cranch, 220–21n89
secularism and secularization: Grasso on, 184–85; secularization, defined, 1; spread of secularism in antebellum United States, 7; in United States vs. Europe, 111–12
Sedgwick, Elizabeth, 124–25
Seven Mile Mirror (Burr), 168, *169*
Shattuck, Harriette Lucy Robinson, 218n66, 219nn68–69
Shaw, Lemuel, 223n2
Shoemaker, Stephen P., 32
Shreve, Grant, 111–12
Simmons, Nancy Craig, 214n17
Skeptic, The (Russell), 161
Smith, Amos, 45, 203n59
Smith, Samuel Abbot, 175
Smith, Susan Belasco, 143
Society for Philosophical Enquiry, 96
Souvenir Festival Hymns, 233–34n2
"Sovereignty of Ethics, The" (Emerson), 200n38
"Spirit of the Hebrew Scriptures" (Peabody), 114–16
"Spiritual Deadness" (sermon, Parker), 165–66
"Spiritual Laws" (Emerson), 15

Stewart, Dugald, 32
Stokes, Claudia, 111
Stone, Lucy, 110
Story, Ronald, 224n7
Stowe, Harriet Beecher, 219n67
Studies in Religion (Clapp), 112
"Study of Religion" (Abbot), 183
Stula, Nancy, 221n89
Sturgis, Caroline, 102, 141
Suffolk Street Chapel (Boston), 168
Summer on the Lakes, in 1843 (Fuller), 101, 119–23, 143–46, *144*, *145*
Sumner, Charles, 175
"supernova effect," 215n31
Swedenborg, Emanuel, 130

Taylor, Charles, 7, 215n31
Temple School, 103, 141, 154
"That Terrible Thoreau" (Gross), 209n62
Third Meeting House in Concord (Wesson), 80
Thoreau, Henry David, 49–91, 93–94; church affiliation of, 50, 56–57, 60, 61, 78–79, 85, 90; Concord's religious schism and, 53–64; as Concord's "village atheist," 9–10, 49–53, 66, 88; death of, 71, 88, 208n53; Emerson's characterization of, 74, 88, 208n53; as Emerson's protégé, 3, 9, 72, 91; family of, 56, 57, 60, 66, 68–70, 126, 203n6, 212n91; as Harvard student, 51, 67, 71–72, 89, 206–7n35, 207–8nn42–43, 208n45, 211n88; legacy of, 93–94, 192; letter to Elijah Wood (October 8, 1841), 78; *Walden*, 9, 51, 53, 66, 79–91; "Walking," 64; *A Week*, 9, 51, 53, 65–79, 82, 89, 91; women's reception of transcendentalism, 126, 129. *See also* Concord; *Walden*; *Week on the Concord and Merrimack Rivers, A*
Thoreau, Jane (aunt), 212n91
Thoreau, Sophia (sister), 126
"Thoreau at Harvard" (R. Adams), 207–8n43

Thoreau's Harvard Years (K. W. Cameron), 207n42, 208n44
Tocqueville, Alexis de, 29
Toward a Female Genealogy of Transcendentalism (Argersinger & Cole), 97–98
Traditions and Reminiscences of Concord, Massachusetts, 1779–1878 (Jarvis), 208n44
transcendentalism: *Dial* as official transcendentalist periodical, 58–59; legacy of, 191–92; Peabody as first transcendentalist, 113. *See also* Emerson, Ralph Waldo; Thoreau, Henry David; transcendentalism, urbanism, and unbelief; unbelief; women and transcendentalism
"Transcendentalism" (Parker), 33
Transcendentalism: A Lecture (Parker), 201n43
transcendentalism, urbanism, and unbelief, 147–86; Abbot's "free" religion and, 154–55, 174–86; as Boston's amusement/entertainment, 150–53, 157, 159–61, 183–86; Chardon Street Conventions and, 159–60, 226n26; Kneeland and, 147–51, 153, 155–59, 179; "Parkerism" and, 153–54, 161–74. *See also* Abbot, Francis Ellingwood; Kneeland, Abner; Parker, Theodore
"Transcendentalism in Print" (Zboray & Zboray), 123
"Transcendentalist, The" (Emerson), 19, 22, 47–48
Transcendentalists, The (Miller), 96–99
Transcendentalists, The (Packer), 223n104
"Transcendental Wild Oats" (L. M. Alcott), 110
"transparent eye-ball" of Emerson's *Nature*, (Cranch), 135–37, *136*
Travels in South-Eastern Asia (Malcolm), 129
Trinitarians: dealings with First Parish Church (Concord), 53–64, 204n12; religious denominations of, 6, 32, 55